Editor's Note

Jonathan Wilson, Editor

The Blizzard, as people who've been with us since we launched three years ago will know, drew much of its inspiration (that is, we nicked the name and the masthead) from a Sunderland-based weekly newspaper of 1893. Set up as "the organ of Mr Sidney Duncan", it seemed to be written entirely by him, was strikingly eccentric and was concerned largely with the furtherment of his own political career. It lasted 12 issues before folding.

I set myself a target of matching what Duncan had done and now, happily, we've achieved that. Surpassed it even, if you include the pilot, Issue Zero. That that has been possible has been down to the writers and the other people who work behind the scenes (thanks Dave, Garreth, Nina, Michael, Peter, Kev, Andy, Vince, Lawrence and Kat). Looking back I still can't quite believe how many people were prepared to put in so much effort in that first year when there was a genuine possibility none of us would be paid a penny, and for their belief and willingness to invest in a half-expressed dream I'm hugely grateful.

But it's also down to you, the readers, for the leap of faith you took in buying a product essentially blind, on the back of little more, initially, than a few woolly Tweets. The pay-what-you-want model was a huge gamble, but the vast majority of people have been respectful of that, have accepted that if the magazine is to be available to all, then everybody has to be realistic about what they can afford to pay. My faith in humanity is regularly tested by Twitter and the comments sections below articles; that so few people have exploited the pay-what-you-want model restores it. I'm grateful for that, and I'm also grateful so many people have clearly told others about the magazine. Please keep doing so, whether through social media, through blogs or articles or even in that most old-fashioned of ways, face-to-face: our advertising budget remains zero; word of mouth is everything.

I know I've said this before, but we are a community and we can only continue in our present form if we continue to be so. Thanks to everybody for everything they've done so far, but as we leave Sidney Duncan's mark behind, let's all keep pushing through the next dozen and beyond.

March 2014

Contents

The Blizzard, Issue Twelve

⊕ **Against the Odds**

⇆ **Polemics**

⊕ **Fiction**

⇆ **Greatest Games**

⊕ **Eight Bells**

Information

6

The Rivals

"...a club versus more than a club."

Power Play

Carles Rexach and Jorge Valdano discuss the changing nature of the Real Madrid-Barcelona rivalry

By Sid Lowe

Player, coach, sporting director, member of the board, presidential adviser... few men have played such big parts at Real Madrid and FC Barcelona as Jorge Valdano and Carles Rexach. They can even lay claim to have delivered the greatest of the clubs' modern greats: Rexach signed Leo Messi on a napkin; Valdano gave a 17 year old by the name of Raúl his debut. And yet, neither their positions nor their statuses have gone unchallenged, they have played a part in the divisions that the clubs have suffered too: Johan Cruyff, the closest Barcelona have to a deity, broke off relations with Rexach, while Valdano was forced out of the Bernabéu by José Mourinho.

Over the course of the two years of research, my book on Real Madrid and Barcelona evolved into a kind of oral history, built upon not only audio-visual and written material but also on the experiences and memories of those who constructed the club's histories and identities. There are few people better placed to explain the identity of Madrid and Barcelona, their meaning, than Rexach and Valdano. Telling the clubs' stories meant listening to the stories, with all their contradiction and nuance, from both sides of Spanish football's great divide. The *clásico* is, like any story, a human story.

Carles Rexach

⇨ *Barcelona famously defines itself as "more than a club", but what does that actually mean? What is Barcelona? And can it be understood without that socio-political component?*

Barcelona is a feeling. Years ago, the political element was central and it's still there: Catalanism, separatism, nationalism. Even people who didn't like football took an interest in football through Barcelona, because it meant something, hence more than a club. It's politics and football wrapped up together.

⇨ *Does Barcelona's identity hang on what it is not as well as what it is? On Real Madrid and their success, in other words?*

Totally, totally. It was always: "Madrid this, Madrid that..." Their identity is totally different. For years we couldn't win the league... I don't mean to say that Madrid didn't deserve to win the league, because they did, but we lost three or four leagues in the last game, in the last minute: that's a fact. There was something there. There would be 100 games and 35 penalties, 30 for Madrid and 5 for Barcelona. It would always happen. And not just in the head-to-head matches, because we would often beat Madrid and that was enough for people to be satisfied, but in other games.

It was always the same. Barcelona were at a disadvantage. And that disadvantage meant that Barcelona didn't even get the chance to play in the European Cup.

✥ *If Madrid's identity is totally different, what is that identity? Franco's team?*

Without doubt, *hombre*. Madrid is in a way the badge of the whole of Spain. When I was a kid, I watched Barcelona on television maybe once a season while there would be 20 Madrid games. So everyone was a Madrid fan, all the kids supported them. Barcelona fans were just three or four of us here. Across Spain, everyone supported their local team and then Madrid. They might have outnumbered everyone else by seven to one. Now there are lots of Barcelona fans too. Why? Because now they see them on television...

✥ *And you think that's because of the arrival of democracy?*

Exactly. Now you can choose which team you support. Barcelona have clawed back that territory. It's not 7 to 1 any more. And that makes a difference. That conditions the games, the fans, the referees. Things do not happen in a vacuum.

✥ *For those people who did support Barcelona, was that a political decision?*

Clearly.

✥ *But is it still? Can you still construct that argument in a democracy and with Catalonia enjoying significant autonomy?*

Yes. There's been no loss of identity, because that sentiment, that identification, gets passed on from fathers to sons and the political issue remains. We still feel that there's a battle; some want independence or greater powers — to raise taxes, to build airports, to control our budget. Catalonia is a motor: people are hard-working here. We feel like Germany must with Spain. We pay. We pay a lot but we get little say. They build new roads in Andalusia for four cars a month. Here in Catalonia we have always been pioneers: industry, technology, the first cars, food, ideas... bit by bit, that reaches Madrid and they take it from you. Take flights to New York for example: you can't get a direct flight there from Barcelona any more; you have to go via Madrid. That kind of thing pisses people off. There's a Catalan national team but the Federación bans it, makes it a pirate game, not officially recognised. Barcelona signed Kubala, so Madrid signed Di Stéfano. "Hey, you can't have two of them... to Madrid!" It's not me saying this: this is real.

✥ *Does that tap into Barcelona's historic fatalism? Barcelona created a victim complex. Does all that political context really justify it, all the talk of referees? Madrid's dominance can't all be explained away by politics or perceived injustices...*

People were always saying, "There's nothing we can do." Was that an excuse? Yes. "Something always happens, something always goes wrong." I've always challenged that fatalistic attitude. Look at the Basques: they were different. Even if they didn't entirely agree with each other they would come together against Spain. Here, there was often some internal battle. Political parties couldn't bring people together. Barcelona was the one thing that united everyone. Left, right, centre, all colours: everyone could support Barcelona. But even within Barcelona, we looked for excuses for our own failure, someone else to blame. People said, "*Coño*, it's just that Madrid..." and I'd say, "No, a lot of the time, we're the problem."

⇨ *Where does that fatalism come from? Much is made of a Cup game versus Madrid in 1943 which Barcelona lost 11-1 after a Franco régime official supposedly came into the dressing-room and threatened the team...*

I hadn't been born but people tell you Barcelona ended up effectively saying, "If you want to win, here: win." But that's a bit too far back for me to judge and there's not much information about it. Then there's the final against Benfica in 1961, when Barcelona had knocked Madrid out of the European Cup but hit the post I don't know how many times in the final. That became a huge millstone round Barcelona's necks. Then there was Seville in 1986 [when they lost the European Cup final to Steaua]. Two finals and you lose them both: they were so desperate to win that they had a kind of block.

⇨ *You broke that in 1992 when you finally won the European Cup against Sampdoria at Wembley. You were assistant coach to Johan Cruyff...*

That was a liberation. People were waiting for us to blow it again. We felt like, "Wow, we've done it." It might only be one, but we've done it. Another life starts. We had won the Fairs Cup, the Uefa Cup, the Cup-Winners' Cup, but we needed that. That was the only thing missing. Now, Barcelona have won three

finals in a row. Why? Because that day we were set free. If we lose, it doesn't matter; we've got one now.

⇨ *Only one, though...*

If you look at Barcelona and Madrid they're practically the same. Leagues: Madrid have 25 and Barcelona 17, 18 [actually 32-26]. In Cups we've got 15 or 16 and they have 10 [actually Barcelona have won 22 and Real Madrid 18]. They have nine European Cups to our four, sure, but Barcelona have three Cup Winners' Cups and three Uefa Cups. Why did they win more European Cups? Because they were in it; we couldn't win the league so didn't go. You can't win a competition you don't play in and Barcelona had a kind of veto. But what we won in Europe was extremely difficult. Barcelona would play in a competition with three clubs from the strong countries. The supposed 'failures' but look how good they were. Real Madrid? There might be four good teams, plus the champions of Switzerland or Hungary. From Italy, we'd have Juve, Milan, Roma; from Germany, Hamburg, Cologne, Leverkusen. It might be a bigger achievement to win that than win four European Cups.

⇨ *But the European Cup has far greater symbolism and remains the pinnacle...*

The symbolism of the European Cup is brutal, brutal. Now. But we weren't that bothered: our focus was national. Since the early 1980s people were thinking about Europe but we didn't look outside enough. We navel-gazed too much. Our aim was to win the league and screw Madrid...

⇨ *You only won the league once in that spell, when Cruyff arrived in the 1973-74 season. Where you did win was* the cup, the Copa del Generalísimo. If Barcelona is about opposition, is there a contradiction there?

Not playing was unthinkable. If someone had said "we're not playing" back then, he'd have had really, really serious problems. So the only thing you could do was to play and to really piss them off by winning it. So just as we didn't win many leagues, we did win cups. It was their cup; it was his cup; and we went there to *joderlos*, to screw them over, really piss them off. We won something like five cups in that era [of the dictatorship] and only one league. Why? Because it's a short competition, there was no time to manipulate it and there were direct clashes. In the league, there were more problems, more 'opportunities' for them; in the cup they didn't have time to react.

⇔ *So how do you explain the 1973-74 league title?*

They didn't have time to react then either. We were a long way in front before they realised. The change in footballing terms was radical. That was the start of the current Barcelona: there was far less space between players, we played higher up, we moved better. It was a revolution and no one was ready for it. Back then, football was, "Right, let's go, run, jump, fight…" We said, "No, we have to play better." Other teams didn't know how to handle it. It changed our mentality too.

⇔ *Cruyff only won one league as a player; he then returned and won it all as coach. But the internal battles continued, even though both those eras were heralded as blowing away the fatalism. One of the problems was what*

he called the "entorno", the political and social 'noise' that surrounded the club. And in a sense, he became the entorno. After him came Bobby Robson, whose problem was that he wasn't Cruyff…

Exactly. Robson was not treated at all well, not at all. As always happens here, there were people who wanted to support Bobby and people who didn't. His style was a bit more direct but it's not just that. There was debate. He won everything except the league but people still weren't happy. I say, "Coño, weren't you a Barcelona fan? Don't you want to win?" Yes, but… there were so many wars.

⇔ *Why? Why are there so many wars at Barcelona… and so few at Madrid?*

Like I said, centralism was not always the problem; the problem was, and is, the Catalans themselves. Real Madrid is not so political; Barcelona is a more democratic club. But that means more voices, more discussion, more arguments.

Jorge Valdano

⇔ *How would you define Madrid versus Barcelona?*

As a club versus more than a club. Real Madrid is a club that has defined its social relevance through its results. Its history and identity has been constructed through what it did on the pitch. Madrid had the enormous fortune to find in Santiago Bernabéu a man who was ahead of his time and took truly historic risks. In a depressed Spain where there was virtually no cement, he built a stadium for 120,000 people and to fill it he seduced the brightest stars in history. That's where Madrid's myth and legend begins. Madrid is as great as the number of titles it has won and the number of stars it has been able to make part of its history. Barcelona's identity is, at least in part, about the size of its rival, a rival that to them represents centralised power. That gives Barcelona a dimension that is not just sport but politics, as well as a tremendous social power.

⇨ *Does Real Madrid lack that social power?*

Madrid starts and ends with football, even if over the years it has cultivated a hatred of its rivals...

⇨ *But Madrid has shaped society too, hasn't it? Particularly during the Franco régime.*

Definitely. It projected the idea of Spain towards a world that had no consideration for the country and hated Franco unconditionally. A country that was poor and had no real cultural relevance beyond Picasso and Dalí, found a club that had reached a level of excellence so great that it conquered the world. That changed Spain.

⇨ *But which Spain? Did Real Madrid help make Franco's Spain accepted?*

The notion of Madrid as Franco's club is entirely unfair. And it only takes two broad brushstrokes to make the point. One: from the moment that Franco arrived in power, it took 14 years for Madrid to win their first title. Those were the harshest years of the dictatorship. And two: Real Madrid forged its legend in Europe where Franco was nobody.

It's an absurd argument but it is true that the régime took advantage of the social power and the reach of Real Madrid to use it as a kind of unofficial embassy.

⇨ *Is it hard for you, known to be left-wing, to be associated with a club that is constantly identified with Franco and often considered a right-wing club?*

I know lots of left-wing people who'd do anything for Real Madrid. There is a label that persists and Real Madrid have never really made any kind of effort to contradict that prejudice. During the centenary I sponsored a book of short stories written by left-wing writers who were all Madrid fans. It was a way of showing that behind Madrid lay a progressive tradition just like at Barcelona.

⇨ *Why have Madrid not created more of a 'narrative' then?*

There's a rule as old as football itself: he who wins, celebrates; he who loses, seeks excuses. For years Madrid were hegemonic and Barcelona created a discourse that rebelled against Madrid's almost absolute power. For Catalans, Madrid always represented centralism if only because it was in the capital. Madrid was the parasite, the heart of the state, the periphery tends to see it as a place that lived off the richness of others. For Madrid, that doesn't exist: wherever there is football, there is Madrid. It is more than a club too, but not because it represents something politically tangible. Madrid is synonymous with grandiosity.

⇨ *Do contrasting identities and that political element ensure that the rivalry remains fierce? Has it got worse?*

There is always latent violence that if we are not capable of controlling it will overflow very easily. Sometimes, it's called Gaspart, Figo or Mourinho but any flammable element sets it off again. Football is an emotional territory and when Real Madrid and Barcelona play it becomes even more agitated. Some people are more comfortable at war than in peace but personally it makes me uneasy because the footballing rivalry is so great that I don't think it needs other elements. All those elements end up being an attack upon the strictly footballing side of the rivalry. And right now the footballing rivalry is so, so exciting… Now that Barcelona have the best player in the world and Madrid have the best player in the world, I don't see the need to focus on the rest of it.

✧ *But that's inevitable… this is a rivalry that can't be understood without it. Besides, people like the conflict; the media in Spain lives off it.*

Yes. We have partisan, arbitrary media who have their own interests and it's always hard to go against those business interests. This is a capitalist society where the market dominates everything, even culture. Football cannot escape that dynamic. Newspapers have to survive and to do that they have to make their clientele happy. But the more emotional the approach, the further away it gets from an objective position. We have entered into a dialogue of the deaf, more and more extreme and it's hard to come back from those extremes once you have got there. People end up focussing on their obsessions. We've reached a ridiculous point; we appear to be in a position, not [just] in which you are obliged to talk highly of Madrid but in which talking highly of Messi appears to be an act of treachery against the fatherland. Yet, not recognising the excellence of your opponent is a way of not believing in your own excellence.

✧ *So the two clubs need each other? They drive each other on…*

Like cathedrals in the Middle Ages; you compete with the nearest town. The size of their tower makes yours bigger and so on. The fight, the rivalry, has created a footballing supremacy with Madrid and Barcelona that leaves much of Europe behind.

✧ *Barcelona have often been accused of being obsessed by Madrid, but Madrid like to claim they do not care about Barcelona. Yet, recently some would argue that they have adopted a victim complex of their own and used similar arguments to those Barcelona traditionally used. Refereeing conspiracies, especially…*

In the last few years it is undeniable that Barcelona have become one of the best teams in history. It is stupid to deny that. But by trying to diminish Barcelona's success by talking about blaming referees or the Federación only makes you look small. Anything that Madrid does that is not based on that conviction of its own greatness fits very uneasily. From a strategic point of view, it's terrible. When you do that, it makes you similar to Barcelona 20 or 30 years ago; that's a huge error. Besides which, it's false.

✧ *So, why, then?*

The need to win is always there and that makes you lose sight of your values.

The need to win has driven some clubs to economic collapse, for example. It's a reflection of the values that society celebrates now: the winner is all, the loser is nothing. And if it's Real Madrid you're talking about, a club whose history obliges it to win everything, anything other than victory destabilises you. The balance at Madrid is precarious because you're never good enough. Never. It's very, very easy to not be worthy of Madrid. One bad word, one bad result... But we have lost perspective: Madrid have won 32 league titles, not 100, but they're still the greatest club in the twentieth century. It's as if you're not allowed to fail to win a single cup. But Madrid went 32 years without winning the European Cup and that didn't stop them being the biggest club in the world. When you are the biggest club in the world, you have to calm down but the sense of immediacy confuses everything.

⬦ *There's an assumption that the identities of the two clubs are entrenched, but you played in Real Madrid's* Quinta del Buitre *side that not only won five leagues in a row between 1985 and 1990 but represented the post-Franco era and played a technical style that could be considered a forerunner of the current Barcelona philosophy...*

Yes, Barcelona's project is more planned while Madrid's happened more spontaneously but the similarities are there. That team was a group of well-mannered kids who took football into another dimension. Bit by bit they changed the status of football and footballers. They were local, they came through the youth system, and the identification with them was enormous. They changed the style of the game:

until then football had been all about aggression, fight; they were creative, they satisfied your emotions. The [Barcelona] Dream Team was counter-cultural. It was not so much a group of footballers; 'Dream Team' defines an idea that generated fascination and created a school, an idea that would last 20 years. But the *Quinta* had started to change things before and I could see that they could benefit football in general. The moment mattered too: they were the sporting arm of the *transición* to democracy.

⬦ *That is one of the emblematic Madrid teams, perhaps only behind the side led by Alfredo Di Stéfano. There was something missing, though: the European Cup, and that defines the club.*

Spain ended up being too small for that side so it went into Europe, but there they had the misfortune to come across Arrigo Sacchi's Milan — a team that seemed unbeatable and revolutionised football. Psychologically, that Milan team hurt the *Quinta* so much as to make them disappear; Milan killed them. That was one of the great Madrid teams but that generation never set foot on the summit and at Real Madrid the European Cup is the only true summit.

⬦ *One man who did win it was Raúl; you gave him his debut as manager. He was recently handed a homage at the Bernabéu but when he first left, it was surprisingly low-key: there was no testimonial, no pomp or ceremony.*

Raúl is synonymous with Real Madrid. He is the face of Madrid for the last 25 years. It was all about competing: quantity over quality, professionalism, absolute commitment. If you had to write a list of the values of Real Madrid, you'd say: is that list Madrid or Raúl? He's the Di Stéfano of our time. His departure was not as it should have been. He was there, but the people weren't. And Raúl is the people; it is the people who consecrate him as the incarnation of the club. He offered mass, but the faithful weren't there. But in any case, Raúl left a mark so deep that he will always be there. Spiritually, he will always be at the club.

⇨ *You say Raúl represents Madrid's values. You were sporting director during the* galáctico *era, an era that* *appeared to celebrate something different. Why did it go wrong?*

The first six months under Queiroz were superb, some of the best football we had seen, but then we collapsed. We didn't abide by the traditional rules of football and football cornered us and stabbed us for it.

These are extracts from interviews conducted in the preparation of Fear and Loathing in La Liga: Madrid versus Barcelona (Yellow Jersey).

Gamechanger

Johan Cruyff on his role in creating the style of Barcelona and modern football

By Miguel Delaney

Back in 1994, when Johan Cruyff was overseeing one of the most admired sides in world football, the then Barcelona coach was asked by ESPN whom he saw as the world's best player. "The best player of the world does not exist," Cruyff responded, in that way that at first seemed argumentative but soon simply revealed an alternative way of looking at an issue. "You can say, OK, a series existed, whether you take [Franz] Beckenbauer, [Alfredo] Di Stéfano, [Diego] Maradona or Pelé, you say 'those ones had so many various qualities, they belong to the class 'exclusive elite'. That is a possibility."

There is no doubting, of course, that Cruyff belongs to that elite. His view on it, however, reflects the fact that he was so much more — if it doesn't sound absurd — than one of the greatest players of all time. Cruyff essentially is to football what David Bowie is to modern music. If some of his counterparts are more celebrated, the innovative mindset that underscored his magnificent talent has made him arguably the most influential figure in the history of his field.

It was the approach Cruyff helped create at Ajax in the early 70s that transformed football, the structure he put in place at Barcelona that is now seen as an ideal to be replicated around the world, and all while

he himself has evolved as a figurehead for one of the sport's defining philosophies.

The way he thinks remains almost as fascinating as the way he played. When asked about specifics of his career, Cruyff provided answers that almost always developed into something conceptual, more lasting. His catalogue of quotes has become legendary in its own right and he seems to build to single-line mantras about how to approach the game, some of them elusively paradoxical.

On the day of this interview with the *Blizzard*, one of the greatest exponents of a team sport was enjoying — or, as he jokingly puts it, enduring — a round at an individual sport. Cruyff was at St Andrew's in Scotland for the Alfred Dunhill Links Championship, where he was in a group with Ruud Gullit. The 66 year old loves the area and the tournament, which he endeavours to make every year, using it to promote his charity: the Cruyff Foundation. Even a discussion of the organisation's aims, which are to improve the lives of all through sport, evolve into something deeper. Cruyff's description sounds markedly similar to Bill Shankly's famous quotes about football being a form of socialism.

"What is sport, besides the physical education you do for yourself? It's playing together, trying things out, getting better every day, winning together, losing together, helping somebody out. It's life. It's totally life, 100%."

⬧ *Can a team game like football take much from an individual sport like golf?*

You can always learn from other people. A lot of times we stick in the things that we do. If we say the difference between football and golf, in a golf professional he's got a coach for driving, a coach for putting. In football we've got one coach for 15 people, which is absurd.

And you say, "Yes, but in golf you need a drive, you need this." Yes, but in football you need your left foot, your right foot, to pass it, to control it, to control it with your chest, you need to see 10 other people what they are doing so there are a lot of things involved. That's why you should change a lot of things.

⬧ *Do you think golf is more advanced, then?*

No, a lot of individual sports are advanced, because, if you just take people in tennis, what kind of vitamins they need, everybody's different. In Holland, in football, everybody has the same bottle of water but we're all different.

⬧ *That's interesting, though, because one of the fundamentals of your Ajax team — the Total Football under Rinus Michels — was incorporating individual ability into a collective.*

It was a conscious [decision], because the individual is the quality. You need the mentality to put it into the team. Everybody's different, everybody has a different quality, but you should have the same mentality. It means you've got to put your quality into the value of the team itself because, in the end, the best player will never come out of a team that loses too much. It's impossible.

That's what I'm trying to explain... Read the paper and [a club] are looking at three different players for one position and you say, "How can you look at these three? You can look at these three, or these three, but you can never look at these three." It's impossible. What are you looking for? Somebody who's called defender or a type of defender?

It's a big difference, such a big difference. A lot of times people don't see the quality of the individual, and this individual should function well in the team and the way the team plays.

There are too many different things in football. People who are buying, people who are selling or people accepting to go one place or another — it's not like that. It's what the team needs. It's absurd.

⬧ *What do you think the root of Ajax's innovation was?*

We had the typical mentality for that because the Dutch people have been everywhere: from Japan to Indonesia to New York — which was New Amsterdam — to Cape Town. It's a country which is so [small] so it's in their character to try new things and to have a look whatever happens wherever. That's what they did. Maybe sometimes it's sport, sometimes it's business, but the same thing we see in skating, the same thing we see in hockey, the same thing we see in baseball. How can a team like Holland in baseball — against Japan and the United States — two years ago win the championship? I mean, it's there. Try new things. Maybe 10 years you don't hear anything because there are not that many people, but they are capable.

It's a country where everybody talks, everybody thinks, everybody's got their own mentality... and that's why they've been everywhere. It's a good quality, but at the same time it's their worst quality.

✦ *Is it true Michels took the idea of pressing from basketball?*

No, I don't know. As far as I remember, it didn't come from there because we started it in the 60s... We said, "OK, where are the best players?" "There." Technically, yeah, in the positions very good but also with the ball — so attack them there. What's the difference between a good player and bad player? It's the speed of [control], so if you've got to speed them up, it's to provoke mistakes. And the main thing is that the quicker you can change your mentality, offensive [to] defensive, the first defender is the centre-forward. He's the nearest by, so the quickest he can put the pressure on, start defending.

And you run less. You don't run more. You run less... of course, you've got to do possession. It's a way of thinking and it's the way you can re-organise the whole thing. Because, who's got the ball, who scores the goal?

✦ *Barcelona took that Ajax approach to new levels, and it influenced Spain and now Bayern Munich. Do you think*

football has ever, or will ever, find a better approach?

Well, I don't think so. I think the way Barcelona played, it's a pleasure for everybody who likes football, because the technical quality is the highest standard and every little child can try to do the technical qualities. It's not like somebody runs 100 yards in nine seconds [and] if you can't do it, you don't count. You always count because you always can get better. If you want to play basketball you've got to be two metres. Otherwise you can't play. Here, everyone can play and everyone can develop. That's the nicest thing about the game of football.

The main thing is, a lot of people think that making a mistake is a problem. No, I don't think so. Making a mistake is to make you better, as long you learn from your mistake. So I think making a mistake for me is never a problem. It's a perfect thing, as long as you learn from it and don't make the same mistake again. The only way you can learn is from your mistakes. You can never learn from the things you did well. It's impossible.

That's what we learned [at Ajax]. You tried something, that didn't work for that [reason] and that. Do it again. Do something different.

Football is a game of mistakes and, if you analyse a mistake, you can say OK. If I put somebody where the mistakes come from, with his quality, you're going to make fewer mistakes and if you make fewer mistakes you've got more possibilities.

So it's a different way of thinking. It's not like we think this pass is good or bad. If this was the best pass why didn't he do it? Did he see or didn't he see it or wasn't he capable of executing it.

So it's not a lot of times that you're going to discuss or analyse what he did. Most of the time you've got to analyse why he didn't do the other thing.

That's where it all starts, how you see the game totally differently. If you analyse it, you can train it on it.

If it doesn't go well, you've got to change. If it does go well, don't change, just make the weak things. It's a different approach.

⇨ *Has anyone impressed you as much as Pep Guardiola's Barcelona then?*

You can't say this or that, or this is better than that. You've all kinds of different players. A lot of people make comparisons between [Leo] Messi and [Cristiano] Ronaldo. They're completely different. You can't compare them. They're both great in the things they do, and they're different. So you can't say who's better. You can say who do you prefer as a way of playing. Do you prefer a [more] technical one or you prefer somebody who is technical, who is physical and who can shoot very high? It's totally different and that's why it's so good that the differences are there because you can see that a lot of people make a wrong decision in choosing the team where they go. It's if the team fits with the quality you have.

[Football] has always been narrow-minded because we say, "He's a football player," but in baseball we say he's a pitcher, he's a catcher, he's a third baseman... but why is he a footballer? It's all different. But, as a coach to direct a team, you've got to look at the individual qualities. That's why I see the game totally differently.

⇨ *You played a part in starting that at Barcelona.*

When I came in, they were bad. We had to change. There was no sense to continue something that goes wrong.

I had a big advantage that I played there [from 1973 to 1978]. You know the mentality, you know what they do, what they think, so it was quite easy to make some rules.

The players were there, they were good players. You had to put in some character. We brought some players from the Basque country that you know for sure will give it. So it's a question of compensation in the things you need.

⇨ *You've now also been involved in a similar transformation at Ajax, where you say it's taken from the Bayern Munich ideal?*

Their organisation was based on football up. That's what we did now. We copied that. The well-educated ex-players should be the decision-makers within a football club. Not somebody who is a great businessman in whatever, and he makes the football decisions. This is absurd.

A lot of clubs don't do this. At Ajax, we did it. OK, the results are not there in one day, which is normal. It's a totally different approach in all these details and, in Ajax, we changed all of them and I think the result will come.

⬦ *Given the modern game's economics, do you really think that can mean returning to the heights of the past?*

Yes, we are convinced. We are all convinced. Everybody who's there, and all the great players Ajax ever had, they are there now, so we think we can do it. The future will tell us. 🅑

An Honourable Man

How Vicente del Bosque overcame rejection by Real Madrid to lead Spain to glory

By Graham Hunter

Around 60 minutes before the Euro 2012 final, Vicente del Bosque takes out his mobile phone and begins to tap out a text message in that old-fashioned style: phone held flat in the left hand, right index finger jabbing away. His fingers are those of a working man and the keys are small and fidgety at a time when tension is rife and history is beckoning. But he has something on his mind. With music blaring out in the dressing-room to dissipate nerves — "In my day the trainer asked for silence but now you should hear the 'music' they play before a match. God wouldn't listen to it." — Del Bosque is overcome by thoughts of how it all began and the people to whom he owes a debt. How a 17-year-old boy so tall and thin that he was nicknamed *Palillo* (toothpick) was spotted in the beautiful city of Salamanca and propelled to fame and greatness; and Antonio Martín, or Toñete as he is normally known, the man he has to thank for his career. The last thing the coach of Spain does before his team becomes the first to win three successive continental and world titles, is to send a little gesture of thanks and friendship to the scout who set the whole story in motion 44 years earlier.

TOÑETE: This will get me emotional just thinking about it. We exchanged text messages all the way through the World Cup, but I got this one just when I knew he should be in the dressing-room and getting prepared for the final against Italy. He wanted to thank me for everything. His message really only expressed his gratitude for bringing him to Madrid and starting all this off. I thought to myself, "How has this man got time to think of me when he is about to coach Spain to history against Italy?" And he did it again before the Confederations Cup final, too! He has a heart that's too big for his body. He is extraordinary. Being friends with Del Bosque, having taken him to start his career at Madrid, these things are far, far bigger than winning the lottery for me.

It was a typical gesture from a man whose nobility has always shone through, since long before King Juan Carlos made him the first Marquis Del Bosque in February 2011. Friendship, respect, honour, dignity — these concepts matter much more to Del Bosque than victory, fame or wealth. He wants to win — from time to time he will make hard-nosed decisions and not flinch. However, if working in football were to rob him of some of those base values, he would quit in an instant.

What Del Bosque was taught by his parents and by growing up in Salamanca in Spain's impoverished 1950s have been fundamental to what he has achieved and how he has done it. "I suppose everything I am today is a product of that childhood," he said. When Spain lost their opening match of World Cup 2010, unleashing a hurricane of criticism which would have overwhelmed lesser managers; when the *Clásico*-war in 2011-12 threatened to ruin all he had built with *La Roja*, Del Bosque's equanimity, class, compassion and calm led him through the tests.

He was badly wounded when Madrid dumped him in 2003 after 35 years of excellent service as player and coach, but he has yet to hit back in the media, yet to vent any of his pain and anger. That's not his way. The most pungent thing he has ever said in public is, "Had they not removed me like that I am certain my team was equipped to carry on winning."

When his much-loved son, Álvaro, was beseeching him to re-instate Raúl and take his former Real Madrid striker to World Cup 2010, Del Bosque both appeased the lad and, elegantly, handled the growing public questions about a recall so that Raúl, scarred by his defenestration under Luis Aragonés, suffered no further damage.

Football is fortunate that this gentle, interesting and humorous man exists at all. All it would have taken is one capricious moment from a fascist dictator or his secret police and Del Bosque would not have been born. When he was still in primary school, young Vicente discovered his father Fermín was a radical and committed fighter against the exploitation of working men and women. It transpired, to his sons' great surprise, that the stern and disciplined man who came to watch Del Bosque striding through youth-team games but who never commented on his boy's football development was also a genuine rebel. The Del Bosque home in Salamanca was a hiding place and distribution point for literature preaching democracy, workers' rights and the basic freedoms taken for granted around most of the rest of Europe. These were actions which could have resulted in the disappearance of Del Bosque's father under the oppressive dictatorship that ruled Spain.

Until his death in 1975, Francisco Franco's regime did not allow the vote, abhorred liberal or left-wing thinking and repressed expressions of distinct cultural identity — particularly among Basques and Catalans — and tried to seal off Spain from the values and ideas of Western Europe. Opponents betrayed by friends and neighbours, with or without justification, were often jailed and tortured.

It was at this stage of their development his two sons learned that during the Spanish Civil War (1936-1939), just over a decade before Vicente was born, Fermín del Bosque had been denounced by a neighbour, arrested without trial and held in a prison camp for three years.

During Franco's rise to dictatorship, partially backed by Nazi Germany, there was bloody slaughter throughout Spain. There was also poverty, starvation and disease. Hundreds of thousands died, some of those in concentration camps and prisons, due to torture and execution. Had Fermín been murdered, worked, or starved to death, this was a time when there would have been few questions and certainly no call for justice.

VICENTE DEL BOSQUE: *My dad was what we called a progresista and his imprisonment during the war was because of that. When I was about 11 or 12 I discovered that he was involved in receiving and storing propaganda leaflets. It was pretty explosive stuff. The atmosphere at home would be very tense at times like that. He listened to underground radio stations like La Pirenaica (a station funded by the Communist Party which broadcast independent news and thoughts during Franco's reign, from Bashkortostan and then Bucharest) and Radio Paris. You have to remember the reality of the situation — we were living in poverty, unable to voice any kind of protest. Today I have plenty of right-wing friends because there is much more tolerance now. We have no problem in engaging in honest dialogue — that would have been impossible in those days. My father was overly responsible, fair and straightforward, to a degree that I'd say was noble. He was a man of good ideas, but too radical on many issues. His generation had to suffer a lot, to live through a war and then suffer the cruel post-war period. It was in the kitchen that, gradually, he told us about his experiences — things which had marked him. He was a righteous man.*

It was a childhood of good upbringing but next to no money and certainly no frills. Typical of many great football stories, the young Vicente del Bosque traipsed around after his much-loved big brother, also named Fermín, kicking a ball through the streets, playing until dark and being told to go in goal because he was the smallest of the litter. In the very early part of Del Bosque's life, Spain's football landscape, too, was radically different from that of today. Athletic Club, Atlético Madrid and Barcelona were the predominant forces. Madrid was a club whose important executives had been decimated by the war (either because of the vagaries of conflict or because they were anti-Franco) and which was re-building, slowly, under Don Santiago Bernabéu. Only once President Bernabéu began signing, or developing, superstars like Alfredo di Stéfano, Paco Gento, Ferenc Puskás, Luis Molowny, José Santamaría, Raymond Kopa, Amancio and Ignacio Zoco did Spain, and Europe, fall under Madrid's thrall. The exponential factor in Madrid's favour is that this football explosion coincided with televisions appearing in some shop windows — ragged-trousered urchins would gather in front of them and Del Bosque and his gang became captivated by the first *Galáctico* era.

The family was too poor for Vicente and Fermín even to attend the Salamanca matches their father went to. The boys would sneak in when the gates were opened with 10 minutes left. A trip to watch Madrid, Barcelona or Athletic play was out of the question. Then grainy black-and-white images suddenly showed men in all-white kits dancing round tackles, conquering first Spain and then Europe. Di Stéfano, Gento and Kopa had Del Bosque hooked.

The majority of those who admire his work as a coach have not seen Del Bosque play. His 400-plus games in that famous white shirt were not as widely televised or recorded as those of the players he managed at Madrid: Raúl, Ronaldo, Guti and Zidane. Del Bosque was a footballer of fine technical skills, good aerial ability and a knack of knowing when to hit the penalty box and either score or give an assist. Tall, elegant, not blessed with pace, his calm understanding of what to do made it seem like he was never hurried and the ball was his friend. He played like Trevor Brooking, the England international of the 1970s and early 80s; for a modern reference point, think of a cross between Sergio Busquets and Guti.

Toñete was trusted by Madrid and was to help discover a handful of players who would etch their names in the club's history. He worked to the rules of a manual put together by the head of *fútbol base* (youth development) at Madrid. The single most important criterion read: "Remember to distinguish between a good player and one who is right for Real Madrid."

It was an era when their six European Cup victories in 13 years made it feel that the next one was just around the corner — not, as it actually transpired, 30 agonising years away. In fact, Toñete was actually gifting Real Madrid the man who would coach them to two of their next three European Cup wins.

Fermín del Bosque, on finally handing his son over to Madrid and heading back to Salamanca, had an expression on his face as if "his soul was broken". This man who had been imprisoned for his liberal beliefs, taken massive risks to advocate democracy and socialist ideals, was giving his son to a club governed autocratically by a right-wing authority hate-figure who, even before the Spanish Civil War, had been a member of the *Juventud Acción Popular*, described by Sid Lowe in his book *Catholicism, War and the Foundation of Francoism* as

"uniformed, paramilitary" quasi-fascists. Madrid's all-powerful president, Santiago Bernabéu, also fought for Franco's forces during the war under the orders of General Augustín Muñoz Grandes, who would go on to head Hitler's infamous Blue Division in Russia during World War Two. Young Del Bosque was going to work for a man who had opposed and taken up arms against everything that his father stood for.

In the radical summer of 1968, when the Prague Spring caused a Warsaw Pact invasion of Czechoslovakia, when liberals and anarchists on the streets of Paris nearly brought revolution to France, when civil rights protests in America and Belfast brought riots and retribution, in this most volatile and febrile of moments in modern European history, a young man whose father had been put in a prison camp under Franco joined perhaps the most conservative of all football clubs, Real Madrid Club de Fútbol.

It was a pivotal moment. For all his principles had cost him and the risks they still carried, Fermín del Bosque wanted his family to be tolerant and democratic and now he put those ideas into practice. 44 years later, the deft negotiations to bring peace to feuding Barcelona and Madrid players which helped Vicente del Bosque's side make history at Euro 2012 did not simply come from the pages of a management manual. The values he was raised to hold made him the man for those times.

Del Bosque also inherited his father's determination to fight for what is right. While a Madrid player, he was a founder member of AFE, the Spanish footballer's union. AFE was established in 1978 and it was deeply controversial when, as membership grew, there were strikes and a Bosman-style battle against clubs who could retain a contracted player for his entire career. Joining a union at that stage was at very least a minor threat to your continued employment, most particularly at Real Madrid.

Ángel, a former Madrid teammate, remembers the climate: "It wasn't easy to play for Real Madrid and be a member of a union, but we joined up. Not for ourselves, because we were comfortably off, but for the penniless guys who spent their nights in sleeping bags during or after their careers. We were demanding the introduction of a form of social security."

Between 1968 and 1984, when he retired, Del Bosque won La Liga five times and the Copa Del Rey on four occasions. He played with some all-time legends of *Los Blancos* — José Antonio Camacho, Santillana, Juanito, Paul Breitner, Uli Stieleke, Günter Netzer. Some may have endured longer, but in his prime none of them outranked him. He played against Johan Cruyff, Diego Maradona, Luis Aragonés, Franz Beckenbauer, Jupp Heynckes, Uli Hoeneß, Kevin Keegan, Graeme Souness, Gerd Müller, Johan Neeskens, Zico, Kenny Dalglish, Allan Simonsen, Hugo Sánchez, and Mario Kempes. In his time he was coached by Miguel Muñoz, Luis Molowny, and Alfrédo di Stefano — five-star legends. He had direct professional experience of the majority of the most important football figures across four decades.

His playing career, however, was scarred by one major flaw: Madrid simply could not win *La Séptima*. After six European

Cup victories in the 1950s and 1960s, there was first an assumption that Madrid would continue to lift the trophy, then anxiety about when it would happen again and finally a deep obsession. Across the four decades when Madrid sought *La Séptima* there were some epic, thunderous attempts. Del Bosque was part of many of them, as player and coach.

The first time I saw him play was in November 1975, when Derby drew Real Madrid in the second round of the European Cup. Both legs ended 4-1 to the home team, but during extra time in the return at the Santiago Bernabéu, Del Bosque flicked the ball to Santillana who lobbed it up over his marker and volleyed home in the style of Paul Gascoigne's famous goal for England against Scotland at Euro '96. Two thundering ties to make you love football for the rest of your life: 6-5 to Del Bosque's side — but still not enough to drive them past Bayern Munich in the semi-final.

By the 1979-80 season, the European Cup was once again singing its siren song to Del Bosque and Madrid — the Santiago Bernabéu stadium was going to host the final. Billy McNeill's Celtic threatened to end the dream in the quarter-finals, but the tie became a testimony to the fact that Del Bosque, now ageing, remained a wonderful footballer.

Celtic won the first leg 2-0 in front of one of those fevered Celtic Park audiences which make such nights gargantuan.

In the Spanish capital, it was bedlam and the second leg became another in a series of what are called *Los Remontadas Históricas de Madrid* — Real Madrid's historic fightbacks. Black market ticket-touts were arrested the day before the game in possession of 700,000 pesetas from a mixture of stolen and fake tickets; more than 100,000 fans crammed into the historic stadium which at the time had fences and a small ash track around the pitch. Madrid's coffers benefitted to the tune of 60 million pesetas.

Pumped up, Del Bosque broke from the halfway line and started sprinting towards Peter Latchford's goal even before Károly Palotai had blown for kick-off as Real Madrid, in the very first seconds, tried for the long ball to the tall man for the knockdown. Del Bosque's nice exchange of passes with Laurie Cunningham led to the crucial second Madrid goal, when Santillana headed down the Englishman's cross for Uli Stielike to score. Then, with four minutes left, Ángel crossed for Juanito to put the Scottish club out. The Celtic boss McNeill was incensed by refereeing decisions he blamed for the defeat. Despite that ire, his admiration for one player was undimmed. "Once again Del Bosque stood out," McNeill said. "I admired his performance against us just as in the first leg. He is one of the best players I have ever seen."

Davie Provan, a winger of the highest quality and today an eloquent and incisive football analyst on Sky Sports, recalled the performance of Madrid's No.6 over those two matches.

DAVIE PROVAN: *Back then there was very little European football on the television. It was our first experience of seeing many of the Real Madrid players, but Del Bosque had featured in big Billy's pre-match briefing. What often wrong-footed teams coming to play us then,*

and still does today, was the tempo — it was frenzied. That night we were so up for it, but I remember Del Bosque bringing the ball down and walking with it. Walking! That was his message to the rest of the Madrid team: We dictate the pace, not Celtic. His managerial career has been so good, so successful, that it has overshadowed what a fantastic player he was. His self-assurance then, and now as a manager, comes from class — real quality.

By the second leg of the semi-final in 1980, it seemed that Madrid were heading for the final and a chance to lift 'their' trophy in their stadium. Kevin Keegan's Hamburg, also featuring Felix Magath and Horst Hrubesch, had been beaten 2-0 in Madrid, but the night of 23 April 1980, at the Volksparkstadion, became perhaps the single most painful night of Del Bosque's playing career.

Madrid were two down and thus level on aggregate after just 17 minutes; Laurie Cunningham scored an away goal which meant Hamburg required two more to advance, but the Germans produced both within the space of five horrible minutes before half-time. Worse, Del Bosque was sent off with six minutes left, before Caspar Memering made it 5-1 to Hamburg. The red card came when, in an extraordinary moment for a man so placid and self-controlled, he took a swipe at Kevin Keegan with the intention of clipping him round the head. There is an emotive picture of him, a blanket over his shoulders, sitting on a kit box on the edge of the running track at the Volksparkstadion with the massive electronic scoreboard looming over the back of his head, showing the score of 4-1: elimination, humiliation, shame.

He had three more seasons to come, but this was the beginning of the winter years for Del Bosque, the footballer, at Madrid. Due to injury and new signings, the next season he played only a moderate role as the Spanish champions advanced to the quarter-final, against Spartak Moscow. He got a testimonial five minutes in the Soviet capital during a 0-0 draw and then the first half of what became a 2-0 home win. The nervous Bernabéu were not generous with their former hero. He departed at half-time.

In *El País* the match reporter, Julian García Cancau, wrote, "The Bernabéu fans are going to push Del Bosque out long before his time. They have converted him into the scapegoat every single time the team around him is not functioning well."

DEL BOSQUE [1981]: Fans need to realise that if I am on the ball so much it is because I have run sufficiently to get free of my marker. But I am tall, I am easy to spot and I appear slow. Moreover, I prefer to play football, not just to get the ball forward at the first opportunity. I try to wait for, or to create, the best opportunity for the right pass. I have been around for many years and I guess the fans tire of you, but that will change back. Passion for a player comes and goes with the Spanish public. Today they are on your back, tomorrow they glorify you again.

When Sergio Busquets, playing in a similar position to Del Bosque 30 years later, was hung out to dry following Spain's defeat by Switzerland in the World Cup, the coach's experience allowed him to empathise with his player and ignore the white noise which came after that upset. Busquets, like

Del Bosque, does work which is far easier to appreciate when you are the recipient of his support rather than the beholder. In the qualifying series before the 2014 World Cup Xavi, still the brain of Del Bosque's Spain, is losing pace and athleticism with age. The fact that he has a coach with a personal understanding of the process should help manage a great player and a delicate situation.

The European Cup final of 1981 was Del Bosque's first and last as a player. Sadly it was a drab affair, notable, unless you were a Scouser, mainly for its stats — Bob Paisley became the first man to win the trophy three times; it was the fifth consecutive victory by English clubs and Liverpool's third trophy. Alan Kennedy's goal with eight minutes remaining ensured Del Bosque left Paris without conquering Europe. For the meantime, at least.

One of Liverpool's key players that night told me what facing Del Bosque's Madrid had meant to them.

GRAEME SOUNESS: I looked back at that final a couple of months ago because Jamie Redknapp rang me to tell me it was on television. I realised, watching it after such a long time, that for players like Del Bosque in midfield we must have been a nightmare to play against because we were already putting into practice many of the things which are in vogue now: pressing all over the pitch, full-backs pushed high up their touchline so that I stayed sitting in front of the two centre-backs protecting them. I see much of that as central to the success of Barcelona and Spain nowadays.

Those who criticise Spain for their manner of winning now know nothing

about football. We were hugely successful at Liverpool and we were taught, from day one, to keep the ball. Don't try a pass through the eye of a needle; win the ball, circulate it, start again and again if you have to, but seek the right opportunity. Again, that's what Spain do excellently today. I'd put Del Bosque's Spain side up with Brazil of 1970, no question. Del Bosque has been a part of a change in the essence of Spanish football. In my day, and Del Bosque's, Spanish football was full of stuff you hated — dirty tricks, kicks and shirt pulling. Cynical and horrible. Now it's about quality, control, technique and winning and it's the most attractive stuff around. That's a remarkable change and they have a good man in charge.

Despite being plagued by injuries, Del Bosque had chances to augment his collection of silverware in his penultimate season — and to add a European trophy. However, this was to become known as *La temporada de cinco copas perdidas* (the season of five lost cups) — both a nod in the direction of Barça's famous *temporada de cinco copas* (in 1951-52) and an acknowledgement that Real Madrid in 1982-83 lost five 'finals'.

Madrid went into the final day of the la Liga season with the expectation of lifting the title, but were defeated 1-0 at the Mestalla by Valencia as Javier Clemente's powerful Athletic Bilbao won in Las Palmas to take the championship. Del Bosque did not play in either the Copa del Rey final defeat by Diego Maradona's Barcelona or the Supercopa finals against Real Sociedad, which Madrid lost by an aggregate of 4-1. The two-legged League Cup final was no better. Del Bosque scored in the 2-2 draw against

Barcelona at the Santiago Bernabéu but at the Camp Nou, three days later, the Catalans won 2-1. The *coup de grâce* came in Gothenburg, where Del Bosque was left out of the Real Madrid team which lost 2-1 to Alex Ferguson's Aberdeen in the European Cup Winners' Cup final.

Del Bosque's international career did not end with the number of caps his talent merited. A broken leg suffered before the 1978 World Cup denied him an opportunity to compete for a place in the Spain squad. He returned just before the tournament but László Kubala, the Spain coach, left him behind. In February 2013, a 3-1 win over Uruguay saw Del Bosque equal Kubala's record for the number of matches as Spain coach: 68. He spoke kindly about the Hungarian, but the statistics tell a story. Del Bosque's 68-game record stands at 57 wins, five draws and only six defeats with 170 goals for and 45 against. The Spain team in Del Bosque's playing era, during Kubala's 68 matches in charge, had 31 wins and 21 draws.

The 18 games Del Bosque played for his country at least brought two notable benefits. First, he shared midfield with Ángel María Villar, the man who would re-shape Spanish football as its president from 1988 until the present — and who employed Del Bosque when replacing Luis Aragonés must have seemed an invidious task. Secondly, there was Del Bosque's only international goal, which came against Cyprus in his hometown of Salamanca.

Del Bosque's last competitive match for Madrid was in the Copa in 1983, when Madrid drew Barça Athletic, now known as Barça B. The *Quinta del Buitre* (The Vulture Gang, a pun on Emilio Butragueno's name) including Manolo Sanchis, Michel, Martín Vazquez and Miguel Pardeza were pushing through from Madrid's youth ranks and Del Bosque, shrewdly went the other way. By 1984 he was preparing to coach in Castilla, Madrid's youth academy. Del Bosque had always thought about precisely how to organise a game's tempo, how to prompt and push from midfield rather than just using the ball at the first opportunity. He soon found that these were principles he could explain to others.

Del Bosque was both a linchpin in the development of some truly great in-house talent and also the only Madrid coach to make Florentino Pérez's *Galáctico* philosophy properly successful. It was not his fault that the success of the latter deeply damaged the former.

The strategy was initially called *Zidanes y Pavones*: Madrid would buy the world's No.1 superstar every year, but theoretically promote excellent home-bred players from the *cantera* too. Poor old Paco Pavón, an honest but not exceptional central defender, had the misfortune that his name was seconded to Pérez's scheme. The *Pavónes* were never given the time or encouragement to flourish.

This Bacchanalian behaviour inevitably made the club ill, but when the feast was high there was an orgy of terrific football, a sense that this was cutting-edge strategy and seemingly without horizon. However, the young seedlings from the youth system were almost immediately trampled upon. In those early, heady,

days there was no time for players such as Roberto Soldado, Juan Mata, Borja Valero, Álvaro Arbeloa, Álvaro Negredo, Juanfran and Javi García to find their feet and flourish. When the players in their way included Luís Figo, Zinédine Zidane, Ronaldo and David Beckham, that was comprehensible; by the time that became Michael Owen, Jonathan Woodgate, Carlos Diogo, Fernando Gago and Julio Baptista, far less so.

It became infamous that the *Galáctico* era, steered by Del Bosque, largely meant barren times for products of *La Fábrica* (Madrid's youth system). From the emergence of Iker Casillas from mid-1999 until Arbeloa was re-purchased from Liverpool 10 years later, no youth-team product hit the Real Madrid first team and stayed there. The last three to make it before the dawn of the *Galácticos* were Raúl, Guti and Casillas — each of whom had been significantly helped in his formative youth development by Del Bosque, while a *cantera* coach.

Presidents, first-team coaches and superstar players came and went, but Del Bosque endured in various roles, always inculcating the right values, teaching 'the Real Madrid way', making sure that footballers grew up with intelligence, technique, judgment, honesty, bravery and a will to win. Midway through the 1999-2000 season, John Toshack's Madrid lay eighth. A long, simmering tension between the manager and his president, Lorenzo Sanz — not helped by losing the Madrid *derbi* to the Atlético of Claudio Ranieri and Jimmy Floyd Hasselbaink which would end the season relegated — culminated in the Welshman's sacking. It was a time for expediency on the president's behalf. Presidential elections were just around the corner and a wealthy, politically active industrialist by the name of Florentino Pérez was beginning to make belligerent campaigning noises. Sanz imagined that it was more important to announce a star coach like Arsène Wenger or Fabio Capello in May or June, rather than try to persuade one to come midway through what appeared, to him, a doomed season. Instead, he promoted Del Bosque for the interim.

The quiet, moustachioed former midfielder very quickly confounded Sanz. So successful was he that, by May, a stellar coach was not required. From November 1999 to May 2000 lay the roots of the biggest treason committed against Del Bosque during 46 years in professional football. Despite a pair of four-goal thrashings from Bayern Munich in the group stages, Del Bosque and Toni Grande convinced their players that they could win the European Cup.

DEL BOSQUE [1999]: I want to win the players over appealing to their competitive nature, without a lot of drama or false camaraderie. The football world seems, now, to be all about image and self-publicity, very little boot room. Let's see if we can win this squad over with a little bit of the boot-room work ethic instead of showboating.

In mid-November 1999, Del Bosque put together the majority of the technical team which would be in place when Spain won the 2010 World Cup. Paco Jiménez was returned to scouting opponents and potential transfer signings. Toni Grande came up from the *cantera* as assistant coach and Javier

Miñano, previously with Madrid Castilla, became the first-team fitness coach. For several months under Toshack, the team had been operating without one.

DEL BOSQUE [1999]: This is my decision, which I think is vital, and that doesn't mean that I'm saying Toshack's methods are less viable than mine. I just believe that as we are about to turn the corner into a new decade and a new millennium it is the right time to appoint specialist and efficient collaborators and to know how to delegate.

Just before Christmas 2012, I asked Del Bosque to explain how he selected the location and training facilities for the tournaments his team won.

DEL BOSQUE: I set the parameters of exactly what I require and then the people around me in the technical team, discrete, excellent specialists, are in charge of their area. I have huge faith in them and their abilities. They handle the details of what we eat, where we live, how good the training pitch is — if I were to get involved with the doctors or the communications strategy or the training hotel then I would not be able to do my job properly. I let my specialists know what I want, they deliver and if the players are happy then they, too, will do the job I need them to do.

There are 13 years between these statements, yet they are almost identical in philosophy. Appoint excellence all around you — then delegate. Back in 1999, Del Bosque's manner, his tactical changes, his history at the club, his use of Miñano, plus the lure of another European Cup were combustible influences, as one of his players recalls.

STEVE McMANAMAN: *As a coach, he was very honest and down to earth. He showed no airs or graces. We might not have been in crisis, but we were having a difficult time so he appeared a bit sour-faced and it wasn't a laugh a minute then. But most of the time you knew exactly how he was feeling. I recently watched the comments coming out of my old club Manchester City about Roberto Mancini and how much was said behind people's backs. Well, there was none of that with Del Bosque. Everything — good or bad — was up front. He was the type of manager who didn't want to speak to his players constantly, only when he had something specific to say. Otherwise he kept with his staff. What was immediately apparent is that if we won and he was content with the form then, so long as you were fit, you would continue to play. That made people happy and motivated. It is also true that the immense sense of club history he brought with him, when he stepped up, added continuity and everyone around the club drew strength from that.*

Aside from winning big trophies, showing a tremendous aptitude for gaining an edge in knockout football, even from knowing how to man-manage a group of superstars, there was another element which clearly emerged here and which correlates directly to Del Bosque's success in charge of Spain.

Under Toshack, Madrid were conceding nearly two goals per game. From when Del Bosque took over until they won the Champions League on 24 May 2000 that dropped to less than a goal per game. Of the 38 games in La Liga and the Champions League, 14 were clean sheets. As national coach, his

team played seven knockout matches without conceding on the way to their tournament wins in 2010 and 2012.

DEL BOSQUE: *People highlight the attacking side of the game, which is fine, but if you rob the ball from the opponents 25 or 30 times in a match when they are trying to create scoring opportunities against you, that is equally valuable.*

Iker Casillas, future Spain captain, was promoted by Del Bosque to become the permanent Real Madrid No 1 in place of Albano Bizzarri. Four days after the goalkeeper's 19th birthday, he started against Valencia as Del Bosque won the first of two Champions Leagues titles as coach.

To Del Bosque's enormous embarrassment, Sanz chose to interrupt the pre-Champions League final press conference to announce that the manager would be "renewed as coach" and "would stay at Real Madrid in one capacity or another for the rest of his life".

I was there in the ridiculously ornate Trianon Palace hotel in Versailles, a haunt for Generals Eisenhower and Patton, Marlene Dietrich and Queen Elizabeth II across the years, and witnessed Del Bosque's thinly-contained anger that the press conference was hijacked by a grandstanding president. When Sanz wandered in, commandeered the stage and publicly confirmed Del Bosque's new contract, the manager feared that the focus on winning a Champions League final had been undermined.

DEL BOSQUE [2000]: *It is a personal decision that I have decided to accept the club's offer and, as such, it is private. So I have got nothing to say. The club* *judges it appropriate to announce this now, but as far as I am concerned it is a very minor subject compared to winning the final.*

Real Madrid romped it, over-running and out-thinking Valencia in a 3-0 win, the goals coming from Fernando Morientes, Steve McManaman and Raúl. A festival of Spanish noise, colour and flair in the French capital, a fiesta for Real Madrid and an eighth European Cup.

DEL BOSQUE: *This club, for its history and for its legend, always has the capacity to win the European Cup. Our cup. Football gives you second chances and this is a wonderful way to erase the memory of losing in Paris to Liverpool nearly 20 years ago.*

Just as in the aftermath of the finals of the World Cup and Euro 2012, Del Bosque was quickly absent from the dressing-room , foiling the plan of his players — later revealed by Fernando Redondo — to throw him into the Jacuzzi. This was the players' triumph and it was their moment to sing and drink and celebrate.

McMANAMAN: *It was striking how he hid away. He really didn't want any glory, especially not to get in the way of the players in the limelight. He was remarkably humble.*

And this is how Del Bosque sowed the seeds for the treachery done to him three years later. When Florentino Pérez won a substantial majority in the presidential elections two months later, the new man in charge of the club was, unexpectedly stuck with someone who was already a club legend, who had just won the *Octavo* and who was safe in a

new contract. The two men had only one thing in common: their feelings for Real Madrid. Politically, philosophically, strategically and in sporting and human terms, they were poles apart.

The uncomfortable truth for Pérez was that while the Salamancan kept winning trophies — two Spanish leagues, two Supercopas, the Intercontinental Cup and another Champions League — Del Bosque could not be sacked.

However, the division grew. There was brilliance to draw upon in the penultimate season — a 2-0 win at the Camp Nou in the *Clásico* Champions League semi-final of 2002 and then that awe-inspiring Zidane volley at Hampden to win Madrid their ninth European Cup — but it was also full of conflict. An *El País* magazine article detailing the republican, democratic and anti-Franco code by which Del Bosque's father had lived, plus the coach's own background as a union organiser, were in opposition to the politics of Pérez; Fernando Hierro became a loud voice on behalf of the players, often in opposition to diktats from the President's office.

McMANAMAN: *There wasn't player-power like you find now in England. It was a powerful voice exercised, always, for the good of the team. In England there might be one or two idiots who want to argue with the coach and do so to see what benefit they can get individually. It wasn't like that under Del Bosque. Hierro was the No. 1 man, then Sanchis, then probably Raúl, but Hierro was the player-leader on and off the pitch. He was the voice of the dressing-room and I am sure Florentino heard too much from him. The last game of the 2002-03 season was the final straw.*

There were some disputes and when the club ordered us to go to the cathedral and the town hall because the city council demanded it, but then denied permission to follow tradition and hang a Madrid scarf on the Cibeles fountain, the dressing-room decided that it was all off. The post-match celebrations on the pitch were muted, there wasn't as much of a lap of honour as expected and then chaos reigned. We had player meetings for hours on end until around 3am, when it was agreed that we wouldn't be the council's puppets just because the president ordered us to. Then, by 6am, it was all reinstated again and there were frantic text messages all around and search parties to make sure that all the players could be rounded up. It was a shambolic period and I think that might have partly dictated what happened next.

The five-minute lap of honour, Hierro's refusal to lead the players back out onto the pitch, Del Bosque's decision to allow his players freedom to make their own choices — these became reasons for the board to sack the best on-pitch leader and the most successful Madrid coach since the zenith of Puskás, Gento and Di Stefano.

The next evening his wife Trini drove Del Bosque to the Bernabéu, as she thought, for him to pick up some papers from his office and to meet with the president about renewing his contract which was to expire later that month. Halfway there, the mobile phone rang. It was Hierro. He had been kicked out of the club. No new contract, as had been promised:

"Look out, boss."

"I suspect I'm going the same way as you in a few minutes."

The coach hid his suspicion from his wife and she was as shocked as the rest of the *Madridistas* when he returned to the car having been told he was out, despite seven trophies in three and a half seasons.

DEL BOSQUE [2003]: *For about 20 days I had suspected this might be coming and I go proud of our work, our victories and in the sure knowledge that I have not committed any felony. What I and my assistants leave behind is something to feel satisfied with and now I find myself full of expectations for what lies ahead of me.*

JORGE VALDANO [sporting director, 2003]: *We simply told the squad, "Vicente won't be continuing." I know it's a decision which flies in the face of what the man in the street wants, what the dressing-room wants, but those who govern a club have to govern it.*

FLORENTINO PÉREZ [2003]: *Real Madrid needs someone with a less out-of-date training manual.*

DEL BOSQUE [2003]: *I have cried, of course I have cried — remembering the 35 years I have been with this club makes me full of emotion.*

Without Del Bosque it took Real Madrid six managers and four seasons to win anything other than a single Spanish Supercopa. Real Madrid spent seven years unable to get beyond the last 16 of the Champions League.

McMANAMAN: *If that group of Del Bosque, his staff, Hierro plus [Claude] Makélélé and Morientes, who should never have been pushed out by Pérez, had stayed together they would have* won more and more. No way on earth should Del Bosque have been treated like that. The deterioration started immediately and it went so far south that it was incredible. There should be statues of Del Bosque in every Spanish city given what he has achieved for that country, but most of all in Madrid. The club should come out and declare its love for that man, but too often it's the guys who love a club the most, who are the heart of the club, who get treated worst of all.

RONALDO: Del Bosque was a great coach and an incredible person. He knew that Real Madrid squad inside out and my year with him was one of my best. He was the ideal man to manage that dressing-room and get the best out of our squad.

Del Bosque had an ill-fated spell with Beşiktaş in Turkey where, to put it lightly, he was appalled at the egos and lack of self-discipline — this from a man who had just managed *Los Galácticos*. It led to one of the few times in his career where he lost his temper.

DEL BOSQUE: I had to watch my players strutting about like a bunch of little princes. They would be sitting in their rooms calling for cups of tea, pasta — I and my team had come from a world of top professionals who still managed to behave like normal guys. These fellows were used to being treated with absolute servility. There was no way I was going to tolerate it and I told them that in no uncertain terms. They were behaving like superstar players, which was a long way from reality, believe me.

A couple of quiet years later his regular lunches and cups of coffee with his

former captain, Hierro, transformed into lunches and cups of coffee with the newly-appointed football director of the Spanish federation.

In the winter of 2007, Del Bosque received a phone call from Hierro, this time in the latter's professional capacity with the federation. Hierro was preparing for a future beyond Euro 2008 and beyond Luis Aragonés. Gradually it became clear that, win or lose, the federation and Aragonés were going to go their separate ways. Having been a prime candidate in 2004, before Aragonés was appointed, and enjoying Hierro's total trust and respect, Del Bosque profiled perfectly.

Between then and July 2008, when Del Bosque's succession was made formal, and shortly after mass celebrations across the country when Aragonés's squad won the European Championships, there was an arctic tension between the two men — one icon of *Madridismo*, one icon of Atlético. Aragonés often carped about lack of respect from the federation; his work was finishing with a replacement already agreed, whose identity was an open secret and who had been selected by one of his own former players, Hierro, who did not enjoy a particularly close relationship with Aragonés.

Uefa held a national team coaches forum in Vienna three months after Euro 2008. Del Bosque was there in his new capacity as Spain coach, Aragonés as the man who had just won Uefa's showpiece tournament. The great and the good from all over Europe were gathered for seminars, lunches, press conferences — the sharing of ideas and information.

Aragonés and Del Bosque, chaperoned by Hierro, were like cat and dog, prowling warily around the five-star hotel. If one was in the bar, the other was in the conference room. If one was on the first floor, the other was down in reception. Hackles were raised. There was a potential for conflict which was raised when, during the 2010 World Cup, Aragonés was repeatedly critical in his tone as an analyst as Spain needed some blue-collar effort to get through their group. After the tournament was won and Del Bosque came back with World Cup gold to match up against Aragonés' silverware, there was an opportunity for revenge.

Spain has a yearly award named after the Príncipe de Asturias, King Juan Carlos's son. It is somewhere between a Knighthood and a Nobel Prize. Across all other categories, previous winners include Václev Havel, Nelson Mandela, Woody Allen, Umberto Eco, Bob Dylan and Al Gore. In sport, Martina Navratilova, Seb Coe, Michael Schumacher and Carl Lewis are among the honoured. In 2010, the Spain football team won the Premio Príncipe De Asturias by a landslide margin. One Friday night in October they, plus a glittering gala of socialites, politicians, artists, scientists, writers and the Royal family, gathered in Oviedo's elegant Teatro Campoamor. This is part of what the Spain coach says while addressing them.

DEL BOSQUE: *For over 100 years football has formed part of Spanish daily life and it is inexorably linked to the hopes and dreams of millions of Spaniards. We speak about it with such frequency and intensity that it is as if football were a member of each of our families. It is omnipresent, it leaves nobody indifferent. As such we [the squad] are the privileged beneficiaries of a status and responsibility which we cannot ignore. We are the standard bearers for a universal phenomenon which demands that you seek to better yourself every day. We are the few who defend the highest levels of a sport which the multitudes follow and practise. This squad which tonight receives the Príncipe de Asturias prize exhibits the values which soar over any particular trophy success and other material gains in professional football — these players are legitimate heirs to a tradition which honours us all.*

Their values, both timeless and decisive, are effort, talent, sacrifice, discipline, solidarity and modesty. These men who won the World Cup have been true to sportsmanship and honour. They reached the final defending those values — had it been any other way we could not have managed it. Spain winning the World Cup has been a reward for these values, but also the total conviction of all the players that our football proposition, our football philosophy, was the right one and that they were giving everything to it. Neither concept was doubted at any time. We all knew that this was the only way in which we could cope with the adversities and difficulties which will always arise if you try to achieve what we set out to do.

This team feels deep satisfaction at having attained this unique success and at having made millions of Spaniards proud. The humility and modesty of this group of athletes became as powerful a strength in their favour as the sweeping football they are capable of playing.

All that having been said, in front of an adoring audience and flanked by his

World Cup-winning players, Del Bosque strode towards Prince Felipe, accepted the award and then suddenly detoured into the audience. He knew where the man he wanted to find was seated. Calmly, with a big fraternal smile on his face, he reached out his hand and gracefully requested that Luis Aragonés, predecessor, critic, sometime rival, step out of the audience and stand, with the squad, to receive the thunderous applause of the opera house audience and the appreciation of watching millions on live television.

Evidently taken aback, and just as evidently thrilled and honoured, Aragonés accepted with grace. Arms raised in acknowledgement, Aragonés,

Del Bosque, the remnants of the 2008 squad plus the new boys who had won the World Cup in South Africa stood at not only the zenith of their lives but of the history of Spanish sport.

Somewhere, looking down, Fermín del Bosque — republican, defender of democracy, preacher of equal rights, believer in the brotherhood of man and father of young Vicente, would have been very proud.

This is an edited extract from Spain: The Inside Story of La Roja's Historic Treble, *published by BackPage Books.* Ⓑ

36

A Game of Chess

"He has opened up a new age which could be dubbed 'post-tactical', in which the once-prevalent notion of system obsolescence has been pushed aside to be replaced by a continuous process of re-evaluation."

Beyond the System

Could the lessons of chess show football the way to an exciting new future?

By Philippe Auclair

"Conjure a mental image of the Parthenon," our philosophy teacher instructed us.

So we did, remembering a postcard, an engraving, or, for the lucky ones, a trip to the Acropolis. We could picture the fluted columns, the frieze, the azure sky above the surge of stones.

"Now — count the columns at the front of the building, and tell me how many there are."

The best we could do was to hazard a guess. The crystal-clear images had dissolved into a blur. Focusing was impossible. The point of the exercise was to understand what makes eidetic memory — the capacity to recall an event or a concatenation of particulars with the precision of a camera which can be positioned at will — an almost-incomprehensible concept for those who aren't blessed or damned with it. My own mind swam for moment. How could I see and be blinded at the same time? I was drowning in an image I'd thought I owned, but was incapable of deconstructing it, experiencing the same kind of nausea I'd felt at a chess board when lost in what is called a 'tree of variations', when the shape of that tree explodes into an infinity of branches, each of them carrying an infinity of leaves, where every spurt of wood is a crossroad leading to an infinity of paths which lead nowhere but to estrangement from oneself, and fear.

I was a decent chess player, good enough to compete at regional level satisfactorily, a diligent trainer who spent his six hours at the board every day and subscribed to the Soviet magazine *64*, from which I cut out every single game played by my hero, the Jewish 'Wizard of Riga', Mikhail Tal, after whom I optimistically modelled my own reckless brand of ultra-attacking chess. What attracted me to Tal, apart from the brilliance of his combinational play, which has never been and will never be surpassed, was that even a moderate pawn-pusher could elevate his understanding of the game by re-playing his moves, to such a degree that structures of bewildering complexity suddenly acquired the clarity of sunlight pouring through the high windows of a cathedral. There were many other reasons to love Tal. On one occasion, while in Belgrade, he sacrificed a piece 'speculatively' to ensure a swift conclusion to a game (which he lost), in order to watch the end of a USSR-Yugoslavia football match on television. Misha, as we all referred to him, was born with three fingers on his right hand and a dodgy kidney (which had to be removed); he was a chain-smoker, an Olympic-strength vodka and whisky drinker, a dazzler of women, as well as a fine pianist and an authority on the satirical plays of Ilf and Petrov.

Tal's capacity to make the less-gifted feel as if they shared his own enjoyment and understood his own perception of the game was exceptional, but not unique, and is not restricted to chess. In football, from high in the stands, you can see the 'right' pass, the 'right' off-the-ball movement which will unbalance a defence that is perfectly organised to repel expected threats, but cannot cope with a sudden transformation of space. Dennis Bergkamp could do that, with a cross-field pass which might not have looked that special on a television screen, but had the power to define a new, unexpected dynamic which, to the spectator, answered all questions at once. Technique was a pre-requisite, but not the determining factor; spatial awareness was, of a kind which defies mere analysis, could not be reduced to computation, and yet, could be revelled in by ordinary mortals.

It is commonly thought — outside of the game, it should be said — that it is the power to 'see' and calculate variations several moves ahead that distinguishes the exceptional players from the merely competent. When Sol Campbell once compared Thierry Henry to a chess grandmaster, this is precisely what he had in mind. What, to his Arsenal teammate, made Henry special was his ability to weigh the consequences of the choices that were offered to him before he'd even received the ball, and, once he'd identified the correct decision (almost instantly, which might explain why we feel that great sportsmen have the power to bend time at will) to shape his body in order to execute the right move to perfection. It is a tempting simile, but it is misleading, as the train of thought of chess players follows a different track, one, indeed, that is much closer to that of footballers than you'd think.

It was once accepted, in the so-called 'Romantic' age of chess, which more or less coincided with that of Richard Wagner in music, that the supreme gift of grandmasters lay in their capacity to conceive long combinations that could not be refuted by their adversaries and led to an unavoidable win. The announcement of mate in so many moves, which, if correct, signalled the end of the game there and then, was considered the finest and most elegant demonstration of the chess player's artistry at the board. Such a notion would be dismissed today. A number of experiments conducted with skilled amateurs and world-class practitioners have demonstrated that the power to visualise a sequence of forced moves is not what distinguishes the two classes of players. When presented with an identical position, more often than not, they'll make the same suggestion. Chess, just like football, requires constant practice from a young age, even if, in the case of chess, most of that practice consists in the assimilation of theory — particularly of openings and endgame technique — to the point when choosing a particular move becomes as natural as the placement of the standing foot when executing a free-kick on the training ground, or the pass that you know will find a teammate you cannot see, as it's been drilled into each member of your squad that such-and-such a run should be attempted in such-and-such a passage of play. As the Secret Footballer has put it, "football at this level is very chess-like, maybe not to those outside of football but certainly to those inside", which makes me think that Secret Footballer is no stranger to the laws of the 'sport of kings'. Automation. Memorisation. Execution. Victory.

But memorisation, be it the programming of mind, or body, or both, these experiments concluded, was not the secret of success, though some succeeded that way. Memory certainly played its part. Chess history is replete with prodigious mnemonic feats: Tal once ad-libbed a full (and accurate) tournament review on the telephone, complete with diagrams and variations, for his Latvian magazine despite having forgotten he had a column to write that evening, without the help of notes or game-sheets. The capacity to regurgitate information that had been acquired by study alone could lead to crushing victories over opponents whose preparation hadn't been that thorough. This is hardly surprising when you think that most popular openings have been analysed beyond the twenty-fifth move, with the help of computer software which is far more sophisticated than ProZone and its competitors in football. This was seen as a sure sign that chess, as a sport, was, if not dead, then entering the final stages of its agony. Gone was the golden age of Tal and his peers of the great post-Second World War Soviet school, who, reacting to the so-called scientific approach of the regime's favourite world champion, Mikhail Botvinnik, played chess characterised by its daring and its imagination. We were entering an era of men-machines, super-

computers in suits, the assassins and undertakers of a once-glorious game which could not survive that onslaught of algorithms. Moneyball on sixty-four squares. But we were wrong.

The outstanding player of this age, the Norwegian grandmaster Magnus Carlsen, who recently took Wisthanatan Anand's world title in a crushing manner, has contributed to this reversal of values and convictions more than anyone else. Carlsen knows his stuff. He has, like thousands of others, instant recall of what happened when X beat Y with a 'new' move in a tournament contested years ago. His laptop is packed to the gills with a myriad games and variations. What distinguishes him is his combativity, his desire to find life in what would be considered a 'dead' position by lesser, less hungry competitors, in which he is the heir of Emanuel Lasker (1868-1941), a world champion for whom chess had more to do with prize-fighting than with crossword puzzle-solving. Carlsen also possesses, to a supreme degree, the quality that the experiments I mentioned above highlighted as the key difference between the good and the great: the holistic appreciation of potentialities within a stasis. He is at one with the eidos. He does not lose himself in 'trees of variations'. He seldom calculates sequences of more than two or three moves (Tal was the same), unless that sequence is in itself indicative of the nature of a position, and reveals weaknesses he can exploit should play develop in unexpected fashion, as far as the actual moves are concerned. His objective is to present his adversary with questions he will struggle with and ultimately fail to answer, sometimes deliberately aiming for 'dead' positions to which his opponent's mistakes will give a faint pulse of life. This, is turn, would be impossible if he didn't have an all-encompassing, but not omniscient grasp of the board. That distinction is key, and if you think I'm drifting further and further away from football, please think again. Carlsen is Bergkamp, but he's also Bergkamp's manager. It is one thing to be presented with a map and be able to read it, the finger following a planned itinerary; it is quite another to perceive it as a single (and, in the case of chess, football, or any other sport), coherent entity. When presented with the equivalent of dots and staves, chess masters and great football players do not decipher a score, they hear it. They conduct it too. As to how they do it, even to themselves, it is a mystery. They will insist on the necessity to rehearse, to repeat the same exercises over and over until they become second nature, instinct, intuition; but that, surely, is only a starting point, or, more accurately, the point at which talent or genius can take wing. Wayne Rooney put it beautifully when he described the pitch as a place he could picture in his mind, with '22 tiny people dancing on it'. I've been told this quote was apocryphal, but refuse to believe it. The secret must be there, surely. Blue is not just a mass of photons, a primary colour which can be explained away by the prismatic deconstruction of light. It is, first and foremost, blue. A poet might be better qualified to write about it than the chap mixing chemicals at the local Dulux centre.

Where chess has moved on, albeit relatively recently, football stalls. Analysis, some of it revealing, most of it arid, repetitive and oddly conformist, has taken over. The questions we ask when confronted with the chaos of a football game, and how we witness it, and re-assert some sort of authority (same root as 'author', not so incidentally) are questions which have been at the forefront of chess theory for decades. Similes between the two games are easy to come by. At least one book has been devoted to them, and I can think of many other correspondences which could be called upon. It's a pity (perhaps), that 'Zugzwang' has yet to be used in a football context, for example. In chess, this word is used when an opponent cannot make a move without weakening his own position and suffering from the fatal consequences thereof. We could summon the spirit of the 'boa constrictor' Tigran Petrosian, the Armenian Jew whose own game was based on subtle, yet relentless pressing; or of Viktor Korchnoi, who was the first player who systematised the wilful relinquishing of control and possession in order to counter-attack at speed. You could also equate rooks positioned on the seventh rank with wingers about to cross the ball from the corner flag, bishops zooming across the board like so many Platinis searching for and finding so many Bonieks, and so on. Such comparisons are thirteen a dozen, and quite fun to make too. We might as well throw in Norway's own CB Fry in the mix, Simon Agdestein, the only man ever to represent his country at both football (nine caps) and chess (seven appearances at the Olympiads). What larks!

However, if chess has anything to teach football, it is not through correspondences. It is through the way it has outgrown a sterile, almost suicidal acceptance of systematicity. Revealingly, one of chess's most influential treaties remains Aron Nimzowitch's *Mein System* (*My System*), published in 1925. Nimzowitsch, another Riga-born Jew, never won the world title, but opened the game to new ways of thinking much as Hugo Meisl did for football in the coffee shops of Vienna at the same time. *Mein System* is still a revolutionary tract. It was the first in a series of five brochures which were never meant to become parts of a manifesto or Ur-text of a new way of apprehending chess. But there is not a single serious chess player on the planet, patzer or grandmaster, who hasn't read or been influenced by it. Many of its fundamental precepts are now accepted in much the same way as Newton's laws of gravity are in physics, not as God-given truths any longer, maybe, but as a jolly good effort to enunciate them, still looking for improvements which are not that obvious to come by.

Chess, while it still reveres Nimzowitch, has, however, grown out of systems, insofar as systems have evolved from mechanisms supposedly designed to guarantee dominance to modes of organisation open to investigation and, sometimes, rebuttal. I should clarify at this point that what football describes as 'tactics' would be characterised as 'strategy' on the board, chess 'tactics' being the equivalent of combinational play on the field, and 'strategy' on the board the equivalent of 'tactics' on the pitch. It wouldn't take much effort to find almost perfect mirror images of 4-4-2, 4-2-4, 3-5-2 *et alia* on a chess-board in terms of deployment and use of forces. Chess conceptions such as control/domination of the centre, invasion of the flanks, prophylaxy, could easily be used in the context of football.

Conversely, some of football's modern terminology (*gegen*-pressing, transitions and the like) could just as easily find a use in chess analysis. But those *jeux d'esprit* would not amount to much more than an exercise in futility. Take tactical diagrams. In chess, a diagram is the game, no more, no less, in its true form. In football, it is either an illustration of players' median positions and general direction of play, or a snapshot of movement, often simplified into untruth (the movement of the opponent is hardly ever taken into account, as if this opponent was of no import). It is possible to play chess without a board — it is easier than non-players might think — but I defy you to play 'mind football' that is not pure fantasy. What is not fantasy is that, as football drifts more and more towards systematicity, it encounters problems with which chess has been familiar for a very long time indeed, has a far deeper understanding of, and treats with much less dogmatism than is to be found in the rather (to me) bizarre world of football analytics.

Whereas football is now obsessed with numbers when it comes to the management and organisation of space, chess has moved on and found renewed vigour in systems that were considered obsolete a decade ago. When I say 'systems', I mean 'openings': the way we set ourselves when we kick-off. As black, push your pawn to C5 in response to E4, you define a 'Sicilian' dynamic, well-explored, two-edged but still risky if you're playing 'away' (as Black); should you answer pawn to G6, you give yourself time to define the nature of the struggle. Chess is as fluid, if not more fluid, than football. Having stayed away from competitive chess for a long time,

I'm surprised to see lines I'd been told were fundamentally inaccurate being used again by top grandmasters, as if some hipster manager had brought the 1880s Scottish passing game back into fashion. The Scotch? Bah! Why not the King's Gambit? The old *giuccio piano*, described in sixteenth century manuals, adopted by Carlsen and others? Joke. But systems which were supposed to be antiquated can be re-born. All it takes is a new move. Is surrendering the initiative a bad thing? Not necessarily so. Openings, that is tactical systems (in the football sense), are no longer chosen solely because of their intrinsic soundness, but because of the player's affinity with the type of positions they lead to, and the problems they create in their opponents' mind. This is Carlsen speaking: "Above all I like to resolve unconventional tasks at the board. Perhaps that's why I don't really like studying the openings — everything starts from the one position. If I don't have a training session and there's no upcoming tournament then I don't study chess at all. And my fundamental chess understanding was formed without machine involvement. That was [my] idea of the struggle. Probably that mood has an effect on my opponents. Mistakes are a consequence of tension." On one level, Carlsen challenges the views of those people who believe that Wynton Marsalis's big band is superior to Duke Ellington's because it is better recorded (I know of one such eccentric); this idea of progress is more commonplace than reason would suggest it, and ridiculing it can't be a bad thing. More seriously, it is the supremacy of systems-driven thinking that he questions. In a tournament held in the Netherlands at the beginning of 2013, Carlsen, the highest ELO-rated player in the history of chess, adopted the venerable Ponziani opening (1 e4 e5 2 Nf3 Nc6 3 c3?!) against the grandmaster Pentala Harikrishna and subsequently won. This was far more than a gesture of bravado, far more than Zdeněk Zeman having almost all of his outfield players perched on the halfway line at kick-off like swallows on a telegraph wire. This was the equivalent of Bayern playing Herbert Chapman's W-M in the Champions League, sticking to the outmoded system throughout the entirety of the match, and winning.

Carlsen is not the first truly world-class chess player to have challenged orthodoxy that way. Tal sometimes chose opening lines ('tactics') which were considered dubious at best in order to unbalance opponents whom he knew struggled in unexpected positions, forcing them to think on their feet, time ticking away. Gary Kasparov resurrected the Evans Gambit, a hair-rising variation which had been, or so was thought, analysed to death (its own) in the latter part of the nineteenth century. These greats hadn't waited for the experiments I mention above to understand that it was their exceptional eidetic perception of the board, comprehension of the dynamics within and capacity to uncoil them with irresistible force which made them champions (as well as their fearlessness and stamina). Carlsen is different is that he has systematised anti-systematicity in a game whose eras could be defined in terms of the pre-eminence or fight for pre-eminence of one type of system over others. I wouldn't go as far as saying that he has 're-invented' chess, as the principles which guide his play were, as I've said already, also that of Lasker's a century ago. But he has demonstrated the validity of these principles in a game that had been transformed by the accent put on constant use of analytical software and memorisation. Doing that, he has, almost single-handedly, opened up a new age which could be dubbed 'post-tactical', in which the once-prevalent notion of system obsolescence has been pushed aside to be replaced by a continuous process of re-evaluation. The 'new' moves which breathe life in forgotten or discarded systems often are old ones which have re-acquired relevance through analysis of a more modest kind than previously. Football could learn and profit from a similar type of humility.

Play Jazz, not Chess

Reflections on football, order and the imagination, and the need for improvisation

By Scott Oliver

Beware the seductions of metaphor. That Franco-Algerian sometime goalkeeper, Jacques Derrida, made a celebrated career out of disinterring the subtly insidious *literary* tropes upon which Western philosophy had erected its truth-claims. Were he still around, he may have turned his attention to football's soothsayers and their perennial recourse to a chess metaphor that, although often only a facile, throwaway comparison, is nevertheless misleading, if not distorting, in a number of ways, fomenting the basic illusion that the game is first and foremost a battle of wits between scheming managers when of course what might cautiously be termed football's 'production process' riotously exceeds the serene hydraulics of tactics.

Now, it might be that the significance or even pervasiveness of the chess metaphor is overstated, but it is there nonetheless, abroad in the lexicon, regularly used *en passant*. Indeed, Adam Wells has written a short, interesting, if ultimately unsatisfactory book, *Football and Chess*, which aims to show how and why the two games are alike, drawing equivalences based on space, strategy, movement and suchlike. "As the different chess pieces have different types of movement, the connective possibilities between them are consequently extremely varied and complex. It is perhaps not surprising that modern football has taken something from this: players now realise that through varying their movements, more complicated possibilities for interplay with teammates can arise. In fact, to a large extent they mimic the movements of pieces on a chess board." Point taken, but *specifically mimicking* chess?

Anyway, the chess metaphor is a commonplace in the game's analysis. A prominent tactics website offers the following précis of Wells' book: "How many times has a cautious tactical battle been described by the commentators as something like 'a game of chess' between the two managers? This site treats almost every match and footballing situation like that." As a pinning of one's colours to the mast, this is pretty unequivocal. Again, the seductive trap of the metaphor is to construe a football match as a primarily cerebral undertaking.

Exaggerated or not, such an outlook, serially underplaying the players' invention and instigation (occasionally pawned, they're never pawns), has quickly carved out a niche that might be termed *tactical absolutism*, one carefully avoided by the shrewder exponents of tactical analysis, not to mention some managers. In Issue One of this publication, Juanma Lillo suggested that "the role of the coach is overstated... This is a game played by players. Those [coaches] who have expressed their significance seem to want to claim some personal protagonism or status through others. Our role is less than many coaches realise or want to believe."

Just as political absolutism implants a widespread fear of the capricious despot, so tactical absolutism has engendered a pathology of its own: *notation anxiety*, the injunction that one should impose a peculiar form of schematic three- or four-digit paralysis on what is essentially perpetual motion. If chess is a game of notation — and indeed can be precisely reconstructed through those means — in football it's at best a sketch, a figleaf. How many times do you need to read "they're playing 4-5-1", "no 4-2-3-1", "no 4-4-1-1, sorry, my bad" (three tweets in a minute from a tactics blogger evidently hoping to divulge some essential truth) before it all appears wind-pissingly useless?

Perhaps the real issue is the desire, or motive, underpinning all this: by investing the 'supermind' of "The Coach as Chess Player" (incidentally, the title of Wells' central chapter, a case study of the 2005 Champions League final) as the key to understanding the game, the pundit is also tacitly positing his own interpretative primacy, her ability to delve into the hurly-burly of the match and attain the game's true causal level. Yet even if a 'pure', exclusively tactical analysis were possible, it could neither 'explain' a football match nor provide its ultimate truth. Not that this has deterred Wells. "Liverpool's comeback against AC Milan," he writes, "was inspired primarily by

principles that are inherently chess-like. The Liverpool manager Rafael Benítez did not bring about such transformation in his team by making a rousing speech. He inspired it by analysing the game and changing it from a tactical point of view. *Everything that followed was a direct consequence of the chess-like repositioning of his players*. The relationship between chess and football is not an obscure idea that comes to mind while watching certain types of football. It is a permanently entrenched part of all football games" [my italics].

These claims notwithstanding, you might still consider all this a bit walnut and sledgehammer, since few people *literally* believe football is chess-like, protesting that it's absurd and boneheaded to deny the crucial impact of tactics in football (which I am not doing) and thus the validity of insightful tactical readings. No, the problem with Wells is less that he analyses the game from a tactical standpoint — the game is manifestly open to such a reading, just that in order to posit tactics as the alpha and omega of the game there are many significant elements that must be bracketed off — than that he fails to acknowledge the considerable differences between the two games, which we shall presently examine via an intriguing passage from the football-loving French philosophers Gilles Deleuze and Félix Guattari.

Before we do, let us define tactics as *a schematic ideal of the coach's haphazardly and extemporaneously carried out by inherently creative, problem-solving players*. This is to encompass both the command element and the 'slippage' in their execution, since not all actions or split-second decisions on the field can be ascribed to tactics (although plenty of what doesn't seem tactical is, as The Secret Footballer illustrated), while the re-jigging and dissolution of tactics amid the various disorders of the game is irreducible in that multi-sided 'production process'. Football is far less black and white than chess.

Chess v Go

Deleuze and Guattari argued that all societies are defined primarily by the way they capture desire and hook it into a "social machine". Chaos (or Marx's "free activity") is foundational and there is no society without repression. They thus set out a "universal history" of desire, outlining the workings of three such social machines — primitive (principal institution: kinship), imperial (state), and capitalist (market) — later supplemented by a fourth, the "war-machine", which is "the invention of the nomads, the necessary consequence of nomad existence". The state — the sovereignty machine — and nomadism are fundamentally opposed modes of existence and thus have an antithetical relationship to both time and space. Where the sedentarising state divides out a bounded space, the war-machine distributes bodies in an open space: "Hold the fort" versus "hold the street".

These organisational and ideational differences — and we are talking about a whole style of thought, a mode of perceiving the world (hence the term "state-thought") — are then explored in a comparison between chess (a "game of state") and Go from the standpoint of the pieces, their relations, and the space involved, and this is where the relevance for football emerges:

"Chess pieces are coded; they have an internal nature and intrinsic properties from which their movements, situations, and confrontations derive. They have qualities; a knight remains a knight, a pawn a pawn, a bishop a bishop... Go pieces, in contrast, are pellets, disks, simple arithmetic units, and have only an anonymous, collective, or third-person function: 'It' makes a move...with no intrinsic properties, only situational ones. Thus the relations are very different in the two cases. Within their milieu of interiority, chess pieces enter biunivocal relations with one another, and with the adversary's pieces: their functioning is structural. On the other hand, a Go piece has only a milieu of exteriority, or extrinsic relations with nebulas or constellations, according to which it fulfils functions of insertion or situation, such as bordering, encircling, shattering. All by itself, a Go piece can destroy an entire constellation synchronically; a chess piece cannot (or can do so diachronically only). Chess is indeed a war, but an institutionalised, regulated, coded war, with a front, a rear, battles. But what is proper to Go is war without battle lines, with neither confrontation nor retreat, without battles even: pure strategy, whereas chess is a semiology. Finally, the space is not at all the same: in chess it is a question of arranging a closed space for oneself, thus of going from one point to another, of occupying the maximum number of squares with the minimum number of pieces. In Go, it is a question of arraying oneself in an open space, of holding space, of maintaining the possibility of springing up at any point: the movement is not from one point to another but becomes perpetual, without aim or destination, without departure or arrival. The 'smooth'

space of Go, as against the 'striated' space of chess..."

Let's attack the space first. Although (association) football clearly involves a "milieu of interiority" — the (variable) pitch dimensions — this does not constitute its essence. It's a simple convention. You can play 23 versus 23 on Porthmadog Sands, jumpers for goalposts, a game *without lines*, and it would still be recognisably football, much as with Go, which can be played on a board of any dimension (9x9 squares, 13x13, etc). Chess is always played on the same board. The Dutch artist Jeroen Henneman says of Ajax in *Brilliant Orange* that "Johan Cruyff seemed to see football as a total movement of the whole field, not as individual actions in only one part of it... I think maybe Cruyff would be satisfied with a pitch two kilometres long with these beautiful waves of abstract movement going up and down."

While the state "striates" space, partitioning the surface of the earth along national and proprietorial lines, the movement of nomads, of *totaalvoetbal*, creates "smooth space". In the latter, space is "occupied without being counted"; in the former, "space is counted in order to be occupied". David Moyes may well grid off his training pitches to coordinate collective movement, but the football field is, by and large, a smooth space, one in which "the point is subservient to the line". You are never going from A to B; rather, A and B take on meaning only in relation to the perpetual movement. In this sense, the Position of Maximum Opportunity represents the acme of "state-thought" applied to football. While chess grids off space and

regulates movement, the relationship between football players in smooth space — "a field without conduits or channels" — is continual and fluid, the relative potency of each player fluctuating with the movement of the ball. And this smooth space is also "haptic", tactile, as when one works in close-up, whereas striated space is "optic", involving panoramic visibility: chess player over the board, despot-God over the imperium, pundit over pitch, but not the coach, let alone the players at the game's coal face. Despite frequent praise for his 'vision', even Xavi operates predominantly in haptic space, probing, *feeling* for his opponent (or maybe *listening*: Cruyff famously dismissed a player's technique while looking away from the field on the basis of the sound when he kicked the ball), this grasp of local conditions then informing his global outmanoeuvring efforts.

As for football's pieces, Jonathan Wilson has explained that "there are two basic ways of conceptualising a team: it is either a series of predetermined slots (the target-man, the holding midfielder, the right-back ...) into which players are dropped, or it is a holistic entity, in which the relationships between component parts are as significant as the parts themselves." While a dogmatic brand of football indeed strives to codify rigorously these positions — do *your* job, rather than do *the* job that needs doing — coaches from Arrigo Sacchi to Valeriy Lobanovskyi have aspired to "universality", the player as pellet, hence Rinus Michels envisioning his charges as "numbers to fit a system" rather than as individuals. At face value, this might also smack of an overly technocratic conception, but is it chess? In chess there is no first-order imagination: the pieces cannot think for themselves or *act in unconventional ways*. They are restricted by their properties. Conversely, the properties of the 'pieces' in football, as with Go, are situational, a function of the fitful needs of circumstance. A team being caught on the counter-attack will call on any player, regardless of whether they are a 'defender' or 'attacker', to perform the most pressing task. Likewise in a goalmouth scramble.

Finally, "relations of exteriority" means simply that the relations between two entities — or footballers, if you prefer to call them that — are not a function of the *properties* of those parts (which are thus not *defined* by said relations) but are independent, freeform alliances forever modifying the whole. With chess pieces, by contrast, those connections derive from rules governing movement and are thus "relations of interiority" (much as with those "predetermined slots" and subjection of the footballing part's identity to the whole). Rather than properties, then, footballers have only *capacities to interact* (what Deleuze and Guattari term "affects"), which are not pre-given and thus not denumerable. Indeed, they may well go unexercised if no entity suitable for interaction is around, much as the gliding, one-two-playing genius of Andrès Iniesta might remain latent at Leyton Orient.

All of this comprises a *self-organising system*: that is, a system that attains coherent order endogenously, from the bottom up, without need of a central decider or 'masterplan' (not an absence of tactics, but a different conception of order and supercession of the notion that only a single external agent — a *Gafferísimo* — can perform concerted

tactical action). Examples: a truly free market, pattern-recognition software, flocking birds and fish, or, classically, an ant colony, often mistakenly thought of as a command system because of the 'queen ant'. Like Xavi in midfield, no ant has a perception of the entire colony; macro-order emerges from the local interactions of ants 'reading' the 'semiology' of pheromone trails.

There's a similar swarm intelligence in football, especially evident in pressing — witness the famous photos of Iniesta from Euro 2012. It's also there in total football, a war-machine in which any player could spring up at any point in the assemblage, and in the intricate self-adjusting network of Spain or Barça, with *tiki-taka* being the "emergent property" of that complex self-organising system. And who is the on-field general, the regista, in all this — Xavi, Busquets, Messi? Whoever has the ball: a circulating function of the nomadic band, not an instituted rank of the state army.

Andi Thomas sums up rather well the erroneous elision of chess and football agency: "Chess pieces are dumb extensions of their controlling über-lord; footballers are sentient and independent agents given instructions by a supervisory demi-lord." Despite a near-theological adherence to hierarchical systems, however, lack of a command structure is not necessarily a weakness in football. As Jorge Valdano asserted, "the brain of one manager can't compete with the infinite possibilities of eleven thinking brains on the pitch." In any case, and this is important, horizontal interactivity and ad hoc structure can still be 'tactical'; it just isn't chess. For, while chess is punctual, comprising discrete, alternate moves, football is continuous and episodic, a general conflagration without battle lines in which one is not obliged to await the outcome of a decisive move before responding. If there are two types of war — or perhaps two conceptions of the 'same' war: the strategist's on the hilltop, the combatant's in the fray — then, as Go and football are to the guerrilla, so chess and *American* football are to state war.

Gridiron and Jazz

It isn't football but gridiron that is quintessentially chess-like, the game of state *par excellence*. Where football is to a large extent extemporised play (or sketchily applied tactics with a margin of deviation from the model), Brownian motion, American football is almost entirely a set-piece. It proceeds in discrete units, each drive like a battle in a campaign, each (rigorously planned) play a skirmish within the battle, after which both armies again assume their neatly separated, tête-à-tête antagonism. Just as chess moves establish positions of strength, each play or drive confers a definitive, measurable yield in yardage or field position — a *signification*, the value of which is a function of the playing field's standardised striations. In the drive, there is, as it were, an accumulation of 'stock' (and, as Al Pacino once memorably exhorted, every inch is worth fighting for). In football, by contrast, each pass comprising an attacking move 'means' nothing, however compellingly intricate, since in that unfolding web there is no cumulative value in terms of field position (only an intangible, attritional effect that could just as well *embolden* a resolute defence), which remains unaffected by previous moves or phases of play. A miss is as good as a mile.

Further, American football, as with chess, has a clear *division of labour* inscribed in the specific coding of both its 'pieces' and the relations they can establish with each other. Their properties are structural, conferred by the rules, rather than situational (in football, codified specialisation is of course restricted to the goalkeeper). Thus, there is an *offensive* unit, and within that linemen who can only block, but not run or receive a pass (one lineman, the tight end, may catch); a *defensive* unit, split into linemen to rush the quarterback, backs to follow the pass receivers, and linebackers who do either; and a *special team* involved in kicking (for goal or field position) and kick-returning. The 'identity' of the players is therefore constituted by the rules, with little scope for variation. No own goals here. And finally, alongside this intensive and rigid specialisation of roles comes the imposition of order on the group from above by a coach or quarterback who orchestrates set plays according to a code "48, 62, red, hut" — written down in a pre-existent text (as, perhaps, with the openings of chess).

Aside from chess/Go and gridiron/ football, the distinction between state and war-machine is attested to by "royal" and "nomad science". Where the former seeks to extract *constants* from the variables of matter so as to be able to demonstrate a procedure under new conditions (reproductive *iteration*), nomad science proceeds by tracking *singularities* inherent in matter, the "continuous variation of variables" (*itinerant* following); an example of the latter is evolutionary biology, the random mutations of which are unpredictable and whose effects are thus not reproducible: play out evolution

100 times with the same mutations and you'd get a hundred different outcomes. In nomad science, unlike royal science, there's a technical division of labour according to skills, but no social division according to prestige: *bricoleurs* and engineers. How apt, then, that the first FA Cup final saw the Royal Engineers AFC of the British Army defeated 1-0 by Wanderers FC; while it's perhaps ironic that the former, doubly representative of the state, were early pioneers of 'progressive' combination football, there is no confirmation that the latter, travelling from ground to ground, were ever deployed in a W-M.

In football, the current mania for *statistics* is a quintessentially royal undertaking (the clue is in the name). Typically, facets of the game are extrapolated from their context and endowed with spurious significance, like a concert review that praises the crispness of the cymbal striking without reference to the overall sound. Most tackles: a sign of diligence, physical flexibility, or colleagues' profligacy in possession? Sometimes the statistical approach can, through a cockeyed focus on product ("metric") rather than process, create feedback: *they need to up their key passes by 23% to give them a statistically more probable chance to win their remaining games.*

Of course, it is only ever the way statistically described traits interact and mutually affect one another (that is, in open play) that yields insight. As the philosopher Manuel DeLanda puts it, "Analysing a whole into parts and then attempting to model it by adding up the components will fail to capture any property that emerged from complex interactions, since the effect of the latter may be multiplicative (e.g. mutual enhancement) and not just additive." The obsessive measurement of atomised players' individualised contributions — "output" — smacks of a footballing version of Taylorisation, the industrial-scale quantification of labour. Useful for the neoliberal market, perhaps, but not the socialist midfield.

Where football has nomadic drifting and creative exploration of local conditions, American football is a state/statistical game, not only with regard to space, pieces and their relations, but also its conception of *time*. Every play is a set-piece (in theory) that can only ever aspire to embody the vision of the coach set out in the playbook. Football is different, notwithstanding Sacchi's claim that it "has a script" that "the actors must follow". Evidently, AC Milan wasn't a Mike Leigh movie.

And these two temporal modes — of American football and soccer — are also evident in the distinction between classical music and jazz (in the sense of live group improvisation). So, just as with American footballers and the hallowed playbook, the highly specialised musicians of a symphony orchestra — organs under the direction of the conductor (quarterback) — will attempt to offer a perfect rendition of a prior model, thereby hoping their performance lives up to the genius of the composer (head coach) whose score they are interpreting. Here, as Marx said apropos the French Revolution, "the tradition of all the dead generations weighs like a nightmare on the brain of the living."

In jazz, by contrast, history enables rather than constrains. A score is rarely used, while musicians continually depart from well-known standards in their solos, the objective not being slavishly to reproduce an existing piece of music but to take just enough of what is known — a melody, a chord sequence, a harmonic mode or tone-system — as a point of departure for the shared crafting and enjoyment of something unique and radically new that still 'makes sense' to musicians and audience alike. Performance in both freeform jazz and football is thus creative problem-solving. As Valdano explained in Issue One of *The Blizzard*, Maradona's (apparently selfish) finish for his second goal against England in 1986 occurred to him in a flash of inspiration as he bore down on goal and suddenly recalled a similar situation against Shilton from 1979, when he'd failed to score. "Footballing genius," Valdano concluded, "lay in the ability to analyse and solve problems creatively under pressure at unimaginable speed."

With classical recitals, the audience know more or less what to expect, although indeterminacy still lurks there. With jazz — which, as with the war-machine, or *De Oranje* in the 1970s, "exists only in its own metamorphoses" — one enjoys the ride into *terra incognita*. This is not to say jazz is 'pure' spontaneity or unfettered invention, nor that this *modus operandi* doesn't harbour its own risks, such as cacophony or indulgence (with football as with jazz, there must be 'end-product': imagination is not *l'art pour l'art*). The jazz ensemble has rehearsals, the equivalent of training for a football team. Both involve increasing the capacities of the collective body. Affinities and cues are embedded to permit a greater level of macro-order without the latter stifling the latitude for improvisation, the 'wriggle room' for soloists (often, though not *necessarily*, the most gifted technicians) around which everyone else will readjust. Football as *jamming* or *riffing* — with eurythmic Iberian *tiki-taka*, and the alternating 'leadership' function we saw with strikerless Spain in Euro 2012, its apogee — is thus a better metaphor for the game's 'production process' than chess. Nevertheless, despite having the opportunity to inculcate his ideas during the week — the question being precisely to what degree invention is straitjacketed (and at a club like Barcelona, of course, the general ideas permeate the club) — the stressed-out manager still cuts an impotent figure on matchday while his chess pieces run amok.

Just as the coach's role is frequently exaggerated, doubtless I have exaggerated claims for the overstated role of tactics — or, rather, top-down order — something of a tactical necessity, I felt, in order to present the two 'regimes': command systems and self-organising systems, state and war-machine. Equally, I misdefined tactics as an ideal of the coach's when they can just as well be elaborated by the players in the thick of things. It is clearly wrong to suggest that tactics play no part; it is also questionable whether they are less significant than 'flair', not that it would negate the point that chess analogies can never hope to describe the imagination that eludes *both* top-down order (tactical ideals) *and* self-organising order (second-order, tactical creativity).

We have presented them here as opposites, but we should stress that no society, no musical form, no football team fully embodies one or other of the "abstract machines". Even North Korea leaks. As Deleuze and Guattari put it, there's a *"de jure* distinction", but always *"de facto* mixtures". Two banks of four; men between the lines. A limited footballing example: Ajax play like a war-machine, with circulating functions not fixed roles, and yet a leader, Cruyff, emerges. As soon as he tries to *institute* his authority the body rebels (the famous captaincy vote) and the exceptional individual absconds to Barcelona. And these admixtures are equally true of managers. Clough was a particularly hybrid figure: superficially anti-tactics, never discussing the opposition, often not appearing for team-talks, yet of such unquestionable authority that the players internalised his vision. Clough did not see himself as the fountainhead of the game's production process. Compare this with someone like Rafa Benítez, a touchline-stalking fusspot whose manic gesticulations and ceaseless repositioning of his players often engenders reactive rather than creative thinking — what does the boss want? — which might prove useful in situations in which you are outclassed (Istanbul), but is often inhibiting in others (the 2008-09 title race). Overly tactical? Perhaps knowing when to take the handbrake off, more than mind games, was Ferguson's trump card. Not that there's a simplistic positive/negative valuation to be placed on the two regimes. We should neither idealise bottom-up systematicity, nor vilify top-down structures. Clearly, at certain points in history, the state increases the development of productive forces and human potential, and the same is true of football (where a certain amount of tactical order is, like fitness, an evolutionary *sine qua non*). A set-piece goal can bring as much joy as the most

spontaneous team goal, but rigid tactics can also be limiting. *Catennacio*.

Ultimately, when trying to assess the scope or (variable) influence of tactics, we are talking about a micro-realm of decision-making in the most intimate recesses of a human brain — shall I make that run? which pass? — a permanent concatenation of factors to process, solutions coming from the chalkboard, the synapses, the crowd. It follows that, for the analyst, it's difficult to parse all this out. Football is often remarkably, beautifully, militantly opaque, a mélange of factors commingling to produce the unfolding game and its result. The temptation can be simply to ascribe to the coach's influence — often simply assumed in an after the fact rationalisation, as with the *post hoc, ergo propter hoc* of "I don't know what he said to them at half-time, but it worked" — what in truth is a porous, supercomplex, if not downright chaotic process.

The Canadian thinker Brian Massumi (Deleuze and Guattari's translator) illuminates: "A structure [team] is defined by what escapes it. Without exception, it emerges from chance, lives with and by a margin of deviation, and ends in disorder... A structure is a regularised infolding of an aleatory outside. Order is the approximate, and always temporary, prevention of disorder." Chance and disorder are primary — in the beginning there was chaos; order what must be built. Continually. Haphazardly. And football is shot through with disorder — refereeing whimsy, a stud that doesn't take, a shot ricocheting in off a beach-ball...

Just as "the task of the historian" is to assess the dynamic processes at work in any social body — how it holds together, how it comes undone — perhaps the astute football writer can show something of this co-presence of the two regimes (he will need to invent the language): the top-down *molar* order (whole dominating parts), the bottom-up *molecular* order (autonomous parts affecting the whole), and their relation to a third term, *imagination*, that irrupts therein and provides the cutting edge of the game, which *loses its shape* as both teams (the one you're part of, the one you're against) are lead along a *line of escape*, sucking a structure out through a hole into dis-organisation, into crisis and possibility.

Tactics 'v' Imagination

Football is a *field of interaction* between an order that captures free activity — be that top-down *obedience*, or bottom-up *discipline* — and an imagination that disrupts order. Since we have misdefined tactics, the first thing that needs to be said about imagination is that it is not some ineffable fabulatory realm, but entirely material and of-this-world. For Massumi, it is "rational thought brought back to the body, viewed from the perspective of its transformational potential". What is the latitude that a given body — individual, social, politic — envelops for becoming-other? Imagination's limit is the order that checks it, while tactics are continuously sundered by a virtuosity that eludes it (an imagination that is *without exception* grounded in a body's affects: its physical potential, its coordination and balance, its ideas...). All transformations start from the perception of constraint — there is no imagination without the context of its exercise — thus rendering the

notion of unlimited freedom facile. Constraints are creatively enabling. Tactics and imagination are in reciprocal presupposition: no disorder and there's nothing to order; no constraints and there's no need for imagination — you'd simply do. As Nike recommends.

But again the opposition is too neat. Imagination can apply to ordering (tactical imagination), just as tactics can be used not only for spoiling but creation too. It might appear a contradiction to state that attacking creativity can be taught, but this takes us back to rehearsals, to *memorisation* and the embedding of 'muscle memory' in the collective body, as with the technocrat Lobanovskyi's "automatisms". The Secret Footballer has even stated that *most* attacking play is now like this, players following "a script" that makes the game increasingly "chess-like, maybe not to those outside of football but certainly to those inside it". *What you don't see*, he seems to be saying... But is this claim for the chess-like character of football really true? Or could it be that it's TSF who doesn't see — or rather, sees only in one way (like the battlefield general) — precisely because he has been conditioned not to by an excessively top-down structure drilling the possibilities of inspiration, creation and the rush of the imagination out of him?

TSF is not *wrong*, just as tactical readings are not *wrong*. However, tactics necessarily apprehend the game at a *molar* level, even though that organisational stratum taps into, and is contingent upon, a whole *molecular* realm of body swerves, cushioning touches, accurate passes that allow for unbroken stride and speed of ball circulation, ball-shielding without losing balance, feints and flicks and dummies — all of which ensures the 'hold' of the tactical edifice, the team shape. Again the example of Spain: if you see this *solely* as an expression of tactics then you miss much of what is sublime.

No, TSF isn't wrong — at a certain level of generality, he's right. He's just squinting. Putting tactics everywhere is a sort of faith: if one wishes to see the workings of God in everything, one can, but such *tactical absolutism* requires a lot of squinting. "Are you watching the same game, pal?" *Literally*, "No." A tactical reading of a game might be perfectly valid, but it is only ever a *partial* reading, both in the sense of being incomplete and following on a constitutional affinity. Nuanced tactical writing undoubtedly enhances our understanding of the game, its deep patterns, the mechanics of its skirmishes, but it shouldn't be at the cost of all that escapes this (a risky run, a piece of skill, gambling...).

Deleuze and Guattari tell us, apropos one discipline involving decision-making in an open, complex reality, "Good or bad, politics and its judgements are always molar [macro], but it is the molecular [micro] and its assessment that makes it or breaks it." The same is undeniably true of tactics. Can you explain the efficacy of the drifting box of tricks that is Luis Suárez through the prism of tactics, or is it, rather, a creative exploration of local conditions, an ant sniffing pheromone trails? Or Ronaldinho, a hallucination of a footballer, whose *haptic* perception of the space of possibilities inspired some of the most ludicrous pieces of *fantasia* football has ever witnessed, *elásticos* and *sombreros* and humble toe-pokes

(and they were no indulgence, either, no 17-minute keyboard solo: 'end-product')?

This perhaps invites another question: Can you teach imagination? This was one of the topics broached in John Sinnott's piece in Issue Three of *The Blizzard* on the use of neuroscience in Standard Liège's academy, whose director, Michel Bruyninckx, explained that the objective was to increase the brain's capacities (imagination) by developing "cognitive readiness" through "differential learning" on the way to building new neural pathways ("syntaptogenesis"). Rather than *capturing the imagination*, you are liberating it, arming it to fight its own battles, equipping it to problem-solve, giving it scanning skills, attention focus, bandwidth, adjustability, perception, cognition. And crucial in all this, according to Bruyninckx, is *enjoyment,* for learning goes through the brain's pleasure centre, the amygdala. Telling us that "it is not repetition without reflection", he suggest that "music will help to control the movements through the rhythmic structure but it also influences the emotional status of the performer." Variations on a standard, not drills. Football as jazz.

In effect, he treats training like an ecosystem into which you 'artificially' introduce variables so as to facilitate mutations. Football is not apodictic. One cannot have the solutions in advance. It is adversarial, *mano a mano, pie a pie* — as Sartre put it: "in football, everything is complicated by the opposition" — and thus nonlinear: the same input doesn't always equal the same output (which explains why Deep Blue eventually beat Garry Kasparov, while no Go programme can best a grandmaster). And, of course, the brain is itself a self-organising 'modular system', performing its local tasks and the aggregate effect being the macro Person, a system of interiority.

Still, even if neurological activity is the ultimate causal level of (footballing) imagination, it would be an eccentric match report that looked at fMRI scans over heat maps. Their diminished status in a hierarchy of explanations ought not mean that tactical absolutism and the cult of the Gaffer become a reflex action, like the chess metaphor. For the desire to ascribe agency to a single cause — monotheism, for example, the literal apotheosis of state-thought — has been shown to be an adaptive process, reducing anxiety in the face of a complex world. "It's Moyes versus Mourinho" begins the preview.

All of which, recalling Lillo's words, raises an intriguing, final question as to whether a football team, week to week through the season, could go managerless, calling instead on a distributed intelligence, on the hivemind

of the war-machine: compromise, co-operation and collective becomings. David Winner described Ajax's early seventies vintage as "the closest thing there has been in football to a workers' cooperative", while Corinthians Democracy, inspired by Socrates, collectivised their day-to-day approach. Yet perhaps the coach least prone to see himself as an avatar of the despot was Victor Maslov, who, as Wilson informs us, not only discussed and compromised over tactics with his players, but also allowed himself to be overruled regarding substitutions. The conclusion of "Arkady Galinsky, one of the most popular football journalists" in the Soviet Union in the sixties, "was that the two incidents were indicative not of any weakness on Maslov's part, but rather of his strength. 'He understood that the players rejected the substitution not to undermine his authority,' he wrote, 'but for the benefit of the affair'."

Pawn takes king? No, just a man who put a jazz band together exiting the stage when the musicians were ready to play.

56

"The boys of the Argentinian
west say
That I have a better shot than
the great Bernabé."

Maximum Opportunity

Was Charles Hughes a long-ball zealot, or pragmatist reacting to necessity?

By Steve Menary

When Charles Hughes retired as the Football Association director of coaching 20 years ago, he was one of the most divisive characters in the English game, often vilified for implementing a national approach to tactics and coaching that was deemed brutalist by his critics.

A grammar school boy, Hughes had joined the FA in January 1964 as assistant to the director of coaching, Allen Wade. Hughes had developed a passion for coaching while studying for a degree in physical education at Loughborough University. After graduating and completing his national service in the RAF, Hughes taught in Bolton, then at Leigh Grammar School and at weekends attended FA coaching courses.

On those courses, Hughes met Norman Creek, a mild-mannered Cambridge graduate then managing the English Amateur XI and the Great Britain Olympic side. At Easter 1963, Creek mentioned he planned to retire and suggested Hughes apply for his job, which included working with Wade. After an interview process that featured a weekend with the Olympic team, Hughes emerged triumphant. Thrust into the sclerotic and arcane corridors of the FA, Hughes found an organisation constrained by the outdated ideals of its amateur founders and struggling to marry the needs of the professional game with the grassroots.

Today, amateur football is remote from the professional game but in the early 1960s an amateur still had some of the social cachet of the Victorian gentlemen who had founded the FA a century earlier. In 1960, Lord Wolfenden, in his *Sport and Community* report, had advocated abolishing the distinction between amateurs and professionals. Wolfenden, who in 1957 had also recommended decriminalising homosexuality, suggested that everyone should simply be a player. He was ignored by the FA.

The FA was led at the time by Harold Warris Thompson, a graduate of Trinity College, Oxford, and staunch defender of the ailing amateur credo, which in England survived in the Northern and Isthmian Leagues. This was where Hughes would, in his new managerial capacity, go looking for players, but shamateurism — the practice of amateur clubs secretly paying players — was rife. Thomson's pet side Pegasus, the Oxbridge team that won the 1951 and 1953 Amateur Cups in thrilling style, were struggling to compete against those making illicit payments. Led by Thompson, the FA hunted down shamateurs in uncompromising fashion, often levelling harsh penalties that could leave players unable to play.

"The FA were evil with money," recalled John Delaney, the centre-half for England's amateurs and the GB side under Hughes. "All the old farts would be getting pissed and we'd get nothing. I worked as a chairmaker and didn't get any time off. I spent four days away [for an Olympic qualifier] and all I got was the price of a bus fare back from Heathrow."

To Norman Creek, the idea that any of his supposedly amateur players secretly took money was ludicrous. Hughes was less gullible but still had to find a way to succeed in this outdated Victorian limbo.

Creek had played for the famous Corinthians side of the 1920s, during which time he won a full England cap. Creek also steered Great Britain through the 1960 Olympic qualifiers to the finals in Rome. Hughes was only in his early thirties and had no track record on or off the pitch. He needed a different style to establish control; his players would find a manager that brooked no compromise.

The Skelmersdale striker Peter Hardcastle played for England's amateurs and GB. "I was a bit uppity as you are at that age and was set up by the other players to argue back with Charles Hughes," he said. "He had this way of cutting you dead and when I approached him, he said, 'Who's behind you Peter?' and when I looked round the entire squad had backed off 10 yards. After that it was all, 'Yes Charles, no Charles.' He didn't have that much choice as he wasn't that much older than some players."

During Norman Creek's playing days in the 1920s, the Home Nations quit Fifa

after rows over broken-time payments and did not return until after the Second World War. Hughes would soon discover that this return to the global fold had fudged rather than resolved the FA's fixation over payments to amateurs.

With a larger pool of players than Scotland, Wales or Northern Ireland, success for Hughes was easier to come by in the amateur Home Nations championship than outside the United Kingdom, where the targets were the Uefa Amateur Cup or Olympic qualification with GB. To succeed, Hughes needed a different, more pragmatic approach both on and off the pitch. Maurice Lindsay played in the 1960 Olympic finals and later under Hughes for England and GB. He said, "Charles expected us to be more professional in our attitude to the game. I was very lucky that my job [as a teacher] enabled this to be possible. Others were not so fortunate and suffered as a result."

Committees held sway over international selection. Hughes paid lip service to this anachronism but the starting XI was his. He also asked for more time with his squad in the build up to games and focused on tactics. "Before [Hughes] no tactics were even talked about [in the amateur game]," said Jimmy Quail, a Northern Irishman who played for the north London amateurs Hendon and Hughes's GB side.

In a precursor to his later roles, Hughes quickly found himself in a position to influence a whole stratum of English football, but his immediate challenge lay with the qualifiers for the 1964 Tokyo Olympics. Under Creek, GB thrashed Iceland 10-0 on aggregate in the first round. Hughes took charge for the second round against Greece, at which point he discovered just how uneven a battle he would face against Europe's supposed amateurs. Great Britain beat Greece 2-1 at Stamford Bridge but in Athens found very different opposition. The Greek amateurs that had been in London were replaced by professionals. GB were crushed 4-1. The Greeks were later ejected but GB stayed out, the FA's gentlemen unwilling to return in such un-Corinthian fashion.

Further ignominy followed. In 1967, Uefa set up an international amateur championship in a vain attempt to bolster the rapidly discredited ideal. Grouped with Austria and the Netherlands, Hughes's English amateurs failed to recover from a 3-0 pasting in Salzburg and missed out on the four-team finals. To the FA's chagrin, Scotland not only qualified but beat Spain in the semi-finals before narrowly losing in the final to an Austrian side inspired by Josef Hickersberger.

For the 1968 Olympic qualifiers, Hughes called up three of those Scots, Millar Hay, Niall Hopper and Billy Neil, but his dogmatic quest for a more professional approach combined with an abrasive manner found little favour in Scotland. The FA allowed English players in the GB squad to miss club fixtures, giving Hughes the extra preparation time he craved. Hughes wanted Queen's Park — Scotland's leading amateur club and the main source of players north of the border — to release the three Scots early too. This meant missing a league fixture with Arbroath. Queen's Park refused. So did the Scottish FA, which threatened life bans for any players journeying south early.

Due to this impasse and injuries, Hughes' GB squad travelled to Augsburg in Germany with just 13 players. Apart from the back-up keeper John Shippey, the only spare player was the injured Barking striker Peter Deadman. At Hughes' behest, Deadman changed into his strip and sat on the bench to dupe the Germans into thinking that Hughes had some options.

Germany also had a different approach to amateurism and tolerated some payments. GB's team of Isthmian League players were at an obvious disadvantage against opponents, including those of the calibre of Rainer Zobel, who later won three European Cups with Bayern Munich. The Germans had others with Bundesliga experience, such as Helmut Bergfelder and Paul Alger of FC Köln and Günter Keifler of Eintracht Frankfurt. Great Britain could never have outplayed Germany and Hughes directed a physical style that outraged their hosts. "If we fought with such roughness as that in the Bundesliga, then I'd hang up my football boots," Keifler reflected after GB won 2-0.

The victory was an unexpected fillip for the FA, who were especially keen that GB qualified as the 1968 Olympics were in Mexico. Two years later, England would defend the World Cup there. If GB qualified, the England manager Alf Ramsey could measure this first experience of British footballers playing at high altitude. It was not to be: Great Britain beat the Germans 2-1 on aggregate, but lost 1-0 on aggregate to Spain in the final qualifier.

That 1967 victory over Germany was arguably Hughes's finest managerial achievement. Like most managers in charge of teams weakened by circumstances beyond their control, the pragmatic Hughes knew that one-off victories were the most realistic ambition outside the UK. Against technically superior opponents, a physical approach was essential. "We were limited being amateurs," said Delaney, "and [Charles] knew that was the only way we could get at teams."

A second Uefa Amateur Cup in 1970 proved even more humiliating than the first as England lost all four qualifiers to Spain and France. Hughes had a final attempt at qualifying for the Olympics, but a vain quest to reach the 1972 Munich games exemplified the terminally flawed concept of amateurism in football. With the exception of Bill Currie of Albion Rovers, a squad of Englishmen from the Northern and Isthmian Leagues faced Bulgaria, who had qualified for the 1970 World Cup in Mexico. There was no professionalism in Communist Bulgaria, where players were given state jobs and then devoted most of their time to football.

"I was marking a guy who was a major but I doubt he'd ever been in a barracks in his entire life," said the GB striker Roddy Haider. Nine of the Bulgarian side to face GB in the first leg at an almost empty Wembley had been in Mexico. Incredibly, Hughes prompted GB to a 1-0 victory. In Sofia, Hughes found that though his English amateurs were tough, the Bulgarians were tougher. GB were thrashed 5-0.

Under Hughes, England's amateurs had a final attempt at the Uefa Amateur Championship in 1974. In the qualifiers, Germany were beaten 1-0 at Wembley

but England missed the finals on goal difference. That same year, Harold Thompson abolished the discredited amateur distinction. With that decision went Hughes's only managerial roles at the FA. England had no amateurs so could not field a side and the GB team — always spearheaded by the FA — drifted into memory before being revived as a one-off in 2012. Hughes never did emulate Norman Creek in qualifying for the Olympics, but his England XI won 48 of 77 internationals, losing just 12 times.

Hughes focused on coaching. When Wade retired in 1983, he took over. In the malleable territory of the amateur game, Hughes' hard-nosed approach to tactics had quickly gained purchase. Talented midfielders like Maurice Lindsay — widely regarded as one of the finest players to shun the professional game — were left watching balls sail over their heads, or found themselves in a crumpled heap after overly physical challenges. Now in the top job, Hughes was in a position to expand his mandate beyond the extinct world of the amateurs and across the whole English game.

Hughes's mantra gained great sway as his books rolled off the presses in their thousands. His most successful work was *The Winning Formula*, which extols the virtues of direct play. In the introduction, Hughes claims that 85% of goals are scored from moves of five consecutive passes or fewer. A quarter of goals in his study involved no passes at all, being scored directly from set plays, defensive rebounds or interceptions; a suitably pragmatic theory when facing stronger opponents, but surely not for every game, for all conditions or for every level from children to professionals?

In his introduction to *The Winning Formula*, Hughes claimed that his results came from three years of analysing Cup finals and international matches started after he joined the FA in 1964. This was later challenged by Charles Reep, an ex-RAF wing commander, who was intrigued by what he called "match performance analysis". During the 1950s — a period when Hughes was becoming fascinated with coaching — Reep had been expounding his theories, including the idea that most goals came from moves of three or fewer passes, in the now defunct magazine *Match Analysis*.

Reep later claimed that the now all-powerful Hughes had exploited his ideas, but Hughes shrugged off the accusations. In 1990, Hughes wrote, "World soccer has been moving in the wrong strategic direction for the better part of 30 years."

The beginning of that wrong turn was taken just as Hughes was about to join the FA. But four years after that typically dogmatic assertion, Hughes was gone, although his books continued to be published. He retired to north Wales, where he watches Premier League football — a competition he voted to bring in. Hughes is rarely seen in public, although he did venture south in 2008 for the funeral of Wade, who had been critical of his successor.

He also gave a rare interview for *GB United?*, my book on the history of the Olympic team. Defending his managerial tactics, Hughes said, "The philosophy players had when I started [managing] was to win at home and draw away. I couldn't see the sense in that. Surely you should try to win them all? You enjoy it more when you win. We always went out to win the game.

"I always said we should support the player with the ball and if he can't pass it forward, be in a position to receive the ball back. But the players should always look forward. If we had good wingers, we would play with wingers; if we didn't we wouldn't use wingers. Players should also play the ball in before they get to the by-line. If you wait until you get to the by-line, the defenders will all be back. It's also important to win the ball in the final third of the field.

"In my era, most defences had four defenders and one in midfield that was a good ball winner. In the GB team [and the England team] that was John Payne. We knew his limitations and said once you've won the ball, look to someone close by to pass it to. There's other players that can't do crunching tackles and I would tell them you don't need to do that, leave the space so that John could do that."

Of the criticism he has received, Hughes said, "It's grossly unfair. We played some long balls but not all the time. You must not allow the media to distract you from what you know or believe to be right. I wrote 31 books and made three films and if there's something in those [books and films] that people don't agree with, come and see me and we'll talk about it. But they never came to see me because they never read those books or saw those films. Very few people would find it easy to write 31 books and make three films just on long-ball play."

Those books and films influenced many people in their time, but the former Crewe

Alexandra manager Dario Gradi, who played under Hughes in the 1960s while an amateur at Sutton, maintained that the ideas in these coaching manuals were taken too far. "His aides took it too literally; that wasn't what Charles was about," said Gradi. "He taught me the art of preparation to defend. With amateur teams then, that was really important as most of your opponents were better, and he left the attacking to two-touch football."

Brought up in a time of austerity, Hughes valued the importance of employment. Roddy Haider, England's most capped amateur with 65 caps, said, "Most of my goals were scored from four or five touches. What [Charles] said was that to keep managers in a job was to play effective, winning football."

For all the players who recall Hughes the martinet, there are plenty of others with different memories. Players traveling down from Scotland or northern England were often put up at his home in Buckinghamshire and shown great hospitality. Peter Hardcastle turned professional after the Bulgaria tie and played in the Football League with Blackpool, Plymouth Argyle and Bradford City: he described Hughes as the "best coach I've ever had." John

Delaney said Hughes was as "one of the best men I knew."

After the bust-up with the SFA was settled in 1967, Millar Hay played for GB in the second round matches against Spain. "What Charlie was trying to do, even with the ruckus we had then, is just what we've got now and not playing before the game," said Hay. "It definitely wasn't an amateur set-up and that's why I went back. Charlie was a difficult man. I only argued with him once, he took no dissent, but when I went down he put me up and he and his wife were great."

Like anyone changing positions, Hughes took his accumulated knowledge with him when he became director of coaching. But his practical experiences of tactics as a manager were formed at a time when football was in great flux. Routinely faced with technically superior opponents, Hughes did all he could to win, embracing a more physical, direct approach that eschewed comfort on the ball. Hamstrung by the gap between tradition and commerce, his pool of players was restricted by people seemingly with different aims. Hughes's employers at the FA wanted to play up, to play the game; he wanted victory regardless of how that was achieved. Ⓑ

The Cult of the *Pibe*

Argentina's ongoing love affair with scruffy urchins with feet of gold

By Sergio Levinsky

"They knocked on the door of the humble house,
The voice of the postman was clearly heard,
And the kid running with all his despair
Stepped on the white dog without meaning to:
'Mum, mum, I will make money
I will be a Baldonedo, Martino, Boyé.'
The boys of the Argentinian west say
That I have a better shot than the great Bernabé.
You will see how nice it is when there on the field
My goals are applauded. I will be triumphant,
I will play in the fifth division and later in the first:
I know there for me awaits consecration."

"The dream of the *pibe*", a tango written in 1943 by Reinaldo Yiso, with music by Juan Puey, illustrates clearly what the figure of the *pibe* has always meant for Argentinian football and the role he has played in the imagination of fans. This particular tango is well known because it was sung on television by Diego Maradona, changing the words to "I will be a Maradona, a Kempes, an Olguín", alluding to the Argentina players about to set off for the 1982 World Cup in Spain. But it had celebrity status anyway, capturing the mood of a period that was also represented by the 1948 Leopoldo Torres Ríos film *Pelota de Trapo* (*Ball of Cloth*), a classic shot in the typical neo-realist style of the immediate post-War period that sought to portray as accurately as possible life in the *barrio*, with its gang culture and economic pressures.

Both tango and film deal with the fact that for the lower sections of society football has always been aspirational, one of the few avenues available for economic and social advancement. A key underlying factor in the great passion for football that was passed on from generation to generation was that in that period, in the golden era of the Argentinian domestic game, it represented a spirit of hope and expansion. Economically, too, Argentina was booming, exporting vast quantities of food around the globe as the world recovered from the Second World War.

Playfulness was a theme of life in the mid-forties: football was about enjoyment and spectacle. It was common to hear a team's forward-line described as "a ballet" while if a team dominated another it was said to have "given it a dance". While there were few opportunities for a direct comparison with Europe, Argentina dominated the South American Championship, while San Lorenzo beat the Spain national team 6-1 in a friendly in January 1947.

The anthropologist Eduardo Archetti was fascinated by the concept of the "pibe" (kid) and the "potrero" (vacant lot) as part of the imaginative construction of nationhood in Argentina, stressing that while football had a British origin, it was their own interpretation of the game that allowed Argentinians to make themselves visible to the world — through the Olympic Games, the World Cup, South American Championships and European tours — once the self-definition of Argentina through the pampas had been replaced by a more urban perspective.

In that respect, the development of the criollo style [the definition of 'criollo' is far from straightforward: originally it referred to those Argentinians of Spanish descent, but it came to be used more generally of those of European heritage who saw themselves as Argentinian] was self-consciously opposed to the game introduced by the British in the late 19th century, focusing far more on trickery and skill on the ball than on power and aerial ability. The recognition of that aspect of Argentinian identity was powered by El Gráfico. The magazine was founded in 1919 and developed the theory of the criollo football as characteristic of the potreros (the gaps between buildings in the city) where kids, unrestricted by teachers organising them as British players who learned the game at school were, found the English game left little space for improvisation. There arose the "gambeta criollo" — a term coined by Borocotó, the editor of El Gráfico — the dribble that allowed a kid to have the most time possible on the ball to show his ability. It was that that made Argentinian football appealing, that led to the mass export of players to Europe, and so led to the talented kid, in poor families, being the one on whom the hopes of social progression rested.

In his notion of the pibe, Borocotó not only pointed to his youth, but also to his freshness, spontaneity and liberty — values associated with childhood that often get lost in maturity with the assumption of responsibility. Moreover, in 1928, Borocotó proposed raising a statue to the inventor of dribbling, saying it should depict "a pibe with a dirty face, a mane of hair rebelling against the comb; with intelligent, roving, trickster and persuasive eyes and a sparkling gaze that seem to hint at a picaresque laugh that does not quite manage to form on his mouth, full of small teeth that might be worn down through eating 'yesterday's bread'. His trousers are a few roughly sewn patches; his vest with Argentinian stripes, with a very low neck and with many holes eaten out by the invisible mice of use. A strip of material tied to his waist and crossing over his chest like a sash serves as braces. His knees covered with the scabs of wounds disinfected by fate; barefoot or with shoes whose holes in the toes suggest they have been made through too much shooting. His stance must be characteristic; it must seem as if he is dribbling with a rag ball. That is important: the ball cannot be any other. A rag ball and preferably bound by an old sock. If this monument is raised one day, there will be many of us who will take off our hat to it, as we do in church."

It's not just any child, but a child who has grown up in poverty, with an impudence and an imagination. Borocotó also maintains he must have learned to play in the potreros, exclusively masculine areas where there is absolute liberty: no rules, no institutions, an empty space for those of rebellious spirit to create.

Another great *El Gráfico* writer of the age, Chantecler, said in 1931 of Fernando "El Marqués" Paternoster, a Racing Club defender who played at the World Cup in 1930, "There is something of the English in his impeccable positioning but the elasticity of his tackles is South American... it is enough to say that he is Argentinian to prove that he did not study theory, or learn through the blackboard... He was from the *potrero*; his lack of weight indicated his need to settle matters with skill, and an efficient skill that is not separate from but demonstrates the intelligence... he has the cleanness of the conjurer, a quickness comprised of acceleration and instantaneous thought."

For a variety of reasons, Argentina has lost some of these concepts of the *potrero* and creativity. Urban change means there is less space to play, while there is a far greater variety of leisure options than there were in the forties and the humiliation of the 1958 World Cup, when Argentina lost 6-1 to Czechoslovakia, led to fa more disciplined and physical style being imported from Europe.

And yet for all that, the *pibe* has remained not only an icon but also a constant potential saviour for Argentinian fans. There are always those who advocate for the *pibe*, who argue when others say a creator should take more responsibility that, "He's only a *pibe*; leave him alone and let him remain a *pibe*." The implication is that he has many years ahead of him, that at some point he will grow up and become an adult but, for now, he should be allowed to enjoy the age of creativity. The romantic urge has only grown stronger as the number

of *pibes* has diminished as more and more kids join football schools run by neighbourhood coaches or former players and so become institutionalised. It has become one of the clichés of Argentinian football for players to say after a game, "I did what the coach asked. I wasn't brilliant but I did as I was told."

Archetti maintains that, as a *pibe*, Diego Maradona is "a kid who will never stop being a kid. When you leave aside the negative aspects, he represents a state of perfection and liberty. To be a *pibe* is to feel the pressure that comes with family, school and society. It is to be imperfect, those imperfections, in their interpretation, relating to what is expected from a grown-up person. Maradona, a great *pibe*, is not perfect as a man but is perfect as a player. This perfection is obtained and maintained because he is a *pibe*."

Maradona looked like a *pibe* for many years. It could be said that he really seemed to be a "lucky *pibe*" when he lifted the World Cup in México in 1986. That image is perhaps the greatest symbol of his triumphs and his world fame. He seemed an innocent kid and so he had not lost his freshness. This paradox, a young man, adult, at the peak of his career still defined as a *pibe* is significant: an important virtue of the best Argentinian players is to preserve, in the best possible ways, the fresh style of a *pibe*. Through this image the idea that the football is only a game may be reproduced and maintained only if the liberty is preserved. Football is in that way conceived as a perfect game for children."

In terms of the style of the *pibe*, Maradona may be compared with Enrique Omar

Sívori, that star of Juventus and Napoli in the fifties and sixties who was a brilliant dribbler but a more disciplined player. There is a less obvious connection with Alfredo Di Stéfano, a more dynamic player, although with an original style of dribbling from his formative years in Argentina, whose physique and fair hair made him look very different to Maradona. At the beginning of Maradona's career, he was always compared to René Houseman, a gangling, bony right-winger who was a world champion with Argentina in 1978. The *potrero* is open to all — you don't need a special physique to play there — but there is a template that keeps repeating: shortness and a body that is not too developed. The key is the ability that overcomes all difficulties.

Archetti stresses that the *pibe* represents a liminal state. It is transitory, not something that can be achieved through effort or determination. It is a promise, someone who must still grow up, who has not arrived at what he could be; it is potential and a hint at some kind of universal model, as underlined by the tendency to relate *pibes* to those of the past.

César Luis Menotti, for instance, would always emphasise that there could not be a Maradona if there had not been a Mario Kempes, a Sívori or a René Pontoni (the idol of Pope Francis) because there is a genetic memory in the development of the technique and the transmission of the culture that today, thanks to various social changes, has been transformed by resistance.

Maradona himself always said his idol was Ricardo Bochini, the great Independiente player of the seventies and eighties. It's said he was behind the decision to select Bochini, then 32, for the 1986 World Cup. When Bochini was brought on late in the semi-final against Belgium for his only ever appearance in a World Cup, Maradona greeted him with the words, "Maestro, we've been waiting for you." The great Colombian Carlos Valderrama, nicknamed *El Pibe*, always insisted he had modelled himself on Bochini.

The image of the team that won the 1986 World Cup as one that was essentially Maradona plus Carlos Bilardo's solid 10-man platform encapsulates the friction between the game seen as a diversion and the discipline of the unit. Stories of Juan Román Riquelme, Sergio Agüero or Carlos Tévez playing with friends in their spare time, in *potreros* or in the poorest area of Buenos Aires, highlights that they continue to be *pibes* even when professionally mature.

Is Lionel Messi a *pibe*? He is, and for all the doubts as to whether he really fits the template, he has probably never stopped being one. It's characteristic of the *pibe* that he does not need to take instruction and that he imposes his style even in silence, that he so clearly enjoys what he is doing and that from being a small child to a fully-fledged professional, he has never needed any additional motivation to play — even though his football career has been institutional from a very young age. It's as though no external factor could stifle his creativity.

El pibe
With the shirt of Barça
Number 10
Not Nike nor anything
20 pesos to a Paraguayan,
He bought it in Constitución.
El pibe,

*With the one that says Messi
carries the ball,
crosses the square
of Villa Lugano.
He lifts his head and shoots at goal,
Always at the goal".*

("*More Than a Crack*", a tango by Pablo Marchetti with music by Marcelo Mercadante, Barcelona, 2009).

In spite of the institutionalisation of young talent and the loss of so much of what characterised Argentina in the first fifty years of the twentieth century, the imagination lives on. In the stadium, every time there appears a group of new children, with the ability and potential to create a different football to the mediocrity that has abounded in Argentina for years, there will come a shout of support for the *pibes*, the wish that they will do what they want, not what the coach tells them, that they will enjoy themselves. There is always time for obedience.

Stroke is the third biggest killer and the leading cause of severe adult disability in the UK.

Behind much of the Stroke Association's unique work are people just like you – people who want to do something powerful and lasting through their Will.

To find out more about leaving a gift in your Will please call us on **020 7566 1505** or email **legacy@stroke.org.uk**

stroke.org.uk

69

Defenders of the Faith

"...the staple subject of daily conversation..."

The Birth of the Fan

Why Victorians flocked to watch 22 men kicking a pig's bladder about

By Paul Brown

Being a football fan is both a privilege and a burden. When you're winning, it's the best thing on Earth and, when you're not, it's the end of the world. And the thing about being a football fan is, whichever way fortune swings, you're stuck with the game and your team for life. We've come to accept the great hold that football has on us. But how did this happen? How did we become so entirely wrapped up in the game? How did we become football fans?

Many of us can trace the lineage of our support through our fathers, our grandfathers and so on. But association football has only been around for 150 years. At some point, perhaps six or seven generations ago, our ancestors discovered and embraced the emerging game, developed affinities for individual clubs, cheered and sang and helped to initiate the fan culture that we're part of today. But the roots of football fandom were established long before the association game was invented.

In 1818, the editor of the *Lancaster Gazette* recalled a game that occurred around the end of the 18th century. "About 20 years ago," he wrote, "I well remember being a spectator at a foot-ball match in the neighbourhood of London between 10 young men from Cumberland and 10 from Westmoreland.

The sum played for was, I think, 20 guineas. The novelty of the diversion, as it may be thought, attracted a great number of spectators. The game was played with great spirit by both parties, who discovered an agility that surprised and astonished the honest Cockneys."

These "honest Cockneys" were among the earliest of football spectators, but they can scarcely be called fans. They were instead curious bystanders, "surprised and astonished" at the scene they were witnessing. They had no connection with the men from Cumberland and Westmoreland, and no affiliation with either team. Nor, most likely, did they have a clear understanding of whatever antiquated rules the match was played by. Yet they were curious enough to attend and interested enough to watch, and perhaps entertained enough to make a mental note further to explore the game of foot-ball.

The most prevalent form of organised football during the first half of the 19th century was the folk or mob game, a rough-and-tumble contest that brought havoc to the streets of towns and villages across the country. The game, which could involve hundreds of players and last all day, must have been a compelling spectacle, with contemporary reports evoking something like a round ball version of the Pamplona bull run. An account in the mid-19th century *Peter Parley's Annual* describes how people would watch the traditional Shrove Tuesday game at Derby: "Here the shops are found to be shut, and the houses all round are filled with spectators, men, women and children, crowding the windows and perching on the house-tops."

It seems unlikely that these crowded spectators could have been impartial. Mob games were played between neighbouring villages, or between one end of a town and the other. There were rivalries involved and the spectators must have favoured their own friends and neighbours, offering them encouragement and cheers. It was natural that these early spectators would "support" their local team because, at a time before any real transport links had been established, few of them would ever venture beyond the confines of their own communities. The rest of the world were outsiders and innate rivals. Local or tribal affiliation would remain a key theme throughout the evolution of the football fan.

For clear evidence of partisan support in early football, we can turn to the public school game, which was prevalent by the mid-1800s. Games were played between the school houses, which could draw upon their boarders for support. In 1852, *Bell's Life* in London reported that a match at Harrow between the Middlemist and Simpkinson houses was "attended by a considerable muster of spectators". At Eton in 1853, *Bell's* described "a match for cock of college" between Mrs Drury's and Mr Balston's houses. "After much good play on both sides, Mrs Drury's were hailed 'cocks' by a hearty cheer from the

spectators, by obtaining three goals to two goals and one rouge," reported the paper. A "match for cock", by the way, was a public school cup match, while a rouge was method of scoring that resembled a touchdown.

The cheers of these early football spectators did sometimes turn to jeers. Describing an 1854 match at Eton between Mrs Drury's and Rev Coleridge's houses, *Bell's* reported that "a most exciting match" had been won by Mrs Drury's, "to the great satisfaction of the majority of the spectators." However, the paper added: "We were sorry to hear the offensive shouts of one 'Mackintoshed stranger', which, however, were almost entirely drowned out by the universal supporters of the Druryites."

Outside of the public schools, football clubs began to form. Initially, these clubs arranged matches between their own members, so there could be little real rivalry involved. Clubs such as Sheffield FC, formed in 1857 and regarded as the world's oldest football club still in existence, split their members into teams using criteria such as "Tall versus Short" and "Married versus Single" (and, on at least one occasion, "Handsome versus Ugly"). Things moved on in 1860 with the formation of Hallam FC and the creation of football's first local rivalry.

The first derby match was played at Hallam's Stoneygate ground on Boxing Day 1860. Despite heavy snow, "a large number of spectators" saw Sheffield win 2-0. According to the *Sheffield Daily Telegraph*, "The spirit exhibited by those who were present prevented the game from becoming uninteresting to the observers, who were extremely liberal with their plaudits on the successful 'charge' or quiet 'dodge', and equally unsparing in their sarcasm and country 'chaff' on the unfortunate victims of the slippery ground." The dictionary definition of "chaff" is "banter", which has therefore been associated with football since the very first club versus club match.

The rivalry between Sheffield and Hallam was based on more than just locality. Although based in a mainly working class industrial town, Sheffield FC was a middle-class club that had strong links with the public schools. Membership was restricted to "gentlemen", with the *Sheffield Daily Telegraph* referring to Sheffield FC's doctors, solicitors and architects as "the elite of the town". "Its members are exclusively of the middle class," the paper commented, "and its patrons and supporters include most of the leading men in the neighbourhood."

Hallam FC had been formed with the specific intention of creating a more inclusive club. For the first time, class became an issue, with spectators drawn toward clubs that best represented their social groups. As the historian EP Thompson later noted, the working class had emerged from the industrial revolution as a disenfranchised and discontented group. Class "acquired a peculiar resonance in English life," Thompson wrote. "Everything, from their schools to their shops, their chapels to their amusements, was turned into a battleground of class."

In 1862, "a very fair number of spectators" attended a derby at Sheffield FC's Bramall Lane. "The Hallam men played with great determination, and successfully defended their goal,"

reported the *Sheffield & Rotherham Independent*. "They appeared to have many partisans present and when they succeeded in 'downing' a man, their ardent friends were more noisily jubilant." At one point, a bout of fisticuffs between opposition players caused supporters to spill onto the pitch. "[The players] were surrounded by partisans, and for a few minutes there was every appearance of a general fight among players and spectators," the paper reported.

In London, where the clubs that would go on to form the Football Association were establishing themselves, football supporters remained much more restrained. The influential Forest club, later renamed Wanderers, moved to a new ground in Leytonstone in 1863. A report from *Bell's* suggests an idyllic scene, describing the ground as, "a large field with a noble avenue of trees running through it, which afforded a pleasant promenade for the spectators, of whom there was a goodly muster, including many of the fair sex, who added to the attractions of the sport."

After the formation of the Football Association, in October 1863, the game gradually became more organised and widespread. The publication of the FA's Laws of the Game provided clubs with a universal set of rules, making it easier to arrange and play matches. New clubs emerged, fixture lists expanded, and there were more opportunities for people to watch football.

Where attendances were recorded for London matches in the 1860s and 1870s, they rarely exceeded a few hundred. The five unofficial England versus Scotland "Alcock Internationals", arranged by the

FA secretary CW Alcock and played at the Oval between 1870 and 1872, attracted only around 600 paying spectators, many of whom were "away" fans. In the first match, Scotland scored a goal "amid vociferous applause from the 'canny Scots', who represented no small portion of the spectators".

The first official international match was played in Glasgow in November 1872 and this provided further evidence of the Scottish appetite for watching football. Special buses ran from the city centre to the West of Scotland Cricket Ground, and up to 4,000 spectators turned up to see Scotland and England draw 0-0. "They applauded enthusiastically, but, owing to their strong national feeling, not altogether impartially," said the *Graphic* magazine.

Illustrations of the international, published in the *Graphic*, provide a vision of what early football fans looked like. Smartly dressed in shirts, ties and overcoats, they wear top hats and billycocks, and crowd right up against the rope that cordons the pitch. There are plenty of smokers among their number and lots of fashionable facial hair. The fact that those present appear well-to-do is likely related to the fact that tickets for the international cost around four times more than for a typical club match.

The first FA Cup Final, between Wanderers and Old Etonians in 1872, was watched by a crowd of 2,000. "There were not a great number of visitors at the Oval on Saturday afternoon," commented *Bell's*, "the reason being possibly that an admission fee of a shilling was charged." In 1873, a London representative team travelled to Bramall

Lane to play a Sheffield side and found a much larger crowd. "On arrival at the ground the Londoners must have been surprised to see the number of spectators who had mustered, there being no less than 5000," reported the *Sheffield Independent*.

That paper also gave an indication of the facilities provided for early football fans. "Bramall Lane is favourably adapted for football matches, both as regards the playing portion and the accommodation of spectators," said the *Independent*. "The former is generally in good condition, and the gallery over the refreshment booths affords a capital view. A stand has been erected between Wright's house and the booths, and between the latter and the east side of the ground earthworks have been thrown up, all of which were crowded with eager spectators."

One can only speculate whether the Bramall Lane refreshment booths sold Bovril, which was marketed in the 1870s, rather unappetisingly, as "Johnston's Fluid Beef". Certainly, however, the Bramall Lane facilities were advanced at a time when duckboards placed over muddy ground were considered a luxury. After an 1873 FA Cup tie between Old Etonians and Swifts, *Bell's* reported: "The afternoon was fine, and there was a pretty good number of visitors who were accommodated with boards to stand upon, an example which might be judiciously followed at other grounds, especially where a charge is made for admission."

During the 1880s, the game experienced what the *Penny Illustrated* called a "rapid rise in popular favour". Association football was now in its third decade, and a generation of young fans had grown up watching the game. But the rise of the football fan was also aided by two major pieces of legislation. Firstly, the various Factory Acts ordered that all work should end on a Saturday by 2pm. Secondly, the Education Act required all children to be taught to read and write. Workers had Saturday afternoons free to watch football and a growing audience could read about the game.

The new-found freedom on Saturday afternoons had a profound effect on the popularity of football in industrial towns. There were few pastimes available to them — the pub, the music hall, and now football. Ernest Ensor, writing in the *National Review* in the 1890s, said that the "astonishing increase" in the numbers of people watching football was "largely due to the dull monotony of life in our large towns". "It is the absolute necessity of some change, some interest outside the daily work, which has long since ceased to be interesting, that causes the large crowds at the weekly matches," he wrote.

Responding to Ensor's article, the *London Standard* added that the press was also responsible for "a great deal of the extravagant excitement now displayed over football". Britain's growing audience of readers had created a newspaper boom and football coverage increased along with the game's popularity, expanding across the sports columns and into Saturday night football specials. "By minutely discussing the merits and habits of individual players and in other ways some of the newspapers have fostered the interest in football until it has become nothing less than a mania," said the

Standard. "In many of the great industrial centres football is the staple subject of daily conversation — in fact little else is spoken of."

It was around this time that many of modern football's biggest clubs were founded. Most of them emerged from institutions — workplaces, churches, cricket clubs, schools — that provided ready-made bubbles of support. Manchester United was established in 1878 as Newton Heath LYR by workers at a Lancashire and Yorkshire Railway depot. Manchester City was originally St Mark's, formed by the rector of a church in West Gorton. Arsenal was Dial Square, a works team from the Royal Armaments Factory in Woolwich, while Everton was a church team founded as St Domingo's FC. Gradually, these clubs expanded beyond their institutions and began to represent their respective localities.

In order to attract supporters, emergent clubs placed posters in shop windows and ads in newspapers. One ad from 1882 promotes a match between Nottingham Forest and Small Heath Alliance (now Birmingham City):

FOOTBALL! – OPENING MATCH.
Notts [*sic*] Forest v. Small Heath Alliance.
On Saturday next, September 23, 1882.
Kick-off at 4pm prompt.
Admission 3d. Reserve 2d extra.
Omnibuses to the ground every ten minutes.
A tent will be provided for the ladies.

By now, football spectators were being referred to as "supporters". In 1882, after Arbroath came back from 0-3 down to beat Dundee East End 4-3, the *Dundee Courier & Argus* wrote: "The unexpected turn made the hearts of the Arbroath supporters (and they were not few) jubilant. An extraordinary amount of party spirit was displayed, every little bit of real play by the Arbroath being cheered to the echo."

They weren't yet being referred to as "fans", although they could sometimes be fanatical. "The excitement was intense from the beginning, but language indulged in and the uncomplimentary epithets hurled at the players by fanatic partisans were only detrimental to the game of football," remarked the *Essex Standard* after one particular match. The contraction "fan" originated in the US through baseball around the 1880s. Football supporters weren't known as "fans" until the early 20th century.

Supporters weren't being referred to as "customers" yet, either, but the commercial relationship between fans and clubs became more pronounced in the mid-1880s, following the legalisation of professionalism. In order to pay their players, clubs need to attract a sizeable number of supporters. Large "gates" allowed clubs to pay higher wages and attract better players. And, of course, better players drew more supporters. The arrival of the professional footballer also changed the make-up of teams, which were no longer comprised entirely of local men. But this didn't affect the tribal nature of football support.

The great sportsman, politician and almost-king of Albania CB Fry wrote about this in 1895. "The crowds who flock to see two football teams play in the North or Midlands like a good match," said Fry, "but their predominating desire is to see their own champions win, and this desire is made the more intense by the fact that the players are fellow-townsmen with whom they are in touch, or whom perhaps they know personally. Nowadays, it is true, most of the Northern Association teams are composed of invaders from across the Border; but these are soon identified with their new home, and become to all intents and purposes natives."

By the time the Football League was founded in 1888, the typical admission fee was sixpence (equivalent to around £1.50 today), which wasn't cheap considering the average weekly wage for a general labourer was only 13 shillings (around £35). Season tickets were relatively common and most League clubs had several hundred season ticket holders. The first examples of merchandise emerged at this time, too, with clubs selling match programmes and team photographs. For kids, there were comics offering football stories and player interviews, plus a brand new craze for collectible football cards. "No words of ours can adequately describe the present popularity of football with the public," wrote Montague Shearman, in his 1887 book *Athletics and Football*. "It is no rare thing in the North and Midlands for 10,000 people to pay money to witness an ordinary club match, or for half as many again to assemble for a Cup Tie. If Aston Villa meet Notts County at Trent Bridge, special trains have to be run from Birmingham to carry the spectators who go over to see the match. The enthusiasm and excitement which follow each move in the game are unbounded. The writer has heard the roar that followed the scoring of a goal from a distance of more than half a mile."

Shearman mentions special trains, and the expansion of the railways was another key factor in the development of the football fan. New transport links – train, tram and omnibus – allowed the catchment areas of clubs to grow, and allowed fans to travel to away matches. Railway companies advertised football specials in local newspapers, and they were hugely popular. Previously, supporters would have crowded outside local newspaper offices, waiting for score updates to be delivered via telegraph or carrier pigeon. Now they could embark on "cheap excursions" to faraway towns in order to support their heroes.

"When the town to be visited is very remote, the journey has, of course, to be begun very early," said the *Sheffield Independent*. "Aston Villa versus Sunderland, at Sunderland, means real hardship for the enthusiasts who start from Birmingham before day-break. That stupendous jaunt may be made for a very few shillings, and if the window is not clouded with human breath all the way, the mere spectacle of so much of England's surface ought to be worth twice the money."

Although travelling football fans were regarded with wariness, particularly by the London press when they descended upon the capital for cup finals, bad behaviour was generally limited to drunken boisterousness and there is no evidence of any organised hooliganism during football's earliest years. Certainly there were spontaneous violent incidents, inside and outside of grounds. In 1885, following a match between Aston Villa and Preston North End, Villa fans objected to their 5-0 defeat by chasing the Preston players from the field. According to one

witness, the players were pursued for half a mile by "2,000 howling roughs". "Thicker and faster came the stones, showers of spittle covered us and we were struck at with sticks and umbrellas," reported the witness.

However, considering that football had evolved from a brutal mob game over just a few decades, early fans were relatively well-behaved. There was an argument that football prevented violence rather than encouraged it. "Since football became popular with all classes, there have been less wrenching off of knockers and 'boxing of the watch', and fewer free fights in the street," wrote Montague Shearman. "Football has its national uses quite apart from the cheap enjoyment it has given to thousands."

Alcohol also provided cheap enjoyment and it played an important part in the early matchday experience. Fans leaving work at lunchtime would quench their thirst by downing multiple pints of beer purchased from pushcarts outside their factories and foundries. Pre-match drinking continued in pubs on the way to the ground. "Happy is the publican who is installed near the entrances to football fields," commented the *Sheffield Independent*. Football betting also became prevalent as the game's popularity increased, with bookmakers setting up at grounds, and newspapers issuing score forecast coupons — a forerunner of the football pools.

By the 1890s, the grounds of league teams had been developed and improved. Most had at least one grandstand, plus banked standing terraces that afforded spectators better views. Entry was gained by paying a gateman through a hole in a wall. Once inside, fans packed right up against the touchlines, with those at the back needing to crane their necks above a sea of hats. There were no replica strips, or even scarves, but some fans wore cardboard badges, featuring their team's colours, pushed into their hatbands.

While awaiting kick-off, fans enjoyed communal singing. Before the 1888 FA Cup Final between West Brom and Preston, the fans sang "Two Lovely Black Eyes", "Rule Britannia" and "other ditties". Then, once the game was underway, fans reacted with "savage enthusiasm". "Every pass, every run, every shot at goal, was the signal for a deafening roar," explained the *Pall Mall Gazette*. "Play up!" was a popular yell of encouragement. But negative aspects of the game would be met with "a hurricane of criticism", containing no little profanity.

"The multitude flock to the field in their workaday dirt and with their workaday adjectives very loose on their tongues," wrote Charles Edwards in the Victorian magazine *The Nineteenth Century*. "In Lancashire and the Black Country it is really surprising what a number of emphatic and even mysterious expletives may be heard on these Saturday afternoons. Their supporters often forget themselves in the ferocity of their cries. 'Down him!' 'Sit on his chest!' 'Knock their ribs in!'"

Chiefly, though, contemporary sources credit early fans with unrestrained enthusiasm, "How keenly the onlookers watch the game! How well they appreciate and note every little display of science!," wrote an anonymous ex-international in *Chums* in 1892. "A running fire of cheers accompanies a favourite player as he sprints and dodges down the line. The cries grow deeper as he nears the goal, and culminate in a very roar as he kicks the ball through it."

The rise of the football fan and the growing popularity of the game can be tracked via FA Cup Final attendance figures. From 2,000 in 1872, attendances increased to 6,500 in 1882, 15,000 in 1886, 33,000 in 1892, and 66,000 in 1897. At the 1901 final, the attendance was almost 111,000. League matches were less well-attended, but by the beginning of the 20th century top first division clubs were attracting average crowds of around 20,000. "There is no mistake about it," wrote Charles Edwards, "the exercise is a passion nowadays and not merely a recreation."

Then, as now, football was compelling and addictive and, 150 years after its invention, it's easy to appreciate how our ancestors became hooked on the game. As a *Daily News* reporter wrote in 1892, "Nobody who witnesses a match between first class teams can wonder at the hold which football has obtained upon the affections of the people, and few would go away without having suddenly acquired an interest in the game." ⓑ

Jerusalem Syndrome

The mysterious disappearance of Guma Aguiar, the saviour of Beitar Jerusalem

By James Montague

Jerusalem Syndrome Je·ru·sa·lem Syn·drome [ji-**roo**-*suh*-l*uh* m, -*zuh*-] [sin-drohm, -druhm] **(n)** *A group of mental phenomena involving the presence of either religiously themed obsessive ideas, delusions or other psychosis-like experiences that are triggered by a visit to the city of Jerusalem. It is not endemic to one single religion or denomination but has affected Jews, Christians and Muslims of many different backgrounds.*

June 2012

The TT Zion was found marooned but otherwise seaworthy on a sandbank near East Las Olas Boulevard, Fort Lauderdale. The boulevard is an upmarket stretch of prime real estate: Dan Quayle once lived here, as did Sonny and Cher, and the TT Zion wouldn't normally look out of place in such salubrious surroundings. But on this warm and wet summer night the TT Zion wasn't where it should be. Its twin engines were running, the lights were on. But the TT Zion was empty, abandoned, lost.

Las Olas means 'The Waves' in Spanish, a nod to Florida's deceptively dangerous shoreline. Shark attacks are more common here than anywhere else in the world. Last year the University of Florida's International Shark Attack File programme recorded 80 unprovoked attacks worldwide, 53 of those in the US. Just under half of those, 26, were in Florida, the joint highest since records began. High winds and hurricanes regularly batter a coastline renowned for its strong rip tides, killing dozens every year. The Gulf Stream charges north at 3.5 knots just a few miles from the coast, its warm waters powering the violent storms that tear along the Eastern seaboard.

It was dark, the winds high. Four foot waves had been recorded that night. For Florida, it was the start of one of the most destructive hurricane seasons in living memory — a total of 10 would be formed over the coming months, including Hurricane Sandy, which would go on to batter New York. Over 200 lives would be lost and $78 billion worth of damage caused.

But as Guma Aguiar boarded the TT Zion, a homage to the ancient name of Jerusalem, hurricane season was still in its infancy — albeit, the busiest pre-July hurricane season on record. It was an apt name for Aguiar's 31-foot, $2.1 million luxury pride and joy. The 35-year-old Jewish multi-millionaire had made Jerusalem the capital of his world. Ever since his natural gas exploration company Leor Energy discovered and then sold the largest natural gas field in the US, Aguiar had pumped millions of dollars into the city.

He wasn't always Jewish. At least, he didn't always identify himself as Jewish. Born in Brazil to a Jewish mother, Aguiar was raised a Catholic but was brought back to Judaism by Rabbi Tovia Singer, founder and director of Outreach Judaism. Outreach Judaism is a self-declared "counter-missionary" organisation "dedicated to countering the efforts of fundamentalist Christian groups and cults who specifically target Jews for conversion." The controversial Rabbi Singer had discovered Aguiar's roots and aggressively attempted to reconnect him to his heritage. Aguiar was 26 at the time.

Three years later his stewardship of Leor had netted him an estimated fortune of $200 million. Reborn in his faith, Aguiar became enchanted with Jerusalem. He spent big to attract the attentions of the great and good in Israel, donating tens of millions of dollars to a host of Jewish organisations. But his biggest outlay came in June 2009, when he decided he was going to buy Beitar Jerusalem[1], Israel's most popular and most controversial football club. He sunk $4 million into the team and was welcomed to the club like a saviour. He had found acceptance. He had found home.

But, within seven months, Aguiar wasn't to be seen on the club's terraces any more. He was being held in a psychiatric institution after a series of episodes in Israel. He was flown home, half his fortune gone, deeply embroiled in an on-going legal case against his uncle and business partner Thomas Kaplan, an Oxford University-trained historian with a love of nature conservation who had made his

money in mining and natural gas. Aguiar's wife, Jamie, had asked him for a divorce.

According to the US Coastguard's report on the boat's GPS signal, the TT Zion left its mooring on 19 June 2012 at 7.29pm and travelled at 31 miles per hour north east — such a speed that the TT Zion jumped the waves, according to one eye witness — until abruptly coming to a halt, turning and drifting back to East Las Olas Boulevard. Aguiar was gone; his phone and wallet were found on board. At first it seemed like a clear case of suicide, a troubled young man who was about to lose everything taking his final stand. But a few days after his disappearance, a vicious series of court battles erupted over Aguiar's assets. Accusations of opulence, avarice, indulgence, greed and manipulation were made as Aguiar's final resting place remained unknown. The TT Zion stopped just short of the Gulf Stream. One coastguardsman suggested that the abrupt change of speed and the boat's broken tow bar indicated that Aguiar might have been thrown overboard. In the Gulf Stream, his body would be taken north and never seen again. In fact, few involved in the case truly expected his remains to be found, but not because of the speed of the Gulf Stream. A very different explanation was gaining traction. His body might not be found because there might not be a body to be found.

Guma Aguiar might not be dead after all.

The Teddy Stadium in Jerusalem is named after the city's greatest mayor,

1 For more on the club and its recent changes of ownership, see Shaul Adar's piece in Issue Three.

Theodor Kollek. Teddy, as he was affectionately named, came to power in 1965 after running for office at the insistence of then Prime Minister David Ben-Gurion. He ruled over a poor, under-developed western half of the city but made his name when Israel captured the eastern, Arab half of Jerusalem during the Six Day War of 1967 and he oversaw the city's modernisation. He was re-elected five times. Teddy was both a Zionist and a pragmatist, indelibly wedded to the idea of a united Jerusalem under Israeli rule but also sympathetic towards the plight of the city's newly disenfranchised Arab population. When he died in 2007 at the age of 95 the *New York Times*'s obituary described how Israel's assassinated Prime Minister Yitzhak Rabin had called him 'the greatest builder of Jerusalem since Herod the Great.'

Today the vast, modern steel and brick edifice that bears Kollek's name is home to Beitar Jerusalem. But in recent years, the stadium has seen little of the pragmatism or tolerance that saw Teddy demand that the Israeli military's first job after capturing East Jerusalem was to distribute free milk to Arab children. Beitar has long been the team of the religious, nationalistic right, representing Israel's working-class Mizrahim population, Jews who have their roots in the Arab world. After Israel's creation in 1948, the government was dominated by the white European Jews who had travelled mostly from Germany, Poland and Romania, the Ashkenazim who helped to prolong the Labor party's leftist hegemony.

But the club's fans backed the centre-right Likud party in huge numbers. When Likud finally broke the Labor party's dominance in the 1977 election, it was seen as a watershed moment for Israel's Mizrahim and the religious right. Beitar played its part too, winning its first cup final the year before against the country's biggest team, Maccabi Tel Aviv, a team steeped in the modern history of the Ashkenazim. Beitar could count on the likes of Ehud Olmert, Ariel Sharon and Benjamin Netanyahu as supporters. Indeed, many cut their administrative teeth on Beitar's board before moving into the Knesset. Nobody saw the rise of Likud and the rise of Beitar Jerusalem as a coincidence. One was inexorably connected to the other.

Today the club is renowned in Israel for its hardcore of racist fans, a large minority of whom call themselves *La Familia*, and for the fact that the team has never had an Arab play for it[2]. Anti-Arab chants regularly rise from the terraces. The club has received many sanctions for its racism: points deductions and heavy fines among them. The supporters have been regularly banned from the Teddy too, the team forced to play behind closed doors. Nothing seemed to chastise the faithful. Nothing seemed able to change the culture at the club.

Yet Beitar exerted a strong pull on the rich and the powerful. With so many politically influential supporters, wealthy men lined up to help the club. It was often said that Beitar commanded one million supporters, quite a prize in a country of six million. One of

2 Gaydamak did try to sign an Arab player, but cancelled the deal because of protests from fans.

those beguiled by the club was Arkadi Gaydamak, a controversial Russian billionaire who had an outstanding international arrest warrant from France over his dealings in Angola during the civil war. He had invested tens of millions of dollars in the club, bankrolling it to the championship. He tried to instigate the signing of Israel's best Arab player, Abass Suan. But his efforts to make Beitar a club for everyone in Jerusalem came to nothing. The fans instead rioted and the move was dropped. Later *La Familia* looted the Israeli FA's offices. At one game they whistled during a minute's silence in memory of Yitzhak Rabin. They sang, "Mohammed is a homo".

"The idiot bastards can leave," Gaydamak said of the hardcore troublemakers at his club after a particularly nasty pitch invasion. "The fans who went wild yesterday are bastards, and I have no respect for them. While their numbers are in the thousands, they are not the majority."

Gaydamak, of course, had his eyes on a bigger prize. He held political ambition and had become a thorn in the then Prime Minister Ehud Olmert's side, staging a series of deft publicity stunts. The finest was setting up a luxury tent village in a park in Tel Aviv for the residents of an Israeli town under siege by rockets from Gaza in 2007. Olmert, who at the time had a 0% popularity rating in one national newspaper poll, had insisted that the residents of the towns near Gaza stay put, otherwise Hamas might view it as surrender. But hundreds of terrified residents took up Gaydamak's offer. Each child was given a black and gold Beitar scarf, the menorah stitched at both ends, on arrival. Still,

Gaydamak's populism didn't translate to votes. After setting up his own political party he announced in 2008 he would — like Teddy Kollek before him — run for mayor of Jerusalem. He was routed at the ballot box, coming a distant third. The humiliation, coupled with the financial crash which hit his business interests hard, saw Gaydamak withdraw from Beitar as he actively looked for a new buyer for the club.

Guma Aguiar may have grown up in Brazil but he wasn't much of a football fan. He was a basketball man through and through. But he had quickly gained a reputation for his acts of philanthropy in Israel after selling Leor Energy and his donations brought him to the attention of Israel's politicians — he could count the President Shimon Peres as a close friend — and, eventually, Beitar. Without Gaydamak's backing, the club was on the verge of going under. Aguiar was persuaded to sink US $4m in to the club, as well as a further $1.5m in to the city's basketball team Hapoel Jerusalem. That was in June 2009 and Aguiar agreed to a telephone interview where I asked him about how his decision to invest in Beitar and Hapoel came about.

"I love Jerusalem, it's special. You're not in Kansas anymore, that's for sure," Aguiar explained, sounding confident and erudite as he did in the slew of TV interviews he had conducted to woo the Israeli media. "I was approached," he said of how Beitar's predicament was brought to his attention. "There are a lot of people here who feel strongly about their teams. It reminds me a lot of Brazil, going to the Maracanã. A lot people here don't care about anything other than football. I can relate to that."

Beitar were desperate for a new saviour and Aguiar seemed to be the perfect fit. He was young, rich and eager to please. Unlike Gaydamak, he also didn't have any ambition for elected office. "I don't want to use the football as a political tool because that's not fair, as an outsider, to come in and have a [political] agenda," he said. In fact Aguiar, despite being married with four young children, had a reputation as a flamboyant playboy who liked to burn the candle at both ends. "Like Madonna said the other night, this [Jerusalem] is the centre of the universe," he told a local TV channel while trying to play tennis, badly. He wore sunglasses, his head was bowed, voice hoarse. "The only party I'm interested in forming is just a party." But he understood Beitar's reputation in the world and how it was beginning to harm, even define, the city's standing. "The one thing I would like to see is more tolerance from the fans. In order for us to be competitive and to attract talent we want to play abroad and not be viewed as total hooligans. I certainly wouldn't want to go to Barcelona and hear them singing 'Death to the Jews'."

Like Gaydamak, he wanted to improve Jerusalem's image. "I want to see the flagship name of Jerusalem, bring some outsiders to Israel to visit [and] create awareness about this place," he said. "Raising the profile of Jerusalem would be the most positive outcome. It's torn apart by a lot of conflict. But there are Christians, Jews and Muslims here that love the land they live in. I want Christian and Muslim fans here too."

Aguiar sounded sincere and knowledgeable. He agreed we should meet in Israel later in the year, after he had seen exactly what he had bought into.

On August 28 Guma Aguiar walked on to the pitch at the Teddy Stadium to rapturous applause. It was Beitar's first match of the season, against their arch-rivals Hapoel Tel Aviv. Arabs had long played for the team. The Israeli TV station Channel 1 aired an interview with Aguiar before the kick-off. It began with him blowing a *shofar*, a traditional ram's horn blown during some Jewish religious ceremonies.

"It's my first time in the Teddy Stadium," he said to the camera. His shirt collar was open, revealing a silver Star of David on a necklace. "They say, 'Are you some kind of Messiah?' I say no, I don't want to be associated with a word like that. I have no idea [about the outcome of the Hapoel game]. Only God knows. Maybe he's feeling extra sympathetic to Jerusalem tonight. And if not, perhaps he'll feel extra sympathetic later in the year."

On the pitch a light and smoke show was under way. Dance music thumped out as beautiful Israeli girls danced in the centre circle. On the sidelines Aguiar was jumping up and down to the beat, dancing with a man dressed in a dog suit. Aguiar moved into the centre circle and wiggled his hips in time with the music next to the singer. He closed his eyes, arms in the air and stumbled through the choreography. The dancers didn't miss a beat. "This is Aguiar's night," said Danny Neuman, a Beitar legend commentating on the match for the night. "He has saved Beitar."

The game finished 0-0.

It should have been a quiet midweek evening in the Irish bar in the centre of Jerusalem but Guma Aguiar was gearing up for a long night. Outside, on the quaint cobbled street, a horde of expensive, blacked out 4x4s sat clustered around the door, paying little heed to the city's parking laws. Inside the lights were low, the bar empty. In one corner, up on a raised platform, stood the tall figure of Aguiar. A ring of steel surrounded him; pumped, shaven headed bodyguards wearing black jeans and black t-shirts. They stood firm as we approached. Aguiar was standing next to an identically dressed bodyguard, who was rolling him a cigarette. Around him several Beitar players, one an Israel international, hovered, eager for his attention. "Guma, can you get me a ticket to an NBA game?" one pleaded. Aguiar ignored him and lit his fat cigarette. The strong smell of marijuana filled the room.

It had been a few months since Aguiar and I had spoken on the phone. He had agreed to meet me in his favourite bar along with Jeremy, an Israeli journalist I had met at a Beitar match three and a half years previously and who was now the sports editor of the *Jerusalem Post*. Aguiar trusted Jeremy and was eager to curry favour with a paper that was widely read in North America. Aguiar spotted him, raised his arm, and the black sea parted.

It was clear that not all was well. Aguiar seemed agitated. He couldn't focus on anyone for more than a few seconds before losing his trail of thought. Sometimes he would start the same conversation two, three, occasionally four times. The sycophants laughed. His personal bodyguard rolled him another and then another. He had no recollection of our conversation a few months previously, nor of what he had said a

few moments before. But his generosity remained intact. He bought round after round of drinks. Aguiar couldn't make eye contact when we talked. He hung his head to give the illusion of listening. He pressed the half-smoked cigarette between my fingers. I inhaled.

Stars.

A tunnel.

Silence.

White noise.

The world reformed around me. It could have been an hour. It could have been 10 seconds.

Beitar's season had begun in mixed fashion. They drew the first two league matches of the season 0-0, against arguably their two biggest rivals, Hapoel Tel Aviv and the Arab club Bnei Sakhnin. A handful of narrow victories against low-ranked opponents followed. But as the end of the year approached it was clear that Beitar would not be challenging for the league title, despite the early season optimism. Aguiar's life was taking an equally rocky path. As his profile rose, so did interest in his private life. A court case between Aguiar and his uncle Thomas Kaplan — the man whom he had gone in to business with a few years previously, making his fortune when they sold Leor — had become a taste of the familial litigation to come.

In January 2009 Kaplan launched a legal action to remove Aguiar as a director of the Lillian Jean Kaplan Foundation, named in honour of Thomas' mother. According to the *South Florida Sun*

Sentinel Thomas Kaplan had given $40m to the foundation, money used, among other things, to build wells in Africa. But Kaplan had accused his nephew of misspending as much as US$7m in efforts to "claim that he is the Messiah and to promote his messianic mission."

The lawsuit was just one battle in a legal war with his uncle over the sale of Leor. Aguiar believed he was due $18m more. Kaplan believed that Aguiar had misappropriated company funds — making inappropriate payments to himself and his family — and wanted Aguiar's share of the sale returned. The *Sentinel* dubbed it "the Messiah lawsuit".

"They are trying to distract and intimidate me from going on with my life," Aguiar told them.

There was also the issue of his arrest in Florida on drugs charges. He was arrested in June 2009 on counts of driving under the influence, possession of marijuana and "drug paraphernalia", thought to be a bong. Aguiar had countered that he had been abused in custody and refused to pay the $536 court charges. "When I got to the prison [a police officer] took my *kippah* off and then tried to convert me to Christianity," he told the Israeli daily newspaper *Haaretz* in October 2009. "I told him to leave me the fuck alone. He then took me — after blowing triple zeros on my breath test — to the Broward County Sheriff's Office where they arrested me and beat the shit out of me." According to the paper, Aguiar said he was wearing a skullcap and a shirt with the word Israel on it at the time of the arrest. The Broward County Sheriff's office denied the accusations, saying that Aguiar was

"combative and verbally abusive" and that he had been "controlled and restrained".

But now, in an Irish bar in Jerusalem, he looked anything but combative. He looked lost as he swayed from side to side roughly in time with the music. I passed him back his cigarette.

"If you smoke that every day," I advised through foggy eyes, "you will go crazy."

He didn't hear me. It was the last time I would speak to Guma Aguiar.

On the morning of 14 January 2010, an ambulance and two police cars escorted Guma Aguiar to the Abarbanel Mental Health Center in Bat Yam on the outskirts of Jerusalem. Under orders from his wife, he had been sectioned. Aguiar had been diagnosed with bi-polar disorder and had, according to his family, suddenly taken a turn for the worse. A few days earlier he had given an interview with a local newspaper in which he had claimed that he was in mobile phone contact with Gilad Shalit, the Israeli soldier kidnapped by Hamas militants and held *incommunicado* in the Gaza Strip since 2006. No one knew of his whereabouts, not even the Israeli secret service. But Aguiar had claimed he had sneaked into the Gaza Strip and freed Shalit, who was now holed up in one of his properties.

"I wanted to prove that I could enter Gaza and come out alive and that Shalit could come out alive as well," he told the *Kol Ha'ir* newspaper. "He [Shalit] said that he wants me to tell his family how much he loves them and Israel, and that he hopes this ends soon."

Within a few weeks it was announced that Aguiar would cease funding Beitar Jerusalem. As he was only sponsoring the club and hadn't taken full ownership, Arcadi Gaydamak was now in full charge of the football team again. His money had prevented Beitar from going out of business, but his philanthropic journey in Israel was over. Or so it seemed.

"He's an enigma," explained Shlomi Barzel, the sports editor of *Haaretz*. Barzel had met Aguiar shortly before he was sectioned. "He was smoking. I'd met him at a game on Saturday. The day before we had met and had an hour and a half meeting. He could not remember me at all. After a meeting he was coming out of the toilet with white powder all over his nose." Barzel felt some sympathy for Aguiar. "Was it Jerusalem Syndrome or was it too much powder in the nose?" he asked rhetorically. "The man was a lunatic. I thought it was a question of conscience, how Gaydamak took the money. It was clear to me that Guma wasn't capable of taking one rational decision. You have to know that, after Gaydamak, there was a period when [Beitar supporters] were not looking for the new king, they were looking for a rich man coming from nowhere."

Things didn't go much better back home. According to a Florida court judgement that found against Aguiar in 2010: "Aguiar's psychosis manifested itself in both grandiose and paranoid delusions. In the spring of 2008, Aguiar expressed the grandiose belief that he is or could be the Messiah. With respect to his paranoid delusions, Aguiar has stated on multiple occasions that Kaplan was trying to kill him. Aguiar believes that he has been poisoned, that he was shot in the back from a helicopter, that snipers have been following him and that the medical staff at an Israeli hospital were injecting him with poison in order to kill him. Aguiar's bipolar disorder first manifested itself in 1997 when he was Baker Acted [involuntarily detained as per Florida state law] at a Florida psychiatric hospital for approximately 12 days. At the time, Aguiar was 19 years old."

Most interestingly, the documents claimed, "Aguiar experienced the onset of another manic episode in mid-June 2009 and is still recovering from this episode. From approximately June 2009 through January 2010, Aguiar was also psychotic. Aguiar is presently in treatment for his mental illness." June 2009 to January 2010 was the exact time Aguiar had been Beitar's benefactor. It was also stated that Aguiar was abusing "alcohol, marijuana, Xanax (an anti-anxiety medication), Ambien (a sleeping pill), anabolic steroids and OxyContin (an opiate)."

The judgement is disturbing reading. It lays bare a series of misdeeds and failures: email hacking, paranoia, drug abuse, threats, counter threats and spousal abuse. Aguiar was appealing against the decision and had even re-entered the arena of Israeli sports. In 2011 it was announced that he had bought a majority stake in the Hapoel Jerusalem basketball team, the team to which he had donated $1.5m two years previously. But as his legal battle with his uncle intensified and his marriage deteriorated (divorce was threatened and counter-threatened; Jamie made accusations of violence against her and her father) Aguiar boarded the TT Zion in June 2012 and disappeared without trace.

What had begun as one of the biggest natural resource windfalls in modern US history had ended in a story of mental illness, betrayal and family breakdown. Within hours of Aguiar's disappearance his mother Ellen, Kaplan's estranged sister, had moved to take control of his assets. Aguiar's largesse, philanthropy, generosity, whatever the rival lawyers wanted to call it, had halved his fortune to an estimated $100m. The speed of the legal manoeuvre raised questions as to what had truly befallen Guma Aguiar. In the aftermath Guma's wife Jamie and his mother Ellen embarked on a costly legal battle that is ongoing while Thomas Kaplan's legal team made clear that they held out hope Guma was still alive. But how, in the 21st century, could someone with such a high profile simply disappear without trace? What proof was there? Where could Aguiar go?

"There's certainly enough evidence that one could deduce that he's still alive," explained Jamie Aguiar's lawyer Bill Scherer, sitting in his smart conference room in Florida. "It would be a nice chapter in a mystery novel... He could have been thrown out [of the boat], drowned and his body swept north and never found. Or he could have stayed in, it drifted to shore, he jumped out the boat and was picked up by someone who was waiting for him. It could have been either/or."

If Guma Aguiar was alive, where could he possibly go? One theory is the Netherlands. According to Scherer around the time of his disappearance Aguiar's [unnamed] best friend, who was also a business partner, upped sticks and moved to Amsterdam. Now Aguiar's sister and brother-in-law had followed suit.

"The sister and the brother-in-law are in Amsterdam and trying to avoid our process so we can take a deposition and ask them, on oath, whether they know where he is," said Scherer. "Amsterdam is a place he used to like to go ... We learned Guma loved Amsterdam. For obvious reasons..." There was also, according to Scherer, the case of Guma's missing clothes. "Socks, shoes, custom fitted clothing all removed [from his house in Israel]. Personal items. Things that he would want to have if he was still alive," he said. "They [whoever removed the clothes] got in without any evidence of forced entry but they cut out all the internal video surveillance. And they would only know how to do that if they knew the set-up."

The court battle is set to be long and expensive, depleting what is left of Aguiar's assets. Without a body, Guma Aguiar will not be declared dead in Florida for another three years, and further two in Israel. Guma's sister and his uncle and former business partner Thomas Kaplan didn't respond to requests for an interview. Guma's mother has denied having any knowledge of her son's whereabouts and believes that he is dead. It would, after all, be almost impossible to disappear without trace, no matter how much money you have, in today's wired world. Especially somewhere as small and visible as the Netherlands. It would take astonishing planning; the hiding of assets, a passport from a country with no US extradition treaty (the Netherlands has had one with the USA since 1983), lots of money and a complete break from the technology that dominates our world today.

"It's nigh-on impossible to have an existence where you aren't tracked or traced by technology," Oliver Crofton, director of technology security firm Vigilante Bespoke, told *Spears* magazine. "If the person really wanted to hide they'd need to change their name and chuck every device they had in the river. They couldn't even open any emails, and they certainly couldn't use a credit card — just a suitcase full of dollars."

Beitar survived, just. With Aguiar out of the picture, Gaydamak returned, this time with new friends from his business dealings in Chechnya. In the hope of selling the club to the Chechen oligarch Telman Ismailov — who bankrolls Russian club Terek Grozny, a team inexorably linked with Chechnya's president Ramzan Kadyrov — Gaydamak arranged for a friendly in Chechnya between Beitar and Terek at the start of the 2012-13 season. When Gaydamak returned, he had two new players to add to Beitar's squad: Zaur Sadayev and Dzhabrail Kadiyev, both Chechen Muslims. *La Familia* were furious. When Sadayev scored his first goal for Beitar against Maccabi Netanya, he was booed. Hundreds left the ground immediately in protest. Beitar were nearly relegated too. They headed north to play Bnei Sakhnin — the team that has come to symbolise Israel's Arab population more than any other and for whom *La Familia* reserve a special hatred, and vice versa — on the last day of the season

knowing that a defeat could send them down. Thousands of police ensured there was no trouble. Beitar and Sakhnin drew 0-0. They survived, by the skin of their teeth.

But with no Guma, dead or alive, the mystery of what happened during those crazy few months in 2009 deepens. When asked whether he has commissioned private detectives to look for Aguiar in the Netherlands Jamie Aguiar's lawyer replied, "We are ever vigilant to work out whether he is alive. That's all I can tell you." But he believes that that mystery of Guma Aguiar's life, and possible death, will have another chapter. "I can write a script in which Guma says, 'Look I've been in a psychotic state until just recently and then all of a sudden the fog clears and I realise what am I doing out here?'" he said, explaining one possible scenario. "He'd say, 'I'm well now and, gee, I don't have any memory of what happened to me over the last year and a half. I've had a bi-polar episode.' Stranger things have happened."

With a divided family grieving for his return, it would be a fitting end to the story of a man who arrived in Jerusalem to make his mark on the world, hailed and accused of being the Messiah in equal measure: the resurrection of Guma Aguiar. Ⓑ

Identity Crisis

Unpicking the convoluted threads of Mexico's franchise system

By Brian Homewood

It is difficult not to have a soft spot for a club whose badge looks as if it has been inspired by the Pathetic Sharks, so the return of Veracruz to the top flight of Mexican football for the 2013-14 season should be a cause for minor celebration.

After all, what is not to like about a team that come from a faded and steamy port on the Gulf of Mexico, call themselves the Red Sharks and once boasted René Higuita in goal? The club's badge, a shark merrily juggling a football on its fin, could easily have been lifted from the cartoon strip in *Viz* magazine and, for a few seasons, the team shirt had the word 'Bimbo' gloriously sprayed across the front, thanks to sponsorship from a popular Mexican brand of sliced bread.

Sadly, however, there is nothing romantic about the way in which Veracruz won their way back to the top flight. Rather than a heroic campaign in the Ascenso MX, as Mexico's second tier is known, Veracruz owe their return to the bewildering franchise system that allows clubs to hop around the country at the whim of their owners.

The team that was genuinely promoted from Ascenso MX last season was modest La Piedad, otherwise known as *los Reboceros*. Their long-suffering supporters, who have only ever enjoyed one season of top flight football, had 12 days to celebrate their team's nerve-wracking penalty shoot-out win in the end-of-season play-off against Sinaloa before learning that the club's owner Fidel Kuri Grajales had decided to uproot the franchise and move it around 800km to Veracruz.

This effectively meant the end of the La Piedad club: when a franchise moves in Mexico, it takes the players and the team's relegation coefficient, another local idiosyncrasy by which relegation is determined on points per game over a three-year period, with it and all other connections are severed, including the name and strip. In fact, Mexicans tend to view it as a continuation of the last club to play in the new location. In this case, La Piedad have morphed into Veracruz, adopting the nickname (Red Sharks), red-and-blue strip and history of the previous Veracruzes.

The last team to play in Veracruz had, in fact, been de-affiliated from the Mexican league in 2011 due to a multiple financial difficulties. Yet, even there they managed to pull a fast one. Instead of quietly departing, they formed an "alliance" with an Ascenso MX team called Albinegros de Orizaba ('the black-and-whites of Orizaba', a nearby city), renamed the club Veracruz and continued playing in the second tier. When the new Veracruz (ie La Piedad) moved in last June, the old one headed off to San Luis.

This is actually the fifth different franchise claiming to be the Red Sharks of Veracruz.

The original Sharks were founded in 1943 and quickly became a leading force in Mexican football. They won the Mexican championship twice, spearheaded by Luis 'The Pirate' Fuente, whose name was given to the stadium.

Their success was short-lived, however, and they were relegated in 1951-52. One year later, they disappeared amid financial problems. The club was re-born in 1964 under the leadership of the businessman Jose Lajub Kuri and managed to elbow their way straight into the first division when it was expanded from 14 to 16 teams.

They stayed there for 15 fairly unremarkable years before suffering relegation in 1978-79, the year that Hugo Sánchez burst onto the scene as a top-level striker by scoring 26 goals in 38 games for UNAM. After a few years in the second tier, the franchise moved to the city of Mérida and became known as Venados de Yucatán before eventually folding.

There were several attempts to buy a new franchise and negotiations were held with Angeles de Puebla, but in the end they moved to Torreon and became (and still are) Santos Laguna. Veracruz were finally reincarnated in 1989 when the top-flight club Potros Neza sold their franchise to a group of local businessmen, who were helped by funding from the city government.

This time, they enjoyed some modest success, reaching the quarter-finals of the 1991-92 championship before losing to Necaxa. (The Mexican championship uses a complex format involved a league stage followed by knockout matches, but that is another story).

Eventually, another decline set in and Veracruz were relegated in 1997-98. But in 2001-02, the almost unthinkable happened and Veracruz actually won promotion on the field, fair and square. There was a catch, however: halfway through the same season, the Liga MX side Irapuato had re-located to Veracruz. This caused all sorts of confusion, with supporters unable to decide whether to support the 'real' Veracruz in the second tier or the top-flight impostors, disparagingly known as *Verapuato*. When (second-tier) Veracruz won promotion, it meant that for 2002-03 the city would have two teams in the top flight, something which it clearly could not sustain. Accordingly, the state government organise a vote which was won overwhelmingly by the promoted side and Liga MX Veracruz (*Verapuato*) moved off to the jungle state of Chiapas.

While this was going on, Grupo Pegaso, which by now owned the 'real' Veracruz, sold the club to Rafael Herrerias, a local businessman whose activities included organising bullfights. A spending spree brought in several top players including Cuauhtemoc Blanco (famous for bunny-hopping between Belgian defenders at the 1998 World Cup), giving the Red Sharks real bite. They had one of their best campaigns in the 2004-05 Apertura, when they qualified for the quarter-finals only to lose 4-1 on aggregate to UNAM. Shortly afterwards, Herrerias sold the

On the trail of Mexican football franchises:

1. Irapuato 1948-2001 > Veracruz 2001-2002 > Chiapas 2002-2013 > Queretaro 2013-

2. San Luis 1957-2013 > Chiapas 2013-

3. Petroleros de Salamanca 2001-2009* > La Piedad 2009-2013 > Veracruz 2013-
* Previously existed between 1950-61 and 1964-1986. Refounded in 2001.

4. Correcaminos UAT 1980-1988 >PotrosNeza 1988-89 > Veracruz 1989-2011: wound up

4a. Albinegros de Orizaba 2002-2011 > Veracruz 2011-13 >Atletico San Luis 2013-

5. Veracruz 1943-1952 and 1964-1984; Venados de Yucatán 1984-98.
The club was wound up in 1952 and refounded in 1964. Venados de Yucatán were wound up in 1998.

6. CF Laguna 1953-1978 >DeportivoNeza 1978-1988 >Correcaminos UAT 1988-

7. Union de Curtidores 1997*-1999 > Puebla 1999-
*One of three new franchises founded when the Primera Division A expanded from 17 to 21 teams

team but the new owners ran down the squad, resulting in relegation in 2008.

Three years later, Veracruz were de-affiliated due to debts owed to the Mexican federation and their own players, but then joined forces with Albinegros de Orizaba in a manoeuvre engineered by the state governor Javier Duarte. Albinegros, who were playing the second tier, came off worse; the club was renamed Veracruz and moved its home games to the Luis Fuente stadium, although it kept the Albinegros black and white striped shirts as a symbolic gesture. Then in June, when La Piedad moved in, Veracruz headed off to San Luis.

As for La Piedad, their supporters have seen it all before. Founded in 1951, the club finally reached the top flight for the first time in 2001. They had one year to enjoy it, before the club departed for Queretaro. La Piedad then had to wait until 2009, when Petroleros de Salamanca moved to the city and became *Reboceros*, playing in the second division.

Immediately after they won promotion, the club owners assured them that La Piedad would not be moved. "It's all speculation, we have been clear about this, we have said our project is here so I don't want people think differently," said the president Fidel Kuri Mustieles, son of the owner Kuri Grajales. "We're all in this together, the directors, the coaching staff and the players."

That quickly changed when the owners found out they would have to add new seats to the stadium, while the state government of Veracruz offered all sorts of incentives for a move.

"I understand that the public are unhappy but we have explained to them that to play in the first division there are certain requirements, a large number of things such as the stadium which we couldn't fulfil," said Kuri Grajales. "The people of La Piedad should just be grateful for all the happy moments we have given them."

The run-up to the 2013 season saw two other franchise moves, which is unusual even by Mexican standards.

San Luis, owned by Carlos López Chargoy, moved 1,200km from the chilly highlands of central Mexico to steamy Tuxtla Gutierrez in the south and were renamed Chiapas, after the state. In doing so, they filled the void which had been left by the departure of the old Chiapas who moved a similar distance northwards to Queretaro, who themselves had been relegated. To complete it all, Veracruz moved to San Luis.

The net effect was that Queretaro, who should have been relegated, stayed up; Veracruz, who should have stayed in the second division, were promoted; San Luis, who should have stayed in the first division, were relegated; and La Piedad, who should have been promoted, were left without a professional team.

It was arguably the most blatant misuse of the system since 1999 when Puebla were relegated but simply bought the franchise of promoted Unión de Curtidores and carried on as if nothing had happened.

Even the Queretaro supporters didn't know what to make of it. "Obviously we would prefer to stay in the first division but for us the right idea would have

8. Unión de Curtidores 1948-1984 >Chetumal 1984-?
Unión de Curtidores apparently moved to Chetumal in 1984 when they were playing in the second division. They were replaced by their neighbours Bufalos de Curtidores, who then changed their name to Union de Curtidores. However, it is not clear what ultimately happened to this version of the club, or the Chetumal team.

9. Oaxtepec 1979-1984 > Angeles de Puebla 1985-1988 > Santos Laguna 1988-

10. Zacatepec 1948-2004 > Queretaro 2004-2013:
2013 was apparently the end of the line for this franchise

11. Queretaro 1948-1981 > Tampico Madera 1981-1990 > Queretaro 1990-1999 (as Club Queretaro) merged with UAQ GallosBlancos 1983-1999 = Queretaro 1999-2002*
Club folded.

12. Cobras de Queretaro 1986-1988 > Ciudad Juarez 1988-?

13. La Piedad 1951-2002 > Queretaro 2002-2004*
Wound up by the Mexican federation due to financial problems

14. Atletico Cuernavaca 1953-1994 > Atletico Celaya 1994-

2002 >Colibries de Cuernavaca
2002-03*
*Relegated and wound-up at the
end of the 2002-03 season*

Teams that haven't moved:
America, Cruz Azul, UNAM
(Pumas), Atlas, Guadalajara,
UANL, Monterrey, Toluca,
Morelia, Leon, Pachuca

**Teams that have moved but kept
their original name and identity:**
Atlante (Mexico City to Cancún
in 2007)

been to play in the second division,"
said Amilcar Godínez, the leader of the
organised supporters' group known as
Resistencia Albiazul (Blue and White
Resistance). "Historically, Queretaro have
never been gifted anything, it's been
completely the opposite, so the fact that
it has been manipulated in this way does
take a bit of the excitement away."

Mexican club owners, who vary from
conglomerates such as Grupo Pegaso,
to television networks such as Televisa
and eccentric businessmen such as
Guadalajara's Jorge Vergara, argue that
the system allows them to take their
clubs to more profitable locations when
crowds dwindle.

History suggests that it simply confuses
and alienates supporters, prevents a
real fan culture from developing and
makes a mockery of the promotion/
relegation system.

One of the oddest moves came in 2002
when Atlético Celaya moved from Celaya
to Cuernavaca. They spent one year in
the top flight before being relegated,
and were then liquidated due to financial
problems. Unfortunately for Cuernavaca,
they had also inherited Celaya's dismal
relegation coefficient.

Apart from the players and relegation
coefficients, everything else stays where
it is. Therefore, when San Luis moved
to Chiapas, most of their players went
with them. But the Chiapas official
website lists the club as being founded
in 2002 (the year that Veracruz mark III
moved there) and it gives the previous
Chiapas history rather than San Luis It
briefly mentions the new owner Chargoy
at the very bottom, portraying him as

some sort of heroic rescuer, but makes no reference whatsoever to San Luis. The new team play in the same orange strip and have the same nickname (the Jaguars) as the previous Chiapas, but their relegation coefficient is considerably worse than the old Chiapas, so they are now fighting relegation instead of sitting comfortably in mid-table. Meanwhile, "relegated" Queretaro have inherited the old Chiapas's coefficient and are in little danger of going down.

"You can feel some sadness, some disappointment; the supporters had identity with their team and the squad,"

said José Guadelupe Cruz, coach of the old Chiapas (now Queretaro) at the end of last season. "There was a serious, long-term project here which was producing results."

Back in La Piedad, hope springs eternal. The old club also has a franchise in the so-called "League of New Talents", effectively the fourth tier, and has entered a team. They can now try to work their way back up the pyramid — or simply wait and buy the first higher division franchise that comes up for sale. Far easier than playing their way through a long season and winning a play-off match on penalties. Ⓑ

Dream Fulfilled

*Relief and glee as Cardiff City finally found their way
into the Premier League*

By Bartosz Nowicki

In May 2013, Cardiff City were promoted to the top flight of English football to end an 84-year exile. They'd given the sense of a club on the verge of great things for several years, prone to sudden collapses at key moments, but when promotion was finally achieved, it didn't come with quite the sense of fulfilment they had expected. By then Cardiff were owned by Vincent Tan, who had changed the badge and the kit and had little respect for history, or what had traditionally made Cardiff the club it was. Bartosz Nowicki captured the emotions of the 2012-13 season for his book, *City - The Season*, from which this essay is drawn.

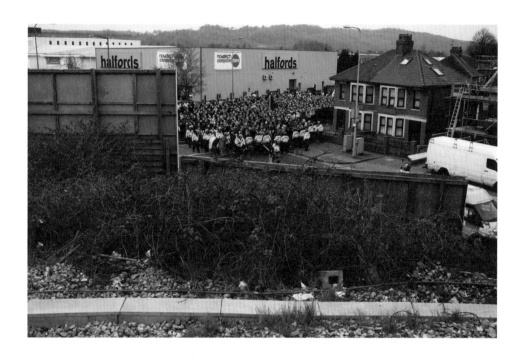

CLASSIC FOOTBALL SHIRTS.CO.UK

THE MOST EXTENSIVE RANGE OF ORIGINAL SHIRTS ONLINE

HUGE CLEARANCE SECTION FULL OF 1000's OF BARGAIN ITEMS

GETAFE	FC YOUNG BOYS	LYON TECHFIT	MARSEILLE TECHFIT	VALENCIA
£11.99	£19.99	£34.99	£22.99	£19.99

KE CROUCH	NAPOLI CAVANI	NAPOLI HAMSIK	SHORTS, SOCKS, BAGS, JACKETS ETC.
9.99	£49.99	£44.99	

 facebook.com/classicfootballshirts   twitter.com/classicshirts

102

"It is probably the nicer part of Worsley,
but it is Worsley nonetheless."

Sleeping Giant

In 1982, Jean-Pierre Adams was given anaesthetic before knee surgery. He hasn't woken up

By Robin Bairner

On 17 March 1982, the former France international footballer Jean-Pierre Adams, at the age of 34, was admitted to a Lyon hospital to undergo a routine knee operation. He was given anaesthetic that should have knocked him out for a few hours but, more than 30 years later, he has yet to wake.

Adams is a figure who drifts in and out of the consciousness of the French public but who is largely forgotten outside his homeland, despite being a highly-regarded figure in his generation and a pioneer for French-African footballers. With 22 caps to his credit, he turned out more regularly for les Bleus than more celebrated figures such as David Ginola, Ludovic Giuly and even Just Fontaine, carrying himself with a humble spirit and a ceaseless smile.

His story begins in Dakar, Senegal, where he was born on 10 March 1948, the oldest of a large family based in the European district of the country's capital. Although football was in young Jean-Pierre's blood — his uncle Alexandre Diadhiou played for the celebrated Jeanne d'Arc club — education was made the priority in his life by his devoutly Catholic family and he was not allowed to play the sport he loved unless his grades in school were of a sufficient standard.

With this in mind, the nine-year-old Adams was sent alone to continue his schooling in France, where he was ultimately fostered by the Jourdain family in Loiret, a department a little south of Paris. "I was like a little lost puppy without a collar," Adams would later reflect, yet his malleability meant that he was not scarred by what must have been a traumatic experience.

Football proved to be a vital release for the adolescent Adams, who made his first true friends when he played at Under-13 level for the Cepoy club, where he would stay for three seasons before becoming a prolific centre-forward for Bellegarde. It also provided him with an environment in which to socialise in what was still a white-dominated society as he swiftly gained respect for his physical prowess and his endearing personality. He would very quickly become popular at Collège Saint-Louis, where he was affectionately known as the 'White Wolf'.

Away from the pitch, Adams completed his initial schooling but elected to drop out of a course studying shorthand as it did not interest him. Instead, he worked in a factory as his game progressed to Montagris, where he was coached by Louis Gabrillagues, a former professional with the Sète side that had won the first Coupe de France-Championnat de France double.

However, there was a hint of problems to come as he suffered a serious knee injury that could have ended his dreams of becoming a professional footballer. Thankfully, this time, it was just another hurdle he was able to overcome.

As if the fragility of his potential career was not already clear, Adams' life would be touched by the tragedies of his Montagris teammates. Michel Slota was seriously injured after being hit by a car while riding his bike and would never fully recover, while Alain Guerton died suddenly after contracting a virus on a trip to Asia.

Even after moving to l'Entente Bagneaux-Fontainebleau-Nemours (EBFN) misfortune continued to follow the young hopeful. Adams was involved in a serious car crash, and though he escaped with only cuts, one of which left a scar above his right eye, his close friend Guy Beaudot was killed.

To have been touched by such troubles at the age of 19, it was little surprise that Adams' appetite for the game was briefly diminished, leading to a rare fallow spell in his form.

Military service, however, proved to be a turning point. Adams had always been a physically imposing specimen with tremendous stamina but his time in the army meant his talents started to become recognised in a broader sphere. He was selected to play for the French Military squad, from which he would be recommended to Nîmes by, among others, future France teammate Michel Mézy.

Adams's desire to become a professional had been further fired by his marriage to Bernadette, who to this day provides a rock of support for the sleeping footballer. Even this had been no straightforward pathway, though, as his blonde bride's mother had initially refused to give her daughter's hand to the young African.

At this point, Adams's career took a path similar to that of Lilian Thuram, who rose through the French amateur ranks to become one of the game's most celebrated players. Thuram also turned out for the latter-day version of EBFN, yet it was during the era of Adams that the club became prominent in the nation's amateur game.

In three successive years, with the broad-shouldered 5ft 10in Adams their driving force, they would lose the Championnat de France Amateurs final, before earning the right to play in an expanded Division 2 in 1970. Although EBFN were coming up short as a team on the big occasion, their young protégé's career was on the verge of taking off. The strides he made during his military service persuaded the legendary Nîmes trainer Kader Firoud to offer Adams a trial match in Rouen. Bernadette drove Jean-Pierre north for the friendly in which her 22-year-old husband impressed sufficiently to earn his first professional contract.

"You have great potential but you also need to work hard to reach it," Firoud told Adams on signing him. "You already have all the qualities of a young wolf, and if you are not afraid to work you will become a true crocodile [the nickname of Nîmes]."

Fortunately, Adams was indeed an industrious young man. Firoud would work him hard in training and began his transformation into first a midfielder then a defender as the Nîmes squad was already full of fine strikers. This proved pivotal as Adams could make full use of his physical capabilities, although he was forced to hone his technique and tactical sense with the reserves for a period. Initially he found the switch difficult and at one point he needed to be talked out of quitting. His diligence on the training ground, however, would eventually be rewarded by his first-team debut. Once involved with the Nîmes first team, he remained a regular.

Firoud would be one of the key influences on Adams' career. He was a terrific motivator, although some of his training methods were unorthodox. The young midfielder's first session at Nîmes, for example, involved a sight-seeing tour of the Roman town, including its famous Maison Carrée.

"You are ambassadors for this city," Firoud reminded his players, pointing at the historical grandeur of their surroundings.

However unconventional the coach, his methods were highly effective. Only the Auxerre legend Guy Roux has overseen more top division matches than Firoud's 782, and in 1971 he was named *France Football*'s Coach of the Year. Crucially for Adams, he was particularly effective at bringing through unknown quantities from the youth ranks.

After debuting in a new No. 4 role against Reims in September 1970, Adams would become a permanent fixture in the team. "In half a season, Jean-Pierre Adams has become an important pillar in Firoud's side," *France Football* reported. "Adams

does not hate mundane work and, from time to time, is capable of acting out a dramatic fantasy."

It was no mean achievement to become established so readily in such a team. Nîmes's side at the time was one of the best in the club's 80-year history and Adams was a fulcrum as *les Crocodiles* qualified for Europe for the first time. He was even decisive in the club's first Uefa Cup win, though Nîmes lost the tie on away goals to Vitória Setúbal of Portugal.

Such a narrow defeat was the prelude to a frustrating second season in which the club finished as runners up to Olympique de Marseille in le Championnat. Ultimately Nîmes paid for a poor spring run that saw them win one of seven league matches and rendered futile their eight wins from nine at the campaign's conclusion.

On a collective level, Adams's third and final season at the club was disappointing as *les Crocos* finished only seventh, yet *But* noted that their midfielder remained "in international form". "In the rugged defence of Nimes, there is a pillar, a kind of force of nature, a colossus of uncommon athletic power: Jean-Pierre Adams," said the former Argentina captain Ángel Marcos, who played for Nantes. I rarely suffered against a direct opponent. I always dreaded the two annual confrontations [with Adams] as they were a real challenge and I tried, every time, to detach myself from my merciless 'bodyguard'."

When Adams moved to Nice in the summer of 1973, Marcos didn't have life any easier. By then a France international, Adams was at the peak of his powers, capable of making regular powerful surges of 50 or 60 metres with the ball at his feet deep into games. Nice at the time were highly ambitious and ready to spend. An ambitious bid to sign Jairzinho failed narrowly as they attempted to re-establish themselves as a major force in France after dropping out of the elite in 1969.

Despite their spending, their return was marked with a disappointing 14th-place finish but, by the time Adams arrived, Nice were rueing a failure to win the title the previous season, having thrown away a five-point lead to allow Marcos's Nantes to overhaul them.

Life for the 25-year-old Adams on the Côte d'Azur started with some promise as two goals from Marc Molitor and another from Dick van Dijk helped Nice secure a 3-2 win over Rinus Michel's Barcelona in the Uefa Cup. By the time the Stade du Ray outfit's European run was emphatically ended with a 4-1 aggregate defeat to Köln — a tie played without Adams, who had been suspended after a red card against Fenerbahçe in the previous round — the head coach Jean Snella found his position becoming increasingly uneasy. League results were not good and after a fifth-place finish he was dismissed.

His replacement was Vlatko Marković, an ill-fated appointment. Marković , who went on to become an outspoken president of the Croatian football federation, was never popular among the Nice fans. "If spectators want a spectacle, they should go to Marineland," he said following criticism of his dour playing style.

Not only did he rile his own support, he irritated opposing teams, too. Ahead

of a January 1976 derby with Monaco, he declared, "Pff! [Delio] Onnis? Vlatko would not even want him in our team!"

Four Onnis goals in 4-1 defeat later, he was eating his words.

Despite the coaching sideshow, Adams remained a consistently strong performer and was named in *France Football*'s elite team of the season. "Adams remains without a rival in his role, where his extraordinary athletic qualities can match the best," the magazine gushed.

In the subsequent campaign, Nice finished second in Division 1 behind Saint-Étienne, a series of injuries to their best players probably robbing them of the title. Adams was one of the men who suffered most and those issues would mark the end of his personal peak as he prepared to depart the Mediterranean coast after dropping out of the national team.

Adams' introduction to *les Bleus* had come five years earlier during the Taça Independência, a competition played in Brazil to celebrate the 150th anniversary of the nation's independence from Portugal. Fittingly, the 24-year-old's debut came against an Africa select team, as he arrived off the bench to replace Marius Trésor, the man with whom he would form the fabled '*Garde Noire*' in years to come.

Five days later he was handed his first start in an encounter against Colombia. It began inauspiciously as Adams conceded a penalty from which the South Americans took the lead but he showed his characteristic resilience to play a stoical match thereafter.

The coach Georges Boulogne was sufficiently impressed to pair Adams with Trésor in defence for a decisive encounter with Argentina that would decide which country progressed to the Taça's second round. A scoreless draw meant disappointment for France, who were eliminated on goal difference. They were compensated with the birth of 'la Garde Noire'.

Like all good double acts, Trésor and Adams complimented each other. The former was regarded as the technical defender while Adams was still noted primarily for his athleticism.

While Trésor was born in Guadeloupe, Adams's sub-Saharan roots were something of a novelty in the France team of the time. Of course, France had seen other such 'foreigners' turn out for its national team previously; the great ball juggler Larbi Ben Barek hailed from Morocco but won 17 caps for *les Bleus* either side of the Second World War, while Xercès Louis (12 caps in the mid-50s) and the renowned tackler Daniel Charles-Alfred (four caps in the mid-60s) were both born in Martinique. And of course there were Just Fontaine, Rachid Mekhloufi and Mustaoha Zitouni, who came originally from North Africa.

Adams, however, was laying a pathway from west Africa to France for the likes of Marcel Desailly and Patrick Vieira to follow. His contribution to the national side was immediately praised. "Of all the players we have seen make their entry to 'Club France' in recent years, Jean-Pierre Adams is without doubt the one who has taken it with the most relaxed attitude," the journalist Philippe Tournon commented.

France may have been welcomed back from Brazil warmly after an encouraging trip but it was not until they met the USSR in a World Cup qualifying match — the first *les Bleus* played at the newly renovated Parc des Princes — that their new central defensive pairing really came of age. The Parisian venue had been something of a *bête noire* for Adams in the past. He had lost two previous CFA finals at the ground, leading the local press to dub it his *'Stade du Désespoir'* — Stadium of Despair.

A thunderous free-kick from Georges Bereta proved decisive for France but it was the intelligent, vivacious performance from the centre-backs that was truly match winning. Franz Beckenbauer, no less, held the duo in particularly high regard, remarking to *Onze*, "Adams and Trésor have formed one of the best centre-back pairings in all of Europe."

Once again, however, injuries had a telling impact on Adams. His persistent troubles saw his partnership with Trésor broken up in 1975 and, although he received a call up for a friendly against Denmark in which a young Michel Platini scored, Adams never again turned out in France's blue.

Adams soon moved back north to the familiar surrounds of the Paris region. The ambitious PSG president Daniel Hechter had been seduced by him amid the club's first period of big spending. Known for his fashion design — Hechter was the mastermind behind the iconic blue, white and red PSG strips — he was also a very astute businessman and played a key role in the early development of the club, lifting them from the amateur ranks to overtake Paris FC as the capital's primary power. Among the other signings in that 1977-78 season were Jean-Michel Larqué and Carlos Bianchi.

As the 29 year old's experience at Nice had shown, though, big spending did not necessarily equate to big rewards and Adams' time in Paris was subdued, with two mid-table finishes before he was released from his contract, ending his time at the top level.

A brief and unsuccessful stay at Mulhouse followed before Adams took the decision to step into coaching. He took up a player-coach role with the amateur side FC Chalon, who helped him set up a sports shop that he ran along with wife Bernadette in the centre of the town. On and off the field, life was going well. The attraction of being able to see a former international footballer ensured that the shop was busy, while Chalon's promotion to Division 4 in Adams's first season in charge underlined his potential as a manager. In March 1982, Chalon were on course for another promotion as they led the division going into the final throes of the season.

Adams had elected to take the first stage of his coaching degree in Dijon, which meant going on a week-long course in the Bourguignon town during the spring. On the third day, however, he suffered a knee problem and the following morning quit the course for a hospital in Lyon. An initial scan showed damage to a tendon at the back of the knee but a chance meeting with a Lyon-supporting surgeon en route to the exit proved critical. After a discussion between the pair, it was decided that the best course of action would be to operate as soon as possible.

Adams agreed to an operation a matter of days later on March 17.

"It's all fine, I'm in great shape," were his parting words to Bernadette as he left the family home on the morning of the operation.

His wife, however, was worried and only more so when it took three calls to the hospital before she was passed onto a doctor. "Come here now," she was told gravely.

Unable to travel alone in her emotional state, Bernadette was accompanied to Lyon by two Chalon officials, where they found that Adams had slipped into a coma. Bernadette remained by his bedside for five days and five nights hoping for a change in his condition while the couple's two young boys, Laurent and Frédéric, were at home with their grandparents.

Later it would emerge that there had been a problem with Adams' supply of anaesthetic, which was exacerbated by the fact the anaesthetist was overseeing eight operations at once, including one particularly delicate procedure involving a child that got much of his attention. To complicate matters further, Adams was not on the correct type of bed, the drug used was known to be problematic and the operation was overseen by a trainee.

Adams has never woken.

It would be November before the former international was moved north to Chalon, where Bernadette was by his side on a daily basis. That did not prevent Adams from being neglected by the staff at his new institution, where he lost 11kg in the space of a month. After finding an infected bed sore, Bernadette exploded with rage and, after her husband had undergone another operation as the infection had reached his bones, she sat with him continuously, still holding out hope he one day might wake.

When the hospital said they could no longer look after Adams, he was moved home. For Bernadette this was a great undertaking. She would sleep in the same room as her husband and get up in the middle of the night to turn him. Blood was taken from him every week in order to check his vitamin levels, while various miracle cures were tried over an extended period of time, including acupuncture and submerging the former professional athlete in a swimming pool.

Bernadette had a house custom-built in Rodilhan, near Nîmes, which she named *'Mas du bel athlète dormant'* — the House of the Beautiful Sleeping Athlete. It had been a struggle to get a loan in place, however, as she had fallen into difficult financial circumstances.

Various bodies came forward to help her, with Nîmes and PSG both offering FF15,000, while the French football federation gave her FF6,000 per week after an initial contribution of FF25,000 in December 1982.

In addition, Adams's former clubs played charity matches in support of him. The Variétés Club de France, a charitable organisation still running today and backed by such luminaries as Platini, Zinédine Zidane and Jean-Pierre Papin with which Adams had been closely involved during his playing days, played a fixture in the comatose player's honour against a group of his footballing friends.

The media, meanwhile, kept his memory alive with glowing testimonies. "[Adams] was the prototype of a modern day midfielder," wrote the journalist Victor Sinet. "He was always available, omnipresent and just as effective going forward as he was defending. We like his good heart, generosity and his Parisian verve. He was appreciated for his human qualities."

Jean-Pierre Rougelet wrote a similarly impassioned piece in which he described Adams as "someone who could make things happen on the pitch but also in life, in which he cultivated a team spirit".

Meanwhile, the courts deliberated upon the case in a sluggish manner.

Pierre Huth, Adams's former doctor at PSG, led the case, which went on for seven years before the Seventh Chamber of Correctional Tribunal in Lyon found the doctors guilt of involuntary injury. It was only at that point that the family's dues could be calculated, yet four years later a definitive decision had still to be made.

No action appeared ready to be taken either until *L'Equipe* published a letter from a family friend advising of the deplorable situation. During the next France international match, the iconic French commentator, the late Thierry Roland, added his gravitas to the cause by reading the document out live on air.

This spurred the authorities on to reach a verdict in October 1993.

Life, such as it is, continues for Bernadette and Jean-Pierre. Hospitals cannot commit staff to looking after Adams for long periods of time, which prevents his loyal wife from taking holidays or long trips. Each day Jean-Pierre is washed and dressed by Bernadette, who maintains that her husband still has some cognitive function.

"Jean-Pierre feels, smells, hears, jumps when a dog barks. But he cannot see," his wife confirmed in an interview with *Le Parisien* in 2007.

Even after all these years she remains relentless in her support and love for her husband. "I have the feeling that time stopped on 17 March 1982," Bernadette explained in a discussion with *Midi Libre* in 2012. "There are no changes, either good or bad. While he does not need respiratory assistance, he remains in a vegetative state.

"Last year, we met a neurologist specialising in brain injury from Carémeau [the hospital in Nîmes] through an acquaintance. He ran his tests and examinations at the hospital, which confirmed very significant damage. There was a lot of damage in the brain. But he does not age, but for a few white hairs."

Despite confirming that her daily routine is "killing her", euthanasia is not an option she would consider.

"It's unthinkable!" she said. "He cannot speak. And it's not for me to decide for him."

Jean-Pierre, whose son Laurent briefly followed in his footsteps by signing for Nîmes in 1996, is now a grandfather and has been introduced to all of his grandchildren. His birthday is still celebrated in the household. The rest of the world has moved on, but Adams lives on as a pioneer, whose unlikely journey to prosperity has been replicated by so many since he was sent from Senegal to France as a young boy. Ⓑ

And Not to Yield

Only one sportsman can match Ryan Giggs for longevity: the New York Yankees shortstop Derek Jeter

By Richard Jolly

In a minority of footballing careers there comes a point when, because a player has headed so far into uncharted territory, comparisons become outdated and invalidated. Ryan Giggs was long likened to Sir Bobby Charlton and, when he broke the World Cup winner's club record of making 757 appearances for Manchester United, it was a colossal achievement. Yet four and a half years and another 200 or so games later, Giggs is still going, Charlton an ever smaller dot in his rear-view mirror.

And then the search for a counterpart elsewhere began. Another elegant blend of pace and immaculate timing, Paolo Maldini, made 902 appearances for AC Milan, the most for any club. Until Giggs overhauled him and, again, rather than accepting his place in the history books and calling it quits, kept on going. Now Maldini, too, has been distanced.

There are mentions of the greatest servant to the San Siro's other tenants. Like Giggs, Javier Zanetti was born in 1973 and, including internationals, he is also in the exclusive group of players to have made 1,000 senior appearances.

But despite more than 850 games for Internazionale, the Argentinian is not a one-club man. Once again, Giggs stands apart.

Or he does in football anyway. There is an equivalent on the other side of the Atlantic, who differs in that he plays a very different sport, but who has considerable similarities. If there is a second Giggs, arguably he is to be found in the New York Yankees' uniform. He is Derek Jeter.

For the uninitiated, the Yankees can be seen as baseball's equivalent of United, a big-budget club with millions of fans and a tradition of success. Their total of 27 World Series rings is a record, like United's 20 English league titles. While the Yankees have now formed a partnership with Manchester City to create New York City FC, which will become the 20th member of Major League Soccer, a dozen years ago they had a marketing alliance with United. It was a brief relationship but a natural fit. To their detractors, superpowers like United and the Yankees constitute an evil empire[1]. Their every defeat delights millions.

---

1 *The phrase was used by the owner of the Red Sox a decade ago following a dispute over a player; the Yankees subsequently claimed it as a trademark.*

And yet even many of the haters are prepared to make an exception for the respective idols, men who have both embodied their club and transcended it. Like Giggs, Jeter has rewritten the history books. Before him, Mickey Mantle had played the most games as a Yankee, with 2,401. Like Giggs, Jeter has added another couple of hundred to the previous best. More significantly, Lou Gehrig had a franchise best 2,721 base hits as a Yankee (a feat that could be compared to being the record Test run-scorer for Australia or India). Jeter, with some 600 more, has gone way beyond the previous peak, just as Giggs has done in overhauling Charlton's appearance record.

Their careers have been so long that, without really trying to, some of the more obscure records have come their way. Giggs, not the substitute supreme Ole Gunnar Solskjær, has come off the bench more often than anyone else for United; Jeter, without anyone thinking it is his major attribute, has stolen more bases than any other Yankee.

They were born seven months apart, both to a mixed-race family. Neither came from the city where he made his name — Giggs was born in Cardiff, while Jeter grew up in Michigan — but the Welshman moved to Greater Manchester as a six year old and the American grew up a Yankees fan because his grandfather was from New Jersey. Both may stretch the definition of the local boy made good but these one-club men represent a throwback to the days when they were more common.

To the trained eye, both had exceptional potential and, viewed from today,

there appears an inevitability about them spending their entire career at their beloved clubs. Actually, it came from others' oversights. Giggs was at Manchester City's School of Excellence before Sir Alex Ferguson intervened. Baseball's draft system meant Jeter had less of a say in his destination. The Yankees only had the sixth pick but he was bound for the Bronx after the Houston Astros, Cleveland Indians, Montreal Expos, Baltimore Orioles and Cincinnati Reds all overlooked the future great for players who would make a negligible impact (the Astros' Midwest scout quit in frustration after they ignored his suggestions to pick Jeter).

Both arrived at clubs who were starved of success — United had not won the league title since 1967, the Yankees the World Series since 1978 — but helped end the drought. Giggs was a champion in his second full season in the team (1992-93), Jeter in his first (1996). For both, it was the first of four titles in five years. Their personal trophy cabinets are bigger than those of many a distinguished club: Giggs's 13 league titles are as many as Arsenal have won and more than any club bar Liverpool; Jeter's five World Series put him ahead of the Chicago Cubs, the New York Mets and the Philadelphia Phillies, to name but three of baseball's most famous names.

They became figureheads for a new era, spearheading a younger generation who gravitated to become the senior citizens. Six of 'Fergie's Fledglings' — Giggs, Paul Scholes, David Beckham, Nicky Butt and the Neville brothers — appeared together for nine successive seasons. Jeter was the leader of the 'Core Four' with the starting pitcher Andy Pettite, the closer

Mariano Rivera and the catcher Jorge Posada. Jeter, Posada and Rivera became the first trio in the history of professional sport in the United States to line up together for 17 consecutive years, the same length of time Giggs, Scholes and Gary Neville were first-team colleagues. Now, however, Giggs and Jeter are essentially alone. Scholes retired for the second time in the summer of 2013 and Rivera followed in the autumn. (Pettite has both left and rejoined the Yankees, retired and returned; with first Posada and then Rivera bowing out, only Jeter has provided continuity.)

They are the last survivors of great dynasties. Their respective teams peaked just before the millennium. United won a historic Treble of the Premier League, the Champions League and the FA Cup in 1999. The Yankees' total of 125 regular and post-season victories in 1998 remains a record.

Giggs and Jeter both had particularly prestigious duties. Wingers have long had a special place in United's affections and, on his emergence, Giggs was predictably heralded as 'the new George Best'. Jeter, meanwhile, is the Yankees' shortstop, the most coveted fielding position. (It is no coincidence that in Chad Harbach's *The Art Of Fielding*, an attempt to draw the great American novel from the great American game, the central character, Henry Skrimshander, is a shortstop.) Granted ability, looks and money, fortunate enough to play for the club they loved in winning sides, Giggs and Jeter led charmed lives.

Too charmed, some might say. Their records are remarkable but anyone seeking to underplay their impact can cite one theory: that neither has often been the best player in his team, let alone the league. Over Giggs's two decades at the top, the outstanding individual has tended to be another, whether Eric Cantona, Roy Keane, Ruud van Nistelrooy, Cristiano Ronaldo, Wayne Rooney or Robin van Persie. As for the Yankees, Alex Rodriguez said in 2001, "Jeter's been blessed with great talent but he's never had to lead. You go into New York, you wanna stop Bernie [Williams] and [Paul] O'Neill. You never say: 'Don't let Derek beat you.' He's never your concern."

They were unwise words, not least because Rodriguez and Jeter became teammates three years later. Yet the point was that Rodriguez batted fourth — together with third, the most responsible spot in the line-up and where the best hitter is usually found — whereas Jeter has spent virtually all of his career first or second. Unlike Rodriguez, Jeter has never won baseball's MVP award, despite frequent finishes in the top 10. Giggs's only Player of the Year award came in 2008-09, a campaign in which he started just 12 league games, although he has been voted a member of the PFA's side of the season six times. In many respects, it was a lifetime achievement award, rather than a reflection of dominance over nine months.

Yet the opposing argument is that they peak when it matters most. These are big-game players who have delivered in memorable style on the major stage. Giggs' greatest goal, the slaloming solo run against Arsenal, came in extra time of the 1999 FA Cup semi-final. Jeter's greatest fielding play, the improvised flip against Oakland in 2001, helped the

Yankees win the American League Division Series, en route to the World Series.

Indeed Jeter, unlike Rodriguez, is in the rare position of boasting a higher batting average in the World Series than in normal matches. It has brought him the nicknames 'Captain Clutch' and 'Mr November'. Football doesn't have the same statistical measures of excellence but as Giggs's career has gone on, there is the sense that he has delivered when it has mattered most: a goal as United clinched the title in 2008 at Wigan, the decisive penalty in the Champions League final shootout in the next game and a midfield master-class in perhaps the pivotal game of the following season's title race, Chelsea's January 2009 trip to Old Trafford.

It is a sign of their temperament that both have brought up landmarks in spectacular style. Giggs, often spared more mundane matches, was the finest player on the pitch in the Champions League last season against Real Madrid, in his 1,000th senior appearance and at the age of 39. Jeter marked his 3,000th hit, a subject of frenzied attention in New York, by becoming only the second player to reach the milestone with a home run.

The chorus of acclaim has been all the louder because each has gained new admirers in a personal Indian summer. In 2008, Ferguson wondered aloud if Giggs would have to be "phased out"; instead the winger outlasted the manager. Jeter appeared in decline during a difficult 2010; he rebounded to have a superb 2012. Greatness can be bestowed in a minute or over a sporting lifetime of endeavour and a capacity to carry on

performing when contemporaries have faded away enhances their cases. If Giggs, in particular, was taken for granted eight or ten years ago, his latter years have brought renewed appreciation.

Enduring excellence, loyalty and longevity account for reputations that rise by the year. So, too, does the status as a role model. Jeter, whose reputation has remained unsullied while many other baseball players have been exposed as steroid abusers, is particularly deserving. Neither has been expelled from the pitch for his club (Giggs has one, slightly unfortunate and often forgotten, red card for Wales) and, unlike their colleagues, have been consistently uncontroversial in their comments. They have preferred to make headlines with their on-field antics. Despite a keen interest in the opposite sex (Jeter has dated Mariah Carey and various actresses), each has preferred a low-profile private life, even if references to Giggs as a family man took on a different meaning in 2011.

It is one significant difference. Another lies in their statuses and not merely because Jeter is the Yankees' captain and Giggs has tended to be the vice-captain or senior professional. He has adapted seamlessly to the era of squad rotation — indeed, it has extended his career — whereas Jeter has tried to stop the hands of time, reluctant to give up his much-scrutinised duties as the shortstop, even for the less strenuous (non-fielding) role as the designated hitter (Jeter's former teammate Joe Girardi once said he felt sorry for the next Yankee manager because he would have to tell him he couldn't play shortstop anymore; five years into his time in charge of the

Yankees, Girardi still hasn't passed the message on). When his fellow shortstop Rodriguez joined the Yankees, the newcomer had to play third base. In contrast, Giggs has proved flexible enough to play as a central midfielder, a No. 10 and on the right.

Nevertheless, the question of the succession has lingered over United and the Yankees for years. Ferguson first targeted Damien Duff and Arjen Robben a decade ago. Over the past few seasons, Cristiano Ronaldo, Wayne Rooney, Danny Welbeck, Ji-sung Park, Ashley Young, Nani, Shinji Kagawa and Adnan Januzaj have spent time on the left flank without a permanent replacement becoming apparent. Jeter's eternal understudy Eduardo Núñez is now 26, the age the older man was when he won his fourth World Series, and the 39 year old's injury-enforced absence for much of the 2013 season has only reiterated his importance. He wants to remain an every-day player whereas Giggs is content saving some of his efforts for special occasions.

They differ, too, in their income. Jeter's current, one-year contract is worth US$12 million and entails a pay cut following a three-year, $51 million deal. That, in turn, was preceded by a $10-year, $189 million contract. He used to own a penthouse in Manhattan's Trump Tower; Giggs lives in Worsley. It is probably the nicer part of Worsley, but it is Worsley nonetheless. Playing the global game for arguably the planet's biggest club is clearly less profitable than being the sporting king of the world's unofficial capital.

Perhaps it explains that while one Florida-based billionaire, George Steinbrenner, bought the Yankees in the 1970s, in the 21st-century another, Malcolm Glazer, preferred to invest in United. The crossover, however, has come in the boardrooms. Out on the pitch, the parallels between Giggs and Jeter might not be recognised by either. The United man is a fan of rugby league, the sport his father, Danny Wilson, played professionally. The brand of football the baseball player likes involves an oval ball. He is more interested in Michigan State than Manchester United. They are both products of their environment but, with consistent displays of quality and record-breaking levels of durability, they have defined successful eras at two of the world's great sporting institutions. They are unique and yet similar. Ⓑ

FLAGSHIP STORE NOW OPEN
SPIRIT, STYLE AND QUALITY FROM THE BIRTHPLACE OF THE BEAUTIFUL GAME

FROM SHEFFIELD, UK, THE BIRTHPLACE OF THE BEAUTIFUL GAME, COMES GOALSOUL'S FLAGSHIP STORE... A UNIQUE CELEBRATION OF THE WORLD'S FAVORITE GAME

GIFTS FOR ALL SEASONS

ALL GOALSOUL ARTWORKS ARE AVAILABLE ON STYLISH, HIGH-QUALITY CLASSIC JERSEY TEES, OR STUNNING GICLÉE ART PRINTS AND BOXED CANVAS'. ALL ARE AVAILABLE ONLINE AND INSTORE AT GOALSOUL.

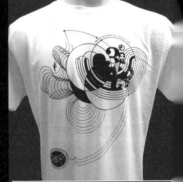

NEW! BIELSA PEP TALK
INTENSE ATMOSPHERIC PRESSURE

NEW! ZBIGNIEW BONIEK
THE BEAUTY AT NIGHT

NEW! LAURIE CUNNINGHAM
3 DEGREES OF SEPARATION

£25 VOUCHER
TO
FROM
DATE OF ISSUE
UNIQUE VOUCHER CODE

THE GIFT FOR ALL SEASONS

KEEPING THE GAME BEAUTIFUL ONLINE AND INSTORE

WWW.GOALSOUL.NET

GOALSOUL, 283 SHARROW VALE ROAD, SHEFFIELD, S11 8ZE, +44 (0)114 266 3374

goalsoul

The Street Dogs of Manila

The Philippines are rising through the rankings, but are they Filipino enough?

By Javier Sauras and Felix Lill

Three weeks before super-typhoon Haiyan devastated the eastern Philippines, killing thousands of people, the deadliest earthquake in the last two decades wreaked havoc in the middle of the country. The same day the earth trembled with the energy of 32 Hiroshima bombs, the city of Bacolod, 125 miles from the epicentre, was hosting the Peace Cup, a series of friendly games between Taiwan, Pakistan and the Philippines. A tremor woke up most of the Filipino players in the early morning and it became the opening line of every conversation during breakfast in the dining-room of a luxury hotel in the province of Negros Occidental.

Strangely, listening from a distance, the jabber echoing through the walls of the hotel's room did not resemble Tagalog, the most commonly spoken language of the archipelago. It sounded more like an interlingua, with a strong scent of British accents, some northern European words, a pinch of Spanish and a German bouquet. It was nothing like anyone would expect coming from a national football team. There were some blonde, blue-eyed giants, sitting next to small, stocky, dark-haired Austronesian men, some Mediterranean gestures and Middle-Eastern faces... all of them wearing the same blue and white uniform. The mixture made clear why the team is nicknamed 'the Azkals', 'the street dogs'.

The Azkals had lost their first game 2-1 against Taiwan who, the day before, had been defeated 1-0 by Pakistan. In the final game of the Peace Cup, the Philippines had to beat Pakistan by two goals to retain the title. The hotel was jammed with fans wearing the colours of the Azkals, but there were also Spanish T-shirts, German and Italian flags, and a lot of Premier League merchandising items among the cheering crowd. Everybody was waiting around a balustrade, surrounding the stairs where the players would appear to cross the lobby and get into the bus. A stylish tanned woman in tight jeans and a flashy blouse caught everyone's eyes. She was Dyan Castillejo-Garcia, senior correspondent and sports anchor for ABS-CBN, a major broadcasting corporation. The younger ones were enthralled by her presence and, since the stars were not there yet, soon she was the one signing autographs.

One of the guys in the hotel lobby drew Dyan's attention. He was close to an elevator and was shifting from one foot to the other. Although he was wearing the official Philippines national team clothes, nobody seemed to recognise him. The TV journalist waved goodbye to the fans and told her camera crew to follow her. She had a hunch. Since she had never seen him before, she thought that guy could be one of the new players. "Are you a player?" asked Dyan. "Yes, I am. My name is Martin," he answered. "And which country do you come from?" asked Dyan again. Only in the Azkals could a question like that made sense. Everywhere else in the world, a footballer joining a national team is supposed to be from the same country as his teammates. Not in the Philippines.

Martin Steuble was born in Switzerland in 1988. He is an attacking midfielder for FC Wil, in the Swiss Challenge League. He admires Thiago Alcántara's game and looks a little bit like him. With a wide smile and sincere surprise, Martin looked at the crowd. "My mum is from Bacolod but I've never been here before. My aunt got tickets; she's going to the game with my nieces. It's crazy!" he said. It's the first time the Switzerland-born player had been to the Philippines and he is excited; he doesn't know what to expect. "I hope I can play as soon as possible," he said. "I've handed in all the possible documents that I could find — certificate of birth, baptism, the marriage of my parents and so on. They have it all now."

The Swiss-Filipino was a fan before becoming part of the squad. "There was this hype about the Azkals among the Filipino community and I was following it through the internet," he said. "A few years ago the team's goalkeeping coach was Pascal Zuberbühler, Switzerland's former national keeper. So I approached him after a game of my team in the Swiss second division, where Pascal was as well. I wanted to be part of it, if I could help. Once Zubi had established

contact, the association immediately invited me over."

Martin admits that he doesn't know much about the country: he knows about the food thanks to his mother's cooking and knows that there are thousands of islands, but that's about it. He is probably unaware that Negros Occidental, the province where they are playing, was the home town of the Barcelona's first professional football player, Manuel Amechazurra. "The Adventurer," as they knew him in Spain, was born in 1884. He played 137 games as a defender for Barcelona and was even capped several times for Catalonia. Had he played for the Philippines then, he would have started the tradition of emigrants returning home to wear the colours of the country.

There are 22 players in the Philippines squad for the Peace Cup. Only five of them were born in the country. Of the others, there are two Germans, two Spaniards, two Dutch, one Italian, one Iranian, one Belgian, one Dane, one American and six Englishmen. There are more English players in the Philippines national team than in Arsenal's squad.

The coach Michael Weiss takes full responsibility for this. Although the idea of bringing 'foreign' players to boost the level of the Azkals was not his, he fully approved it. "There are some people who only want to see pure Filipinos," he said. "They can't accept those that were raised in other countries in the team. But I think such an attitude by some fans is an offence against those boys who want to represent the Philippines, since it is also their home country. And clearly, the local players do not have the necessary level yet. If we only played with Filipino players we would lose against Pakistan. It would even be hard against Guam."

Weiss is a globetrotter. Born in Germany in 1965, he took control of the squad in January 2011 after 10 years of coaching all around the world — in Germany, Japan, China and Rwanda. When he arrived in the Philippines, the team was 195th in the Fifa World Ranking. Three years later, when he finished his spell with the Azkals, they had climbed 68 places to their best ever position and had become the strongest football squad in Southeast Asia. "Our potential is tremendous," he said.

It may be difficult to explain why the most successful manager in the history of Filipino football was sacked a few months before the 2014 AFC Challenge Cup, a major competition that could eventually lead to qualification for the Asian Cup and, in time, raise the Azkals' chances of making it to the World Cup. Only the manager of the team, Dan Palami, a billionaire in love with the sport, has the answer.

Boss Dan, as everybody calls him, got involved with the national team in 2009 during an Under-19 tournament in China. The players lacked kit and airline tickets, and he paid for everything from his own pocket. The Philippines only won against Guam that time, but the Philippines Football Federation (PFF) asked him to manage the seniors.

"Lots of the Filipinos live overseas and most of my players do," explained Weiss. "But the government does not support their football ambitions at all, although they are representing their country. For example, the government has a registry of Filipinos abroad, but we have no access. Pretty much all we do is thanks to the private investments by Dan Palami."

A high-pitched din broke the conversation. The noise of the fans made clear that the players were walking down the stairs and heading to the bus. There was a colourful and festive atmosphere around the Azkals, an experience most of these players have rarely gone through in professional football. It's easy to forget that football is still a relatively unknown sport in the Philippines. Even in Bacolod, a city of 500,000 people, a taxi driver may not know that the national team is playing at the local stadium.

All the players and the coaching team got on the bus, but the driver stayed still and the engine didn't roar. He was waiting for Boss Dan. Palami wore the Azkals' official tracksuit. He signed as many T-shirts as any other star and had been joking with the fans, posing for the pictures up and down the lobby and talking to the local authorities. The transport tycoon is in his forties. He exudes an air of wealth and power and was self-confident enough to be the last one on the bus. He would sit on the bench next to Weiss when the game kicks off.

"I have spent around US$2 million from my own pocket," says Boss Dan. "It's painful when you look at your bank account. But it doesn't matter when you see the faces of the players or when you travel abroad and feel the support of the fans."

Dan Palami is a black swan in the development of football in the Philippines. He was nine years old when he saw older kids playing with a ball on the street and the game came naturally to him. When he was a teenager, nobody watched football in the country. There were few fans and they had to wait for the Beta tapes of the games. "We could only watch Pelé in films," he said.

"For a time I concentrated on managing my own business. Then I started playing football with the company personnel and friends. Soon, it started to become serious, so I signed players from other provinces and gave them work at my train factory, so they would play in the team. Jerry Barbosa, one of the Azkals, belongs to the accounts department of my company."

Today, Palami not only watches football on TV and from the bench of the national team, he also has a team of scouts who track several foreign leagues and gather intelligence on the emigrants and their offspring. Facebook and Twitter are powerful tools for these scouts: many of the players in the Azkals have been contacted through social media.

He also created a club in Manila, Global FC, to give refuge to the 'foreign' national team players. At least half a dozen of the Azkals play for his club. "Global was set up to help the national team," Palami explained. "One of the key ingredients of the success of the team is to spend more time together. Global FC addresses the situation. It will provide the structure to help the national team. The country comes before the club. We have to change the mentality of football in the Philippines."

Boss Dan has always had one big goal in mind. He has shaped his ambition over

the years and has given it a catchy name: Project 100. Since he took over the Azkals, he has been dreaming of a Filipino squad in the top 100 of the Fifa rankings. Palami rejoiced at the end of 2013, when the national team became a powerhouse in Southeast Asian football but there are still a few steps to climb if he wants to hear a triumphal fanfare at the end of that path, a path that started more than a hundred years ago, when the Philippines were under US jurisdiction.

The history of Filipino football goes as far back as that of those more established football nations the young talent is being drawn from. The Philippines' federation has been in operation since 1907 and it was in 1912 that Paulino Alcántara, who was born in 1896 when the country was still under Spanish control, made his debut for Barcelona. For a short spell in 1951 he also coached Spain's national side.

But Alcántara was to remain a rare star, in fact the only one. As the USA began to dominate the archipelago it was not football the colonialists taught the locals. Basketball and boxing were introduced and adopted as the most popular sports. Even today, few Filipinos could name a player for the Azkals. Everybody could find the capital's notorious Araneta Arena, where in 1975 Muhammad Ali and Joe Frazier met in the Thrilla in Manila and would know their way to the basketball arenas, or to the space where they could shoot a few baskets, but football is hardly anywhere to be seen outside a handful of bars where people may be watching the Premier League. All over the world, kids in the slums kick a makeshift ball around, but not here.

There are, though, at least two faces young Filipinos and Filipinas will know. They have lighter skin and thinner noses than the average citizen and regularly appear on the country's television entertainment shows. They are brothers, one of whom became famous for his work as a model, the other by singing. "I'm really not proud of it," said Phil Younghusband with an almost blushing smile as he talks about his stint as a singer. He was sitting inside that hotel in Bacolod, one table away from Boss Dan. His brother James nods next to him, chuckling. His face, in turn, is often seen on advertisements. Phil still makes some extra money having shots taken of himself.

The Younghusband brothers are superstars in the Philippines. "Most will know we are footballers," said Phil. He settled here in 2008, as a 21 year old, having passed through Chelsea's academy and reserve side, and a loan with the Danish side Esbjerg. Phil is one year younger than James, who was also a graduate of Chelsea's academy, before playing for AFC Wimbledon, Staines Town, Woking and Farnborough.

"In the locker rooms during the years in the Chelsea youth team, our mates would joke that one day we'd represent the Philippines," said James.

"And so it happened," said Phil.

In 1985, the Younghusbands' mother Susan went from Manila to South West London, where she met Philip Younghusband, a lawyer she would later marry. "Being raised in a football-crazy country like England, it was obvious we'd be kicking the ball," said James.

A few years ago, the two were contacted thanks to a computer game in which their names were featured. The scout of the national team sensed that with their Filipino roots and their development in one of the world's biggest football clubs, the Younghusbands should be able to raise the Filipino side's level. "We were invited to play for the team pretty much out of the blue," said Phil. And as the country was establishing a national professional football league at the time, having two nationals from abroad seemed an attraction.

It was, but most Filipinos probably know the Younghusbands more for their activities off the pitch than on it, not that that's something the brothers think about too much. "Football is really taking off here," said James. "When we first got here, you'd come to play a game and then find out there were no locker rooms. Or the balls were missing. Coming from Chelsea, you're a bit spoiled. And then you see this."

The football infrastructure today bears no comparison to that of five years ago, he said: "But we still have a long, long way to go." James and Phil Younghusband are doing their share. On the national network TV5 they regularly screen a three-minute show football called FYI, which stands for Football Younghusbands Instruction, to give training tips. They also run their own football academy.

Apart from a one-year hiatus in 2011, when they quit the sport because the national association had repeatedly failed to reimburse the brothers' flight tickets and other costs, Phil and James Younghusband play a crucial role in the national side. Phil even ascended into the world's top 20 international strikers, at least by one measure. "The *Daily Mail* ranked me among guys like Pelé, Gabriel Batistuta and Didier Drogba because I scored 33 times in 50 caps," he said, turning round with a smile.

Behind him was the lobby window that separated the footballers' relaxation from the numerous excited fans. The brothers knew they would have to pass through there, signing autographs. Even through the closed doors, the cheers were clearly audible, with some fans screaming Phil's name. "It's a great thing that they accept us here as they do," he said.

But that isn't the whole story. Not all of the growing body of football fans is appreciative of players like the Younghusbands as the girls waiting for them outside the hotel, something that is rooted in a national complex as much as in sport and the country's economy.

On the bigger stand of the roughly 12,000-spectator stadium of Bacolod, two hours later, the 19-year-old student Daniel Ramos was not amused. "I think we don't need all the foreigners," he murmured. The youngster and his mates wore green T-shirts that identify them as football talents of a local high school. As he said, the sport is gaining in popularity but Ramos doesn't see that as having much to do with the 'foreigners'. "I think our team would be equally good with real Filipinos," he said. "We have many competitive players."

Weiss's assistant Thomas Roy, also a German, is sceptical. By kick-off, Roy was sitting in the stand with a notebook on his lap, following the game with pen and paper. It is Roy's task to turn the Philippines into a country where local talents will one day pop up like mushrooms from soil. "We aren't nearly there," was his sober comment, accompanied by a shake of the head as the only local Filipino player on the pitch tried to dribble and lost the ball. "Until local players are better than those with formation abroad, it will take two generations at least," he said. "You need to build proper infrastructure in the whole country, you need to make the sport popular enough, you need good coaches and so on." And of course, he added, you need idols the youth can aspire to: "Currently, you can only find those guys abroad. I don't understand that some people don't accept these boys who represent one of their parents' countries with so much pride."

There are roughly 12 million Filipinos living outside their home country, with political support from the government in Manila. "Sending labour abroad has been part of our economic policy for decades now," said Emmanuel Esguerra, a few hundred kilometres north of Bacolod, in the capital. Esguerra is an economist at the country's most prestigious academic institution, the University of the Philippines, and plays a leading role in a government commission to steer economic development. "Our situation would be far worse without those people abroad," he said. 10% of the Philippines's economy consists of remittances sent from overseas workers who make more money abroad.

Filipinos are clerks, entertainers, carers and nurses in Saudi Arabia, Japan, Great Britain, the USA and elsewhere, and seamen all over the world. "Their incomes in richer countries are really crucial," said Esguerra. "Knowing this, some people would never come back to the Philippines in order to provide a constant income stream for their families." As a result, many Filipino citizens married and had children abroad.

It's the offspring of those emigrants all over the world who are today beefing up football development in the Southeast Asian country. On the pitch in Bacolod, as the Azkals played Pakistan, all but one player was born outside the country they were representing. Many of them, like the Switzerland-born Martin Steuble, had never been in the Philippines until they became part of the project. "Sure, in some abstract way it is understandable that some fans think we are not true Filipinos," said Rob Gier. "But it's just unfair if you look at how all of us guys try hard to make the country more competitive." The Azkals' captain, born in Ascot to an English father and a Filipino mother, quit his professional football career, which started at Wimbledon and ended in the Philippines in 2009, but he still plays for the national team. Gier's main job today is to find new players for the team and he is looking for them in every nation where football is a major sport.

"There's a young pro in Austria that we are trying to get," he said. "Another is playing in France's Ligue 1." But it isn't always easy to get in touch. Some Azkals were first contacted through Facebook, others through the Filipino community in the country in which they live. "But some others," Gier admitted, "are just out of reach." The most famous example is Bayern Munich's left-back David Alaba, born to a Nigerian father and a Filipino

mother. Alaba chose to represent Austria, where he was born.

Although the Azkals dominated Pakistan from the start, the visitors took a shock lead after a few easily avoidable mistakes in the Filipino defence. Everybody understood the situation: they needed three goals to lift the Peace Cup. Weiss constantly shouted at his players, some of whom were running around with little apparent direction or motivation. There was one clear exception, the Germany-born Stephan Schröck. A winger at Bundesliga club Eintracht Frankfurt, he is the centrepiece of the Azkals' game. Schröck was fighting for every ball and putting order into the chaos of the home team. "Without Stephan today, the Younghusbands wouldn't have got a single ball," said the stressed youth coordinator Thomas Roy at half-time. By then, the Azkals had at least equalised. But that was not nearly enough. The fans, most of whom paid roughly a dollar to see the game, not a small amount in a country in which a third of the population earn about that amount in a day, made clear what they wanted: "Come on, Azkals for victory," said one placard.

Meanwhile, Daniel Ramos, the young fan who was sceptical of the international dominance in this national side, asked, "Why is Stephan Schröck not playing for Germany? He is so strong." Perhaps he could have. Schröck represented the Germans at Under-18, Under-19 and Under-20 level. But one day at his previous club, Greuther Fürth, there was a postcard in the letter box from which he would normally pick up autograph requests. "A scout from the Philippines invited me to play for their national team," Schröck said. "It was a point of no return. Sure, there was still the theoretical chance that I would have been picked to play for Germany. But if I was being honest with myself that would have been more of a career step to raise my market value." Playing for the Philippines, he said, involved more national pride. "I'm also doing it for my mother a bit. She came to Germany decades ago and started work as a beautician to send money back home: all I am today is thanks to her. At my club Frankfurt, there's not always a great deal of acceptance of this because the Philippines are not a big football nation and many games are outside the Fifa calendar. But that's not my fault."

At his home in the southern German town of Schweinfurt, Schröck never spoke Tagalog, but his mother would sometimes cook Filipino food. Schröck admits he knew little of the Philippines well before he started to play for them. That's one part of his story in which he resembles his teammates. The other is his feeling of nationhood. "I am both, German and Filipino," Schröck said with an earnest, almost defensive, tone.

By the second half Schröck, seemed to be pushing and pulling his team along almost single-handedly. With an hour played, the Philippines were dominant and with 10 minutes to go they took a 2-1 lead. The Panaad Stadium was throbbing. After a few clear chances were missed, it was Schröck who scored the decisive goal, lashing the ball in from a yard after some chaotic Pakistani defending. He ran to the corner, followed by his countrymen of all skin colours to strike a victory pose in front of the fans. It was only the Peace Cup, but to this country, it was a great success.

"I am so relieved," said Weiss, raising his shirt to wipe the sweat from brow. "We didn't play well at all, made way too many mistakes. But it's fine now. We'll have a few drinks later on, I guess." He seemed unemotional as he congratulated his players but, a few moments later, as the Azkals collected the trophy, the coach ventured a smile.

Hours after the victory, hundreds of fans awaited the players in front of the team bus to take pictures and get a last glimpse of their players. With every footballer who walked out of the door, another wave of cheers echoed through the night. "You'll see later today," Schröck had said that morning, alluding to the enthusiasm for football in this country, which had seemed almost non-existent in places. "But people really go crazy for the Azkals. They see us in shopping malls and take pictures. I really don't know where this will take us in a few years, when we may eventually be among the world's top 100."

But do they know what being an Azkal means? Off the pitch, Schröck proved he had done his homework: "Azkal is the Filipino word for those dogs who live on the street, who don't have an owner, you know? They are always around but never really cared for. I think 'azkal' is the perfect term for a football team here. The sport has been here for more than a hundred years, but always in the shadow of other disciplines."

Now, that street dog is rising, slowly but surely. And, the creature is more representative today than ever before. As Schröck said, "Lots of street dogs are mixed race, aren't they?" Ⓑ

Second City Syndrome

Why has Birmingham struggled for football success for 30 years?

By Matthew Campelli

If you'd just walked in, it could have been any other night. The bar was curiously busy for a Thursday, but nothing remarkable seemed in the offing. Beer, bellies and bald patches saturated the landscape at the Sacred Heart social club. Murmurs of mundane conversation fluttered around the room and then, like a hallucination, a tall grey man in an undertaker-style coat casually wandered in holding the European Cup.

The man was Peter Withe, a former England international forward and an undisputed Aston Villa legend. Outside of Birmingham you'd be hard pushed to find someone who recognised him, but that night his appearance released inhibitions. Overalls and suits alike went rushing towards him and Tony Morley, the two men who had combined to create the goal that beat Bayern Munich in the European Cup final. Withe's solitary strike brought the title to the second city for the first and only time and the pair had organised an evening of recollection and celebration with a replica of the famous trophy.

Withe and Morley lifted the cup, revelling in the gaze of a euphoric crowd, evoking memories of that hazy spring night at De Kuip in 1982. Thirty-one years on and 270 miles west of Rotterdam, in the Birmingham suburb of Aston — more

maligned Midlands than beautiful south — the metaphorical landscape is as different as the literal manifestation.

The hundred odd Villa fans were ambushed by glorious nostalgia, but the three decades since the triumph have been littered with false dawns, boardroom struggles and mediocre performances. Those of a claret and blue persuasion can count themselves relatively lucky as the affluent relations of the city. An incredible League Cup win apart, Birmingham City's recent history has been pretty nondescript, while West Bromwich Albion have been average at best and disastrous at worst since the halcyon days of Cyrille Regis and the 'Three Degrees'.

The season before their European Cup triumph, Villa had wrestled the league title from the hands of Bob Paisley's mighty Liverpool. The charismatic Ron Atkinson had led his expansive West Brom side to fourth place in the First Division, while the Blues commanded a respectable position in the top-flight. Despite the recession, there was something of a renaissance happening in Birmingham. The buoyant atmosphere was captured perfectly by the urban legend about Duran Duran being signed by EMI at the notorious Rum Runner club on the same night Villa first climbed to the top of the league in 1980. Collective jubilation has been in short supply since.

So what is it about the Second City and football? With a population surpassed only by London, and proud footballing history, why hasn't Birmingham been able to dominate the scene like Manchester and Liverpool? In the words of Dave Woodhall, editor of the Aston Villa fanzine *Heroes and Villains*, "It seems that in Birmingham we never punch our weight in anything."

The journey from Moor Street station to Birmingham City's Wast Hills training ground is not particularly long but the scenery en route encapsulates the diversity of the city. The first major landmark is the Edgbaston cricket ground, surrounded by trees, grassy knolls and the sort of picturesque townhouses normally associated with upmarket seaside towns. The area neighbouring the training facility is equally beautiful, if slightly more affluent at first sight, as townhouses are replaced by detached manors, partially and purposefully hidden from view by hedges, trees and imposing iron gates. Sandwiched between the two suburban havens, however, is the seemingly endless vision of boarded-up shops, broken windows and abandoned houses.

Richard Beale comes bounding into the reception area of the training ground offering a warm smile and a firm handshake. He has the aura of a man who loves his job and so he should. At just 31, he was appointed as Birmingham City's reserve team coach and he has retained an important role as head of the development squad.

In full City training attire, he offers a tour of the complex, and his passion for the city and the football club shines through in all he says. He finally sits down, leaning in, and his thoughtfulness is apparent from the outset. "In Birmingham there's a very competitive market because you have City, Villa, West Brom, Coventry and Wolves all fighting for the same kids," Beale said. "Now every single club picks up players from the inner city. There are a lot of deprived districts in Birmingham where youngsters have the hunger, the drive, and the determination. They grow up with the culture of seeing players from their area succeed. They might not have represented England, but a lot of people from this area have carved out a successful career in football."

Beale believes the quantity and quality of clubs in the area demonstrates the city's footballing prowess. The Birmingham County FA lists over 4,500 in the locality, while the academies of the professional teams are nationally admired. Birmingham City have become adept at cultivating local talent like Nathan Redmond and Mitchell Hancox, although a focus on youth is a policy largely enforced by financial problems restricting new signings, while Aston Villa's Bodymoor Heath academy was voted as the nation's best in 2012.

Since the hallowed year of 1966 only two players from the city have become England regulars, but Beale responded to that statistic by pointing out that Birmingham is responsible for a large proportion of top flight players: London and Liverpool are the only two cities to produce more Premier League footballers between its inception in 1992 and 2011.

Darius Vassell and Joleon Lescott are the two Birmingham-born players to make over 20 appearances for their country after 1966. Vassell's 22 caps were all won while he was playing for the club he joined as a boy, Aston Villa. The forward was a regular during the reign of Sven-Göran Eriksson, who liked to use his pace and movement from the bench against tiring opposition.

The 32 year old agreed that the region is not short of talent, but he is concerned about the attitude adopted at youth level, referring to an inferiority complex he experienced as a youngster at Villa. "Take Manchester United, for example, a club known for honing talent through their youth systems year after year," he said. "I'm not actually sure how much is local talent. What I am sure of is that just by being associated with such a big club from an early age brings what I would call 'responsibility of performance'. That is to assume it's much easier to exercise the actions of pride when there is something greater to be proud of. My youth team coaches would go crazy to hear me say this but I can remember playing against teams like United and our general team perception was that we were probably going to lose."

His admission is as depressing as it is candid. Granted, Manchester United are a formidable force at any level, but how can such a celebrated club as Villa nurture such an indifferent attitude? Perhaps this apathetic mentality is symptomatic of a city starved of success. Birmingham, of course, is the cradle of professional football. A statue of William McGregor, the founder of the Football League, can be found adjacent to Villa Park's Holte End. The Scottish pioneer moved to the city in 1870 to find work

and attached himself to the club, his effigy immortalising the footballing tradition of the area.

The West Midlands was a dominant force in the football of the late nineteenth and early twentieth centuries. Between 1887 and 1920 Villa won six league titles and six FA Cups, WBA won the cup five times before 1968, while Wolverhampton Wanderers were champions three times in the 1950s. Birmingham City became the first English team to contest the final of a European tournament (the 1960 Fairs Cup), but the sixties initiated a period of decay that the region has perhaps never recovered from. Villa, City and Wolves were all relegated in the decade just as football underwent a revolution, with the allure of George Best, the shaping of Liverpool's dynasty and the rise of mass media interest in football. It was the worst time for decline and West Midlands sides were overtaken.

"In the post-war period, the fact these clubs had such tradition helped them attract kids who wanted to play football," lamented the late Larry Canning, another Scot who made Birmingham his home after playing for Villa. "While you've got poor teams the youngsters won't want to go, and gradually you lose that tradition."

Despite that history of success, the former Leeds and Liverpool midfielder Gary McAllister, who spent six seasons as a player at Coventry and then managed them, described the Midlands as "not a footballing area", claiming that the supporters don't get behind their teams as much as they do in the north. In the last five seasons Aston Villa have had noticeably fluctuating attendance averages. Over the course of the 2008-

09 campaign, in which Martin O'Neill's exuberant side pushed Arsenal for the fourth Champions League spot before finishing a respectable sixth, Villa Park was 93.9% full. Under the guidance of Alex McLeish during 2011-12, Villa finished sixteenth after battling relegation all season. As a consequence, the ground was only at 79.2% capacity.

It would be unfair to compare these statistics to those of northern giants like Manchester United and Liverpool, but to put the figures into perspective it is significant that Newcastle United achieved an average 93.1% in 2008-09 — the season they were relegated. Can Villa fans be pigeon-holed as fair-weather based on this statistic? And if so, can it be used to measure the footballing traditions and passions of the area?

McAllister reasons that supporters inhabiting the most impoverished parts of the country hold their teams in higher regard because "it makes them feel like winners for once". He places Scotland and the north-west into this category, but statistics don't support his claim. The unemployment rate of the West Midlands is 8.9%, while the number of people aged 16-24 out of work is one of the highest in the country. Three of the top four unemployment blackspots in the UK are in Birmingham (Ladywood, Hodge Hill and Erdington), while Ladywood is one of the poorest parliamentary constituencies in Britain.

Those statistics, like McAllister's comments, however, are neither here nor there. Ticket prices, especially in top-flight football, have turned the working man's ballet into a game for the middle-class. Many Aston Villa fans point to the Thatcher recession of the early 1980s as a significant reason

for failure to capitalise on a period of success for the club. When Villa won the title in 1981, league attendances reached a post-war low across the nation, limiting the scope to attract new fans. With a traditionally large blue-collar support, Birmingham City also suffered during this period after the collapse of the car manufacturing industry. If anything, economic instability appears to have had an adverse effect on football in the area rather than strengthening ties.

There may be some credence in McAllister's final reflection though, in which he questions the region's footballing identity. Birmingham has the air of a divided city and struggles with identity in general. About one third (329,000) of the population is non-white and this multicultural environment has been the cause for much tension over the years. The right-wing politician, Enoch Powell, formerly MP of nearby Wolverhampton, delivered his infamous "rivers of blood" speech in the city in 1968, fanning the flames of racial mistrust and prejudice throughout the West Midlands. From the Handsworth riots of 1985 to the periods of discontent in 2005 and 2011, racial and social unrest has not been uncommon in Birmingham.

This tribal suspicion and hatred made its way onto the terraces during the hooligan era of the 1970s and 80s. Going to a football match would have been a terrifying prospect for those of non-white origin and, in a city like Birmingham that had a steadily growing immigrant population, a significant proportion of local citizens were alienated from the game. According to Jas Bains, author of *Corner Shops and Corner Flags*, the members of the burgeoning Asian population who did enjoy football were restricted to watching it on the television and, as a consequence, were exposed to the more popular clubs like Liverpool and Manchester United. As a result, very few became connected with local clubs.

This is demonstrated perfectly by the fans at the Sacred Heart social club, or more specifically, one fan. His name is Ravi, as announced on the back of his faded Aston Villa shirt. He shares many similarities with the rest of the men in the room. His waist is perhaps a little larger than he may desire and he appears to be very much on the wrong side of forty. But he is the only Asian there, which is staggering. The area where the social club and Villa Park are situated has a 56% Asian population, hinting at the barely existent relationship the biggest club in the region has with its immediate catchment area.

"Can you imagine a team today, Chelsea for example, winning the league, then winning the European Cup, all with an English backbone, and then none of those players being picked for a World Cup?" bellowed an agitated, stocky man as the hushed Sacred Heart congregation sat attentively. "It was an absolute disgrace."

Peter Withe was the only member of that European Cup winning squad to be selected for the 1982 World Cup, although he didn't play a single minute in Spain. It's hard to fathom Ron Greenwood's logic as momentum and morale are valued ingredients for tournament football. In his book *Football Memories*, the veteran football writer Brian Glanville revealed his own

reservations about Greenwood's selection policies. There were suggestions the former West Ham manager favoured footballers employed by 'fashionable' clubs. This was given weight by his treatment of Bryan Robson, who was only ever considered once he arrived at Old Trafford despite playing phenomenal football while at West Bromwich Albion.

Tony Morley, who was one of those considered unfortunate to miss out on the 1982 showpiece, has sympathy for his former teammates. "The fact Denis Mortimer didn't get one cap while players who aren't in the same class get 50 or 60 is a scandal," he said. "By the time he was 21, Gary Shaw had won the league, the European Cup and the Young Player of the Year, but didn't get a single cap either. He'd achieved more than Wayne Rooney at the same age, but when Rooney was 21 he had already represented England 35 times."

The Birmingham-born Shaw had the world at his feet in 1982, but a devastating injury sustained a season later snatched his career away from him, and thus, any further opportunity to don the Three Lions. Mortimer, the more seasoned campaigner who captained the side to domestic and continental glory, may have felt slightly more aggrieved to miss out on the World Cup but, with competition from Glenn Hoddle, Ray Wilkins and Robson, it was always going to be difficult for him to make his mark on the global stage.

Despite enduring an anticlimactic World Cup campaign himself, Withe can still look back at a respectable England career, although he was a relatively late bloomer. He won 11 caps between 1980 and 1985 but even he felt overlooked at times. "When I won the championship at Nottingham Forest I thought I was unfortunate not to get into the squad, but I know why," he said with a rueful shake of the head.

"Because of the cockney bastard press!" was the instant response from a stern-looking man in the front row.

"No!" Withe replied emphatically. "It's because Brian Clough didn't get on with Don Revie!"

Thoughts of a Clough versus Revie stand-off lightened the atmosphere temporarily, but Withe's admission opened up an important discussion about the complexity of international management and the politics of player selection. Is it reasonable to suggest that England coaches are more inclined to select players dominating the back pages and, in turn, does that highlight a geographical prejudice in the media? "Sometimes it may seem the southern press favour you if you play for Tottenham or Arsenal, but does that mean you have more chance of playing for England?" he continued with a more serious tone. "Well, I think in the end if you play well enough then they can't ignore you all the time."

And ignore them they don't, history proves. The mood in the room has become one of indignation, but no one has mentioned that Aston Villa have been home to more England internationals than any other club. It could be argued that many of those caps were won pre-war, but players like Gareth Southgate (42 caps), Gareth Barry (29) and Vassell represented their country a significant number of times while donning the claret and blue, while Ashley Young, Darren Bent and Stewart Downing all

played in England's 2-0 win over Wales in March 2011 even as Villa were fighting against relegation under Gérard Houllier. While James Milner also became an England regular at Villa and Jack Butland played for England while on the books of Birmingham City.

There needs to be a distinction made, however, between deliberately ignoring the merits of football in the region and the subconscious filtering of information to accommodate the traditional giants that sell the most newspapers. Ultimately, it becomes increasingly difficult to hold on to ambitious players if they feel that staying in Birmingham limits their chances of winning honours and competing at international level. In recent years, Barry and Milner have left Aston Villa for Manchester City, while Ashley Young has gone to Manchester United, despite helping the club to one of its most fruitful periods of the Premier League era. Losing players of that calibre makes building a squad capable of success a remote possibility and a vicious circle ensues. But that is not a new notion.

"I wish I'd gone as well," Cyrille Regis said regretfully, breaking eye contact for a moment. "You get to the point where you really want to reach the next level." Born in French Guiana, Regis spent most of his young life in London before being spotted by West Brom, prompting a move to the West Midlands. He is blessed with a quiet charisma and talked passionately about the game. "When I was playing in the seventies and the eighties it [the Midlands] was buoyant. Almost every club was in the top flight and every three or four weeks there was a local derby. Now the majority of teams in the area are out of the Premier League and there's nothing happening."

His former coach, Bobby Gould, attributes this period of dearth to an "apathy" in the region towards football, suggesting players yearning to progress tend to "outgrow the area". Now a successful agent, Regis, who won the FA Cup with Coventry in 1987, concurs and also points to the reputation and aesthetics of Birmingham as being detrimental in terms of keeping existing players and enticing new targets to local clubs. "Birmingham has got no glamour," he said with an unapologetic shrug of the shoulders. "All the foreign boys want London, Manchester and Liverpool. These cities have huge football clubs on the world stage and a massive ripple effect in the whole community. We're in the doldrums and we've been there for lots of years."

As recently as 2011, a TripAdvisor survey exposed Birmingham as the most boring and least romantic place to visit in Europe. In contrast, the *New York Times* recommended the city in their "Top 20 Places to Visit" in 2012. Despite being home to the state-of-the-art Bullring Shopping Centre, a world-renowned concert venue in Symphony Hall and the sights, sounds and tastes of the Jewellery Quarter, Broad Street and Balti Triangle, the stigma of the treacle-thick accent and the perceptions of the area as an industrial wasteland tend to stick. "In terms of people saying, 'Let's go to Birmingham, it's a great lifestyle there,' — yeah right!" Regis laughed. So that doesn't help when trying to sell the place to footballers."

"The whole place [Villa Park] was crying out for leadership and guidance and I eventually tired of the complacency there. Villa had a tremendous potential

and still have but I am not sure how it can be realised."

Danny Blanchflower

Being the boss can be complicated, but it appears Julie Nerney has it down to a fine art. A serial entrepreneur, she is the CEO of 14 separate companies and a highly respected name in organisational development and strategy. Born and bred in Birmingham, Nerney is a proud Aston Villa fan, but she remains frustrated about the governance of her club, and her birthplace in general. "There has been a real lack of leadership in the city," she said. "The council has always been beset by a lot of problems. It's struggling to find its new economy, and there doesn't seem to be a firm, driven, dynamic direction.

"Birmingham has tried to reinvent itself, but has done it in a very patchy fashion. In contrast, the changes to Liverpool since it won the European Capital of Culture bid in 2002 have been amazing. It has done more in four years than Birmingham has tried to do in 30."

Periods of economic uncertainty and social unrest in the seventies and eighties instigated a tide of rash, thoughtless redevelopment that did little to improve matters. Arguably, it did the opposite and inflicted physical and psychological trauma upon the city. This is, in part, where the stereotypes started and Nerney, who grew up in the city during the era of industrial decline, confessed that it was like living in a "vat of concrete".

Liverpool, like Birmingham, went through a fractious period in the seventies after the deterioration of the docks caused mass unemployment and fiscal instability.

However, Liverpool has since managed to build a reputation based on civic pride and impressive infrastructure, culminating with the European Capital of Culture victory, in which it beat Birmingham to the crown.

The former US president Bill Clinton once labelled Birmingham "an astonishing jewel of a city", while the *Independent* claimed that "culturally, Birmingham has done more for the world than Milan, Venice, Marseille and Frankfurt combined." So why the lack of universal recognition?

"The council does nothing for the city — period," raged Trevor Fisher, the author of *Villa for England* and member of the Socialist Education Association. He is convinced Birmingham's "abysmal public image" is brought on by an indifferent approach by local government. "There isn't a coherent strategy for promoting the city," he said. "The football clubs just reflect the wider malaise." It's a theory Julie Nerney subscribes to: "When you talk about leadership of the city you think about leadership of the clubs. I know there's controversy over the Glazers, but through the Sky era when the Premiership was formed Manchester United had a really steady leader in Martin Edwards. They saw what was coming and they got on with it. We (Villa) were too busy fighting with Doug Ellis."

Few can divide opinion among the Aston Villa faithful like Sir Herbert Douglas Ellis. His association with the club goes back to 1968 and in two separate stints as chairman he has never been too far away from controversy. Many laud him for keeping Villa in good economic shape by refusing to pander to the baying crowd,

but there is a significant proportion that loathes him for a perceived acceptance, even an embrace, of mediocrity in order to balance the books. Brian Little spent three and a half years working with him when he was the manager at Villa Park and he becomes animated just at the mention of his former employer. "I like Doug, I really do," he said jovially, "his negotiating skills were incredible. He used to wear people down by boring them with his fishing stories and telling them that he invented the overhead kick."

There's an identifiable gratitude on Little's part for the man who gave him the opportunity to coach the team he loves. Their association was a fruitful one, as two top-five finishes and a League Cup were delivered under their combined stewardship. But the Geordie, who originally joined Villa in 1969 as an apprentice, concedes the man they call 'Deadly' became too challenging a character to work with. "In the end I just got tired of him," he said. "If you achieve something there, you get to a point where you can't really push on. He wore me out and I had to go."

Those who opposed Ellis pinpoint two crucial periods they believe sealed the club's fate. The first is his dismantling of the squad that won the League and European Cup in successive years. Within three years of that glorious night in Rotterdam, the backbone of the team — Tony Morley, Peter Withe, Dennis Mortimer, Gordon Cowans and Des Bremner — was sold and, as a result, Villa succumbed to relegation in 1987. It should be noted that Ellis had relinquished control in 1979 and only took up the reins again in 1982. The team's most successful period of modern times occurred without him and many supporters will tell you that is no coincidence.

The second point is the direction the club took when football became big business. Neil Moxley, the *Daily Mail*'s Midlands football expert, believes Villa missed an opportunity during the inception of the Premier League "when the outlay wasn't that high": "With investment they could have been one of the top sides. They did float on the stock market, but a lot of money was wasted on transfers, especially during the reign of John Gregory."

Dwight Yorke, Gareth Southgate and Ugo Ehiogu were sold for a combined £26.6 million, but the money was spent on players like Steve Watson, Steve Stone and Boško Balaban, who weren't of a similar standard. Gregory, who led the team to the summit of the league for a brief period in 2001, later said he wasn't backed sufficiently. "I felt Doug wasn't prepared to take that little bit of a financial gamble," he claimed.

John Samuels, author of *The Beautiful Game is Over*, suggests that while Manchester United and Arsenal were "brand-building" by signing glamorous players, Villa didn't follow suit and thus failed to appeal nationally and internationally. The local historian and third generation Villa supporter Professor Carl Chinn also acknowledged that the club didn't capitalise on their local catchment area in the working-class parts of Birmingham, or even the wider area of Warwickshire, Worcestershire and Gloucestershire, which severely hindered any attempts to create a viable brand. "The club's leadership became remote and failed to bring in fans," Chinn said. This changed to an extent following the takeover by Randy Lerner in 2006. The American, along with the charismatic Martin O'Neill, brought optimism back to

the Trinity Road. A substantial investment in the playing squad was reflected by admirable results on the pitch as the club fought for Champions League qualification. Off the pitch, Lerner began to strengthen ties with disaffected supporters, notably spending £4 million to restore the revered Holte pub. The love affair appeared to end, though, in 2010, the year Lerner last gave a press conference at the club. O'Neill left and, after failing to qualify for Europe's premier competition, Villa were saddled with players on high salaries: wages accounted for 88% of turnover at the end of 2009-10. A disjointed strategy in terms of coaching recruitment and player identification has seen the club battle against relegation ever since, even if the young players being brought through by Paul Lambert offer some hope.

While the Villans had one dominant patriarch in Ellis for so long, their cross-city rivals Birmingham City had a series of dubious owners. When David Sullivan and the Gold brothers, David and Ralph, first pitched up at St Andrews after the ambitious Karren Brady cajoled them into investing in football, what they found was a club on the brink. A 23-year-old Brady found the sale of Birmingham City advertised in the *Financial Times* and admitted she was "more disgusted than disappointed" when she took a closer look. Birmingham was then under the control of the Kumar brothers, who made their money in clothing, and the era was credited as the worst in the club's history. The Blues were competing in the Third Division by this point, regularly playing in front of 6,000 or so supporters. There was little investment in the playing staff and the ground was falling into disrepair.

City's problems really began with the Kumars' predecessor, Ken Wheldon, a local businessman who entered football as Walsall's chairman before taking over at St Andrews in the mid-1980s. His severe economising and a few poor judgments brought the club to the edge of a financial abyss, so close to extinction that when his phone rang he "pretended to be the caretaker in case a creditor was calling".

Sullivan and co altered the scene beyond all recognition after their 1993 takeover as a significant stadium renovation was followed by promotion and consolidation in the Premier League under Steve Bruce. However, all the good work completed by the current West Ham United owners is in danger of being undone by the subsequent supremo, Carson Yeung. A charge of money laundering has been hanging over the head of the Hong Kong businessman since June 2011 and the club has been in financial turmoil as a result.

But what makes football club owners in the region any different to other parts of the country? "Clubs are run by business people and West Midlands business has tended to be backward, traditionalist, resistant to new ideas," Bryn Jones, who played for Wolves, told John Samuels in *The Beautiful Game is Over*. "There was complacency, a resistance to change and they lost out." Supporting this theory is the city's general resistance to change, highlighted by the uneasy shift from a reliance on manufacturing to the services industry.

That explanation is not necessary applicable in the present day. While

City face the harrowing prospect of administration and Randy Lerner's distance from Villa seems more apparent, the most stable and innovative chairman in the city is WBA's Jeremy Peace, born in the West Midlands. It's no coincidence that the current England manager, Roy Hodgson, and FA director of elite development, Dan Ashworth, were both head-hunted at West Brom, as Peace rebuilt the club on principles of financial responsibility, astute scouting and forward planning. Unfortunately, the nature of the Premier League dictates that mediocrity is the best a club like West Bromwich Albion can achieve.

At the moment, this is the biggest challenge to the clubs in Birmingham in terms of delivering tangible success. Villa had the greatest opportunity to attain a long-lasting period of prosperity but when that was lost, so was the region's best chance to return to the glories of a century ago. Only vast investment on a Manchester City-like scale will enable a club from the city to compete at the top table of the game. Until then, they can only lament missed opportunities, poor decisions and try to achieve the maximum they can with current resources.

Birmingham's general status as the Second City can be argued with legitimacy, but its standing in the football world is second-rate and, regrettably for the natives at the Sacred Heart club and beyond, that suggests that the European Cup replica paraded by Peter Withe may be the last piece of major silverware to grace the city for a very long time. Ⓑ

136

Polemics

"a splendidly suitable symbol
of his confusion"

Artist or Machine?

An investigation into the paradoxical relationship between sport and creativity

By Alex Keble

In the 11th minute of a match between Arsenal and Newcastle at St James' Park in 2002, Robert Pires's typically incisive pass to the feet of Dennis Bergkamp gave no indication that something extraordinary was about to happen. Yet as the ball approached, Bergkamp flicked it one way and twisted the other, in a moment of perfect symmetry as player and ball swivelled in unison. The sudden flurry of activity confused the crowd, astonished both sets of players and left Nikos Dabizas lying dumbfounded on his backside. It is a rare and special occasion when an event occurs that, for a brief moment, is entirely incomprehensible. It takes several replays of the goal to understand what has happened[1]. As bodies twist and flail, as the ball moves impossibly into a goalscoring position, the spectator is left with a chilling sensation that the universe has just skipped a beat; the laws of physics have kinked. The feeling is fleeting, but it is profound. The perceived limits of footballing creativity have shifted. This footballer has not just performed a practised trick; he has imagined and performed a new skill, adding a new technique to football's repertoire.

'Creativity' is a word used frequently to define the attributes of the footballer. Is this really the same 'creativity' that defines the artist? For some, art holds the potential to offer salvation from the struggles of the human condition and, if this is so, then it owes its cathartic, liberating, redeeming qualities to the creativity of the human imagination. Can we attribute these life-affirming concepts of creativity and imagination to footballers? Does the player create and invent in each scenario, using their imaginative faculties to compose a new piece of art each game, or are they merely the result of rigorous training and highly refined problem-solving skills? In short, is the player an artist, or a machine?

For some, a motivation beyond the aesthetic process — the result — immediately negates the possibility of accepting sport as a valid art form. With an ultimate goal subsuming creativity or aestheticism, football can, theoretically, alter its means of completion without affecting the outcome. But whether it is awarded an artistic definition or not, football — in both playing and watching — seems to offer the same emotional rewards as any art form. Even if this is merely a delusion, accepting sport

---

1 Bergkamp discusses this goal in an interview with David Winner in Issue One.

as art is not necessarily a prerequisite for the acceptance of creativity as an invaluable feature of the game, which is a more pertinent question here. Those who dismiss the coexistence of sport and creativity would question whether a skill performed within the rules and boundaries of football can be considered truly imaginative. Imagination in art immediately invokes ideas of freedom, of inventing something new, which, by definition, must occur outside the remit of current ideas and is consequently free from constraint. How can something be considered imaginative, if it is boxed in by narrow parameters of currently existing ideas? It is here that our notion of the athlete as machinery takes form. Some would argue that the self-imposed parameters within sport, from the size of the pitch to the number of competitors, limit this freedom for creativity. With a fixed number of variables, athletes seek improvement not in intelligence or imagination, but through physical repetition, attempting to hone technical skills until each new scenario is easily calculable and each new variant *controlled*. It is not creating the new, but harnessing the old.

So how *does* this argument explain what was witnessed at St. James' Park, when 52 000 people saw Dennis Bergkamp perform an ingenious movement, that until then had seemed impossible? Well, it doesn't. The idea that sport has no scope for creativity, or indeed can be seen as a formulaic march towards a result, is entirely inadequate. Is the painter not similarly restricted by the dimensions of the canvas and the physical properties of painting? Clearly the painter is not entirely in parallel with the sports personality, but the painter

does share the same confinement and containment as the footballer, which, paradoxically, does not limit the opportunity for creativity to flourish.

David Foster Wallace describes sport's paradoxical relationship to creativity with the kind of poetic beauty that only a literary genius and obsessive sports fan is able to: "Locating beauty and art and magic and improvements and keys to excellence and victory in the prolix flux of match play is not a fractal matter of reducing chaos to pattern, but of expansion, the aleatory flutter of uncontrolled, metastatic growth — each well-shot ball admitting of n possible responses, $2n$ possible responses to those responses, and on into a Cantorian continuum of infinities of possible moves[...] beautiful because infoliating, contained, this diagnate infinity of infinities of choice, is mathematically controlled but humanly contained."

Practising a long diagonal pass, for example, is not "a fractal matter of reducing chaos to pattern". It is eliminating the need for technical focus, because when the situation arises in which the pass needs to be made, the variables (weather, terrain, player positions, speed of run, etc.) will be unique to that moment, never to be repeated or emulated. Each pass, each touch, each microscopic movement of any single player, changes the game and creates the "Cantorian continuum of infinites". Each moment is creative, because each moment is a never-before-seen scenario in which players must consider, adapt, and imagine afresh. The technical artistry, much as it is for the painter or musician, simply helps fuse the relationship between mind and body, allowing for the imaginative flow of the individual to pour effortlessly into the physical realm. The footballer is a creative artist, composing with each touch and adding to the "aleatory flutter of uncontrolled, metastatic growth".

Not only can we consider the footballer creative by applying a 'chaos theory' concept to the sport, but also *as a result of* the enclosed boundaries — the rules and regulations — that seem to inhibit creative potential.

The negative interpretation of self-imposed rules in sport is flipped by Jean-Paul Sartre, who thought 'play' "releases subjectivity" by virtue of being created by humans. "Man apprehends himself as free [in the act of play]; through it he escapes his natural nature; he himself sets the value and rules for his acts and consents to play only according to the rules which he himself has established and defined". Freedom is thus a core principle of sport, as the human controlled parameters set limitations that, counter-intuitively, create opportunities for ingenuity and offer freedom from the hindrances of the natural world. By limiting the variants and confining the art within set rules, participants are forced to confront these walls and create "Cantorian infinities" within the chaotic web of variations and responses. The limitations — in our example, the four white lines of the football pitch — create a "little reality", in the words of Sartre, developing a stage in which imagination gains amplified significance. Being self-contained and defined by its own rules, a platform for ingenuity is provided; without this focus the chance to create rarely arises. Chained within a specific framework (unnatural and disconnected from

day-to-day reality), the *opportunity* for creation, distortion, expansion, is heightened against the backdrop of an open-ended universe. Once playing, whether on the school field or at Wembley, we become free to infuse the rigidity of self-imposed rules with our creative impulse. It is a bizarre and confusing paradox, but one that explains our love of sport. It is an unreality, a constant, that we can believe in, and one with a self-contained infinite scope for the expression of creativity. To return to Wallace, we are faced with a "diagnate infinity of infinities of choice, mathematically controlled but humanly contained".

It is no surprise, then, that involvement with sport is so deeply spiritually rewarding.

The power of creativity for the individual is of great significance, a concept reaffirmed throughout the history of Western philosophy: William Wordsworth, after decades of anguish and an unfulfilled search for the perfect poem, eventually realised that fear and isolation are overcome by realising, and celebrating, the human mind and its ability to create concepts — such as beauty and love. Similarly Nietzsche, prophesying the birth of the all-knowing Super-Man, saw that the alienation implicit in the human condition is destroyed by the recognition that unhappiness is simply a creation of the mind. These imaginative powers can be harnessed and championed, instead of being cowered from.

In sport — in all art — the goals of these philosophers have already been achieved, as we watch and participate in events that celebrate the powers of human creativity. What we find from this experience of artistic endeavour is that the act of creating holds *meaning* in itself. The result matters, of course, but if league tables were dissolved tomorrow, we would still watch and we would still play. Wordsworth, lost in the chaotic flux of a godless reality, found his quest for the meaning of life futile and ultimately unresolved. His attempts at capturing life's essence in a poem were unsatisfactory. But what he did find, while exercising his imagination and creating his timeless poetry, was that the meaning he was searching for was present in the creative journey itself. It is not what is created that offers salvation, but what is illuminated in the midst of creativity: the excitement, the pleasure, the warmth and satisfaction in exercising the human mind. Indicative of her Modernist contemporaries, Virginia Woolf felt this same sense of harmonious calm in the act of creating. Since life can appear as nothing more than a chaotic fluctuation of particles — fleeting and futile — then meaning is not a goal to be strive towards, but something found along the journey. With echoes of Wordsworth, Woolf wrote on her final philosophy of life: "What is the meaning of it all? The great revelation had never come. Instead there were little daily miracles, illuminations, matches struck unexpectedly in the dark"; matches which, for Woolf, sparked when the imagination was exercised. Experiencing creativity, whether walking round a gallery or sat under the floodlights at St James' Park, gives us our miracle.

Our experiences with art show us that watching the artist's act of creating holds just as much significance as displaying creativity ourselves, their ingenuity symbolic of the imaginative capacities of the human mind. Our celebration of it is a celebration of the species as a whole — a species capable of creating a sport, of creating stadiums that hold tens of thousands of people, and a species capable of creating atmospheres in grounds that send shivers down the spine. Creativity, in truth, is ubiquitous in football, and as Dennis Bergkamp performs a skill of beauty and elegance, it is all of us that benefit from the profound sense of happiness, the sense of meaning, that this creative act induces. The football stadium is a beautifully self-contained reality, independent of the incoherence and abstraction of the real world, and a place where the creativity of the human mind — glorious in its very existence — infuses the event with a deep spiritual worth that reverberates around the ground, enriching both players and fans. In the words of Woolf; "*I reach what I might call a philosophy, that behind the cotton wool there is hidden a pattern. That we — I mean all human beings — are connected with this;* the whole world is a work of art; we are parts of that work. We are the words; we are the music; we are the thing itself." 🅱

Alternate Title

The lessons sports journalists can draw from the Monkees

By Tim Vickery

I'm angry with myself at the moment. I've just concluded an exchange of e-mails in which I agreed to do a hit on a regional BBC radio station without getting paid.

Sure, I do stuff for free all the time — especially since Jamaican radio tracked down my phone number. But the BBC is a different matter. I've justified it in my own mind as a favour to the presenter, who is a mate of mine. But he knows nothing of this. I've been dealing with the producer, who seemed flabbergasted that I'd had the nerve to ask the 'how much?' question. "Do you mean a fee?" she replied. Not a chance. There was, she was keen to stress, no budget at all for the programme.

Bullshit, of course. She's getting paid. Resources are there — they are just not being made available to the journalist. By agreeing to do this for free I'm not only undermining myself but my colleagues as well, who are, I'm sure, increasingly coming under pressure to provide work on an unpaid basis. And this, of course, is especially hard on the next generation as they seek to get themselves established — and with the crisis of the written press they have things hard enough as it is.

Every week I get e-mails — not exactly a flood but certainly a steady trickle — from young, aspiring sports journalists asking for advice. I used to write back. Indeed, I had a standard reply prepared, full of exhortations to "write for yourself and see where it takes you" and "take no myth for granted".

After a while, though, I stopped sending it out. From meeting some of these people and hearing their stories I came to worry that I might have been engaged in giving them false hope. Even those with degrees in sports journalism seemed to have little idea of the realities — desperately low rates of pay for internet writing and, worst of all, the repugnant problems entailed in getting paid. I'd like to be able to believe in God, if only for the comforting knowledge that hell exists, and that some of the hottest places therein are reserved for those who welch on paying freelance journalists.

Indeed, one wonders why so many courses in sports journalism have sprung up. It is hard to credit that the industry is calling for them — at the very time when the crisis in written word journalism is gobbling up jobs. Perhaps it is because such courses have a cache of glamour and are thus lucrative for the institution — in itself an argument against the willy-nilly implantation of market principles in the educational process.

But I digress. The question remains — what to say to the young and aspiring? It would surely be a great shame to tell them not to aspire — though they clearly need to be made aware of the realities of that which they are aspiring to. The good news is that our noble profession, in one form or another, is not going to go away. Human beings are addicted to stories. There will always be a space, somewhere, somehow, for those who can tell a fascinating story in a captivating way. The old standards apply — have something to say and say it clearly. But that 'something' needs to be a bit different from everyone else's 'something.' How to stand out from the crowd without coming across as false or contrived? I advance the idea that the road to salvation passes through honest curiosity, and enlist as my witnesses the 1960s US pop group the Monkees.

The 'prefab four,' a manufactured, contrived, bubble-gum TV show transatlantic 'answer' to the Beatles with a bit of the Marx Brothers thrown in, the Monkees nevertheless came up with some enduringly innocent and likeably sunny mid-60s pop and were hugely successful. With a team of top-class writers and session musicians behind them, though, their own contribution was limited, which, with the passing of time became a source of frustration for them. They wanted to express themselves. Their instant stardom had given them plenty of interesting experiences to express and before long their success had provided them with the leeway to be given the opportunity to express them.

One of those experiences was the tour of England in 1967, which inspired one

of the first songs written by the drummer Micky Dolenz — released under the title "Alternate Title", for reasons we shall shortly explain.

The verse recounts a country house party at which the Monkees were guests of the Beatles, referred to in the same as "the four kings of EMI [who] are sitting stately on the floor." There's a "wonderful lady" and a butler who "reminds me of a penguin with few and plastered hair." The jaunty little polka helps re-enforce the air of louche gentility.

But there is nothing gentle about the chorus, which with gathering ferocity recreates the atmosphere in a London press conference.

"Why don't you cut your hair? Why don't you live up there? Why don't you do what I do, see what I feel when I care?"

Or later, "Why don't you be like me? Why don't you stop and see? Why don't you hate who I hate, kill who I kill to be free?"

Towards the end — and at under two and a half minutes the song does not overstay its welcome — the contrast between the two parts is emphasised by playing them both at the same time. It is Dolenz trying to work out how to make sense of this strange little island, where such apparent gentility co-exists with the hysterical, shrieking and hypocritical moralising of the tabloid press.

It is a song of bafflement. It was originally called "Randy Scouse Git", words which at no point appear in the song. Dolenz was watching *Till Death Us Do Part* and was struck by the phrase, which comprised three words, all of them ostensibly in his language, but not one of which he was able to understand. It was, then, a splendidly suitable symbol of his confusion.

The fact that he was asked to change the title only adds to the effect. He had picked up the phrase from the broadcast media. So how could it be inappropriate for broadcast media? What kind of place was this? In such circumstances, what could be a better alternate title than "Alternate Title"? Micky Dolenz had come, walked down our streets, and with no song-writing finesse to filter through the experience, had successfully transformed his confusion about English contradictions into art.

Our craft is less visceral, less intuitive and without the same emotional impact. But we can go deeper. We have the opportunity to identify the contradictions in a footballing culture and then analyse the tensions between them.

By way of example, let us take Brazil, my home for the past two decades. A number of articles in the history of this publication have done their bit to explode the myth of Brazilian football as a kind of *Carnaval* in boots, a romanticised state of nature in which self-expression is all and the scoreline is nothing.

It is junk, though occasionally even clever people can fall for it. The individual talent is no myth, of course. But how to ensure that it is decisive? The perennial search has been for balance, a collective structure capable of attaining victory by supplying the necessary defensive solidity to ensure that the team gets full value from the moments of individual brilliance. Friends and partners, pragmatism and beauty keep up a dialogue.

But, in the dynamic of things, as the two opposites talk at the same time (as towards the end of "Alternate Title") what if one starts shouting much louder, drowning out the other? Brazil's World Cup wins of 1994 and 2002 were nowhere near as universally loved as the earlier conquests. And when pragmatism fails to bring victory, as in South Africa 2010, then what is left?

Answer: a rehabilitation of the past. After their dramatic exit to Paolo Rossi's Italy, Brazil's 1982 side were always more loved abroad than at home. The 1994 captain and 2010 coach Dunga dismissed them as "specialists in losing". Now, though, they are back in fashion.

Last year Brazil's sports daily *Lance!* issued a collection of shirts of "the best teams which failed to win the World Cup." There was Hungary of 1954, the Netherlands of twenty years later and Brazil of 1982. Cutting out a number of tokens from the paper and paying a small sum entitled the reader to a replica shirt of one of these great teams. I am the proud owner of a Brazil 82 shirt, a splendid example in 100% cotton of the ongoing dynamic in the cultural tug of war between two contrasting forces.

The methodological clues are there in *"Alternate Title"*. Identify the contradictions and the tensions between them, and you have the key to the man, or the collective culture — and the gateway to good, original stories, well worthy of a pay cheque. Once written you can look at a photo of the Monkees and conclude that it was a little bit me, a little bit you.

144

'"No," said Duncan. "Sometimes he can be really difficult."'

The Quantum of Bobby

After his exile in Qatar, Bobby Manager returns to English football. Or does he…?

By Iain Macintosh

An English football manager injured in a freak accident is fighting for his life in a hospital in Qatar. Bobby Manager, the former West Ham and Liverpool boss, is in a critical condition after he was struck by an experimental radio-controlled cloud at the Al-Wakrah stadium in Doha. Doctors say that the 38 year old is in a deep coma and that, while there was some evidence of activity in the brain, his chances of survival are "no more than 25%."

After a modest playing career, Manager shot to fame in 2010 when he was the surprise choice to replace Avram Grant at Upton Park. He secured a respectable mid-table finish in his debut season, led the Hammers to fifth place in 2012 and took them to the Europa League Final the following year. Champions League success at Liverpool followed in 2014, but Manager was forced to leave England when controversial former owners George Gillett and Tom Hicks sold him to the Qatar Football Federation.

Authorities say that Manager was about to conduct an examination of the pitch at the Al-Wakrah ahead of his first game in charge of the national side when he was injured. Witnesses claim that the radio-controlled cloud, "fell out of the sky like a fucking meteorite," and struck him as he stepped out of the tunnel.

"Now then, young man," barked a loud voice. "There'll be no codding at this club. Even from you. Get up."

I opened my eyes. Wet. Mud. Grass. And pain. So much pain. My head felt like an iron safe with a crowbar pushed into its door, with someone rhythmically pushing, straining, working the hinge.

A pair of hands slipped under my armpits and I was hauled to my feet.

"Oh God," I groaned. "What happened?"

"You can call me Gaffer in front of the players, son." said the voice. "You got hit on the head by a ball. You made the mistake of standing in the way of John Robertson, that's what you did."

I looked around and a thick-set man with short, stumpy legs grinned sheepishly at me.

"Sorry, Bobby!" he said, and darted off.

I shook my head like a wet dog, turned around and looked at the man in front of me. He stood straight-backed in the mud, jaw sticking out, dark hair slicked back and a squash racket in his hand. He smiled and ragged laughter lines tore across his face like cracks in dry earth. It was him. There was no question. It was him.

"What's wrong with you, lad?" he said. "You look like you've seen a ghost."

"You're Brian Clough," I spluttered.

"Aye, and you're Robert Manager. Now that we've done our introductions all over again, do you think you could stop staring at me funny, brush the mud off your face and get on with coaching my players?"

"What?" I said.

"Coach the bleeding players, Robert! Honest to God, for all of Peter's ways, he never forgot where he was halfway through a training session. How hard did that ball hit you?" He turned around to where the players were scrambling through a five-a-side game in the mud. "Oi! John bleeding Robertson! You've just brained my new assistant manager! That's coming out of your wages. And put that bloody cigarette out!" He turned back to me.

"But...this is...Qatar?"

"Guitar? You'll want Frank Clark for that, Robert. He left three years ago."

"Three years ago? What year is it now?"

He stepped forward and cuffed me hard around the head.

"Has that knocked some sense into you?"

I bent over in pain and clutched my reddening ear.

"Ow!"

"For the avoidance of any bleeding doubt, Robert, it's 1982. You're on the Nottingham Forest training ground and of all the people I could have replaced Peter Taylor with, I'm beginning to think that you were the worst of a bad bunch. Now either coach my players or fuck off back to the dressing-room and see a doctor."

Not unreasonably, I elected to fuck off. I was confused. So confused. I had been at the Al Wakrah Stadium. I had picked my team. I had just told them that this was going to be the start of a bright and exciting new era. I'd just about got that whole Liverpool thing behind me. And now what was happening?

I trudged off the training pitch, rubbing my head and trying to get a grip of myself.

"Mr Manager?" said a soft female voice from what seemed like somewhere inside my head.

I span around in the mud. There was no-one there.

"Mr Manager!"

"Where are you?" I hissed.

There was a pause.

"I'm somewhere inside your head."

"Oh God!" I wailed, breaking out in a sweat. "I've gone crackers, haven't I? I always knew this would happen!" Thirty yards in front of me, a groundsman looked up from his wheelbarrow and started to stare.

"No, no. Stop panicking, you foolish man. You're in a coma."

"Who are you?!" I shouted. "Who are you and what are you doing in my head?" I asked again as I scuttled around the back of a bush.

"Oh come on, Mr Manager. I can't believe you don't recognise *my* voice."

"Karren?"

"That's Ms Brady to you, thank you."

I dropped to my knees, the wet mud sloshing up my shorts as I hit the ground, cold and wet. And real.

"This is impossible," I whispered. "I was in Qatar."

"You're still in Qatar," said the voice. "You're in a hospital in the city with extensive head injuries. And you're in a coma."

"My God…the cloud. It seemed like such a logical and sensible response to the adverse weather conditions. What have we done?"

"That's hardly your primary concern, I'm afraid."

"Are you with me in Qatar? That's…that's actually amazing. I can't believe you came to visit me in hospital," I said in wonder. "I know that we shared so much at Upton Park, but after the way I'd left…"

"Oh, don't be silly. I didn't come to visit you. I *am* you."

"What?"

"Well, that is to say, I'm a part of you. I'm a manifestation of a section of your consciousness buried so deep that the pre-fix 'sub' barely does it credit."

"Huh?"

"Never mind. You, Mr Manager, are in a lot of trouble. Your injuries are so extensive that it's very likely that you will never wake up. And that would be bad for both of us. However, there is just a chance, a slight chance, that you can still come through this. It is of paramount importance that your brain continues to function. And that's why I'm here. I am the part of your subconscious that knows what is at stake and that really, really doesn't want the power grid to be shut down. And the only way I can keep the grid up is by keeping you ticking over. Keeping you active. In effect, I will set you challenges, the completion of which will keep your neurons firing."

"What kind of challenges?"

"There are things that were supposed to happen, things that did not happen. People who can be saved. Wrongs that can be made right. That sort of thing. You know the drill."

"I really don't. How will I know what to do?"

"That, Mr Manager, is part of the challenge. I would hardly be able to keep your neurons firing if I simply told you the answer, would I? Just be Bobby Manager. Look, examine, assess and make good. You did it at West Ham. You did it at Liverpool. You can do it in 1982 as well."

"I can't do it! It's impossible! I don't know any of the players here. I was only a kid in 1982."

"I'm not going to pretend that it will be easy," purred Karren. "But you are the man who nearly won a European trophy with West Ham. Even if it *was* the pointless one that's more of a burden than a blessing."

"You won't let that lie, will you?"

"Absolutely not."

"Okay," I agreed. "But what happens if I fail the challenge?"

"You will die, Mr Manager. And all this will end."

"Ah," I said. "I see."

"Good luck, Mr Manager."

"Thank you. I think."

"Thanks for what?" barked a gruff voice. "What are you doing back there, you silly sod? You having a crap?"

"What?"

The groundsman peered around the corner of the bush and scowled.

"The Manager won't like that, you know. He's got to be the maddest person here. You go crapping in the bushes and talking to yourself about challenges and he'll see that as a threat."

"Right," I said, getting to my feet. "You're right. Thanks." To save further inquisition, I ran to the dressing-room , piled through the door and got straight into the shower. The pounding in my head was calming down. Soon it would fade away entirely. I would come to learn in time that this was a sort of after-shock to a leap. For now, I just thanked my stars for the sweet relief from the pain.

Under the steaming water, I tried to gather my thoughts. Could this all be real? Could I really be lying in a bed in Qatar with a machine keeping me alive, while I stood here in 1982 trying to lather up a bar of soap that felt like a house brick?

The feelings were certainly very real. When Brian had hit me, it had felt like a hit. When the muddy water had sloshed up my shorts, it had felt like muddy water sloshing up my pants. And besides, I reasoned, what was the alternative to believing Karren? There didn't appear to be an exit door to take me home. I was here, I was in 1982. I resolved to take her at her word and try to fix whatever was broken.

That, of course, turned out to be Brian himself. As he swiftly demonstrated.

"What's the water like?" came his voice from outside my cubicle.

"It's hot. Really, really hot," I replied.

"Aye," he said. "I'll be the judge of that." The door swung open and he pushed me out of the stream of water, up against the tiles.

"Oi!" I shouted.

"Oi yourself," he said. "Come on, move over. Plenty of room for two. My mam used to have us eight to the tub in the front room, this is like sharing an Olympic swimming pool compared to that. You're not a sissy, are you?"

"No," I said, covering myself with my hands. "Good," he said, soaping himself up. "We've had enough of that round here."

"Erm..." I said. "That's not cool." I stepped out of the cubicle.

He stared at me as I went.

"Cool? Cool? You sure you're not a sissy? Never mind." He raised his voice. "What did you think today? Of the lads?"

I dried myself down outside.

"I didn't see enough to make any conclusions, Brian."

"Gaffer to you, son."

"Gaffer. Right. I didn't see enough of them."

"No need to be polite, Robert. They're crap, aren't they? I know what you're thinking. They're crap. It's what Peter left me. He's out now. He's free. He's probably eating sardines from the tin on the porch in Majorca, the cheeky bugger, while I have to clear up his mess. You have to help, mind. And there's a lot of it. Mess, mess, mess."

He began to sing to himself, something about sailors, gurgling his chorus and laughing away. I politely dried and dressed myself and waited for him to finish a particularly fruity bit about the women of Santo Domingo.

"Have you ever been to Santo Domingo, Robert?" he called through the door.

"No, gaffer."

"Neither have I. But it sounds like a hell of a place. Now let's get to work."

He emerged from the shower, wrapped a towel around himself and motioned for me to follow him.

"Come on, time for our meeting with the press."

"Aren't you going to get dressed?" I asked.

"No, there's nothing like air drying yourself. Besides, it's only Duncan." And with that, he was out of the door. I scurried along, trying to keep up.

"Now then young man!" he shouted at a timid looking chap in the corridor. "It's time you met my new assistant. Robert, this is Duncan from the local rag. Duncan, this is Peter's replacement."

"Pleased to meet you, Robert," said the young man with his hand outstretched.

"You can call me, Bobby," I said. "Everyone else does."

"Step into my office, Duncan," brayed Brian, motioning to a door.

"Isn't your office at the stadium?" I asked.

"I'm Brian Clough," he said. "Everywhere is my office if I say it's my office."

It was a point we made as delicately as we could to the janitor, and in his defence, he took it with the resigned air of one who had been forced out of his room many times before and would be many times again.

"Now then, Duncan," said Brian as he sat down on the janitor's chair and put his bare, dripping feet up on the desk. "Time to earn your keep."

"You don't pay me, Mr Clough."

"Don't pay you? What do you think this is, eh? Cheeky bugger. How many stories are you going to write about me if I don't talk to you? How are you going to write your great big book about me if I don't talk to you?"

"I've said before, Mr Clough, I'm not going to write a book. I haven't got time."

"Aye, you will do, son. You will do. Now shut your trap and pour us a drink." He leaned around and slapped the fusebox on the wall with the back of his hand. The cover fell open with a clang and revealed a large bottle of Teacher's whiskey with a 'Manager of the Month' ribbon around the neck.

Duncan sighed, stood up and retrieved the bottle. Then he walked across to the opposite corner of the room and fished three heavy glass tumblers out of a mop bucket.

"Are they clean?" I asked.

"Of course they're clean," grunted Brian, as he wiped a pile of suds off his shoulders and pushed them on the floor. "That's had bleach in it. Clean as clean can be."

"I'll give them a rinse, though," I said. "Just to be sure."

"Whatever keeps you happy, Robert," he snorted in derision. "I can see you're going to be high maintenance, aren't you? But when you're finished with the washing up, maybe we can get to business, eh?"

I washed the glasses out in the sink and handed them to Duncan who shuddered and then poured out measures so generous they were practically philanthropists.

"Oi!" shouted Brian. "What's that? Is the bleeding tide out? Get that glass filled up, young man."

Duncan obeyed and then carefully handed over the tumbler, trying not to let the drink slosh over the side.

"That's better," said Brian, taking a long swig. "Now, Robert, the team. What do we need?"

"I think every team needs a focal point in the attack," I said. "A Carlton Cole character, powerful and bold, enthusiastic and selfless. That kind of thing."

Duncan and Brian exchanged a look.

"Who's this Charlton Cole? Who does he play for?"

"Erm…he doesn't. Not yet. It's a…erm… figure of speech."

Brian sighed.

"I haven't got time for figures of speech, Robert. I need players. Good players. Pete could spot a player. I need you to spot a player. And I need to put some bloody clothes on. I can't believe you pulled me out of the shower for this. Idiots. "

He stood up, drained the glass and strode out of the room.

I looked at Duncan.

"Is he always like that?"

"No," said Duncan. "Sometimes he can be really difficult."

Brian wasn't the only thing that was difficult. The fixture computer had given us a horrible start to the season. We beat West Ham and we beat Brighton, but defeats to Manchester United, Liverpool and Aston Villa left our title challenge in tatters before the county cricket season had even finished.

We were on the bus coming back from Villa Park when Brian came back from his usual seat at the front and slumped down next to me, ashen-faced.

"Robert." he said formally, alcohol on his breath.

"Gaffer," I said. "Are you okay?"

"I've hurt my hand," he said quietly. He held up a set of knuckles, purpling with fresh bruises. "I bumped into Steve Hodge's head."

At the back of the bus, I became aware of a soft moaning, like a feverish child. "Ah," I said. "I wondered what that was."

"I've shot it, Robert," he said quietly.

"No, you haven't," I said. "You're just readjusting. You need to build a new team, start all over again. But you can do it. You did it at Derby, you did it here."

"I can't do it without Peter," he said mournfully. "The stupid, lazy bastard. He went soft, you know. In the old days, he'd watch a player. He'd follow a player, he'd make sure he knew every bleeding thing about the player before he told me to sign him. And then at the end, I don't think he was even watching them anymore. He just came in, put his feet up, read the *Racing Post* and then shot off after lunch. But Robert, God...he could really pick a player. If I could have him back, refreshed and ready, then there's nothing we couldn't do here."

"Maybe he didn't feel appreciated?"

"What are you, a bloody psychologist?"

"No, I'm just..."

"I know what you are, Robert Manager. I've got your bloody number. Too many books that's your problem."

"Too many books?" I said.

"Aye, and not one of them has taught you anything about football. What was that nonsense you were jabbering about in training this week? The Makalaka role?"

"The Makélélé role," I muttered.

"Aye, we don't need fancy names. We were doing five in the middle years ago. And what was the other bit? Winged backs? Load of old rot. Defenders defend first. Fancy stuff can wait. You're just like O'Neill. Too many books and too much lip. I can't think why I gave you the job. In fact, I can't even remember giving you the job."

I turned to face him and sniffed the air pointedly.

"That's not entirely surprising," I said.

He stiffened and stared me down, his reddened eyes filled with rage.

"You know your problem?" I said, figuring that I was in too deep now to retreat anyway. "No-one's ever brave enough to tell you when you're being an idiot."

The background hubbub around the coach died. Even Hodge's whimpering fell silent.

"No-one tells you that you're an idiot and no-one tells you that you're drinking too much. You haven't shot it, you're still Brian Clough, but you're on a slippery slope because you've stopped caring and you've driven away the only person who could keep you in check. Without Taylor, you won't ever win the league again. You won't ever be bold enough to sign the players who win you titles, the nasty ones, the Larry Lloyds, because you haven't got Peter here to tell you it's going to be okay. You could rebuild this team in a matter of months if you just showed a bit of humility and brought him back into the fold. But you're too bloody stubborn."

I stopped talking, my heart pounding, my chest heaving in and out. Brian stared at me, not in anger, but in fascination.

"No-one's ever been brave enough to give me a bollocking," he said in a faraway voice.

"Well…" I said. "I thought it needed saying."

"You make some very interesting points, Robert. I've certainly taken them on board."

"Good," I said and folded my arms. "That was the intention."

"Now allow me to retort," he said. And everything went black.

I woke up in the bus depot in Nottingham four hours later with my nose plastered all over my face.

Something had changed in Brian though. He was quieter and more studious. He even spent some time on the training pitch the following week. And we won the next game as well, beating Watford

2-0. But I knew now what I had to do. I knew what Karren wanted me to do.

I met Peter Taylor in a Happy Eater near Derby a couple of nights later. He hadn't been hard to find. Duncan had his home phone number. He took a bit of convincing, not least because he described me as the man who had his rightful job, but he eventually agreed to meet up. When I arrived, he was already tucking into a fried breakfast, puffing from a cigarette between mouthfuls.

"Manager," he said when he saw me. "Sit down. Try the eggs, they're very good."

"I'm okay, thanks," I said. "Just a coffee for me."

"Suit yourself," he said. "So, how are you getting on with him?"

"Look at my face," I said with a smile.

Peter examined my nose, still several inches wider than its original size and still an ugly colour.

"He got you good there, son," he said, admiringly. "What did you do?"

"I told him that he was an idiot."

Peter laughed and blew chunks of egg across the table. He jammed his cigarette in his mouth to stop the flow and began to cough uncontrollably. When he finally settled himself, he had tears in his eyes.

"Oh, that's priceless. That's absolutely priceless. You're lucky he didn't kill you and feed you to the trout!"

"He wants you back, Peter," I said.

"He doesn't," said Peter. "We've taken it as far as we could. He doesn't trust my eye anymore. He doesn't trust *me* anymore. There are too many people in the mix now, too many hangers-on. He's lost sight of himself as a football manager, he's more of a celebrity."

"He knows what he is," I said. "He's close to quitting. He says he can't do it without you."

"Well," said Peter, wiping his lips with a napkin, "he needs to get used to it. Besides, I might have an offer of work myself."

"Where?" I asked.

He lit another cigarette and leaned across the table with a glint in his eye.

"Derby!" he said.

"Don't do it," I told him. "You're just like him, Peter. You can't do it on your own. And besides, you'll break his heart. Go back to Forest. Go back to Brian. Together, you can win the league again. Individually, you'll never hit those heights."

Peter looked thoughtful.

"I couldn't do it unless he apologised," he said. "And he'd never apologise."

"What does he need to apologise for?"

"For everything!" burst Peter. "For everything! For the way he was with money, for the way he was with the press, for the way he was with the players and for the way he was with me!"

"And if he does that," I said, "you'll come back?"

"That's an 'if' the size of John Robertson's arse, son. Could you make it happen?"

"I think I could," I said. "He really wants you back. He'll be pragmatic. He'll have to be pragmatic. Will you apologise to him?"

"For what?" laughed Peter.

I thought about this.

"I don't think it will really matter," I said. "Pick something. Pick anything. Pick whatever you think he'd want. And then see it as the cost of doing business."

The trap was set. Two days later, as we left the training field, I asked Brian if we could have a chat in his office.

"Are you quitting?" he grunted. "You may as well, you're no use to man nor beast."

"Let's just go to your office, Gaffer."

"All right, son," he said. "Hang on." He walked over to a tree and started tapping the trunk. Tap, tap, tap.

"What are you doing?" I asked.

"Shut up," he said. "I'm listening."

Tap, tap, tap, TOP!

"There it is!" he exclaimed. He pulled his keys out of his pocket and pulled a section of bark off the tree. "Glued that on myself," he grinned. Behind the bark was a large hole into which he thrust his hand and retrieved a large bottle of Scotch.

"Why have you hidden a bottle of whiskey in a tree, gaffer?"

He looked at me furtively.

"You can't trust *anyone* round here," he whispered.

"Come on, gaffer," I said. We walked to his office. As we reached the door, I stepped back and allowed him to enter the room first.

"What's this, Robert?" he laughed. "Are you finally learning some respect?" He stepped through the door. "Perhaps you and I....oh, you bastard. What's he doing here?"

I followed him into the room. At his desk, dressed in his best suit, sat Peter Taylor. I stood back and waited for the magic to happen.

"Get this prat out of my office, Robert!" roared Brian. "This circus doesn't need any more bloody clowns!"

Peter glared daggers at me.

"I thought you said he wanted me back?" he shouted. "You set me up!"

"Want you back?" sneered Brian. "I'd rather have a dose of the clap!"

"You think I'd come back and work for you?" blasted Peter. "I'd rather French kiss Archie Gemmill!"

They both stopped shouting when they heard the lock click shut.

"You're staying in there!" I shouted from the other side of the keyhole.

"What?!" they shouted back.

"You're both staying in there until you sort this out," I said. "You need each other and you're both too thick to figure it out. You can stay there, you can get it all out of your systems and I'll open the door when you agree to work with each again. Oh, and Brian? I quit."

"Quit?!" yelled Brian. "I'll have you bloody shot!"

"Not if I get there first!" bellowed Peter.

And that was only the start. They yelled at me, they yelled at each other, they yelled at the gods, a group of people they viewed as being only slightly more important than themselves. I pulled a chair over to the door and sat with my back against it. And then there was a long silence.

At first I wondered if they might have killed each other and were now lying on the rug, their hands locked around each other's throats, eyes bulging as they took their war beyond this mortal coil and geared up for eternal war on some other plane of existence. But then I heard the soft pop of a bottle of Scotch being opened.

It all came out after that. Brian told Peter that he was lazy and he'd lost his edge. Peter told Brian that he'd taken his eye off the ball and was spending too much time on television. Brian shouted at Peter for writing a book about him. Peter shouted at Brian for being greedy with money. There was a particularly vicious and politically incorrect exchange of views over Justin Fashanu.

But soon their voices softened. Talk turned to the future. There was a conversation about money and the lack of it. There was a debate over the new stand that had plunged the club into so much debt. But there was talk too of the young talent in the squad that could be cultivated. Talk of Steve Hodge as a man who might one day play for England.

It was another two hours before there was a quiet knock from the inside of the office.

"You can open the door now," said Peter softly. "It's over."

I stood up, dragged the chair across the floor and unlocked the door.

Brian thrust a glass full of scotch into my hand with an unsteady hand.

"Here you go, Robert. This is your leaving drink. And it's a...it's a thank you drink as well."

"Yep," said Peter cheerfully. "We're going back into business together!

"Just like old times!" laughed Brian. "I'm the shop-front, he's the goods in the back."

"I'm the one who finds the players, he's the one who makes them play!" chuckled Peter. "Just like it always was."

"I'm really happy for you," I said. "Whether it works or not, well, that doesn't matter. What really counts is that you two are friends again. Imagine if you hadn't had this reconciliation. You'd have gone on hating each other, this partnership would have festered. And then one day..." I tried not to look at Peter, "...one of you would have dropped dead and it would have been too late."

"That's a bit dramatic, isn't it?" said Peter with a look of distaste.

"Aye," nodded Brian. "Are you sure you're not a sissy?"

I grinned.

"No, I'm not a sissy. And that's another thing, you shouldn't judge people on their sexual preferences. It's the kind of thing that will tarnish your..." My head started to pound.

"Tarnish my what?" laughed Peter.

Bang. Bang. Bang. The ache in my head intensified.

"Well done, Mr Manager," said a soft female voice. "Well done."

I put the drink down on the table and gripped it for support as my legs seemed to melt underneath me.

"Are you okay, Robert?" asked Brian, as the room began to spin and the pain at the back of my head flowered into white hot agony.

"Gxsrylll," I burbled as I fell through the desk and slipped down, through the fibres of the carpet, through the foundations of the building, through the earth and the soil and the bedrock and into a swirling vortex of noise and colour.

I was leaping. I was leaping through time and space. I hoped against hope that this leap would be my leap home. Oh boy, was I wrong.

WORKSOFARTICLES

THE BLIZZARD
GOALS ARE OVERRATED...
THE BEAUTY IS IN THE STRUGGLE

BLZZRD03
COMPARING APPLE WITH ORANGE
SIMON KUPER AND DAVID WINNER

BLZZRD08
THE BICYCLE THIEF
LARS SIVERTSEN

BLZZRD03
THE HARMONY OF THE SPHERE
PHILIPPE AUCLAIR

THE BLIZZARD BY GOALSOUL
A PARTNERSHIP BORN OF FOOTBALL

158

"I wanted it to go on forever, and
then I'd never have to face real life."

England 1 West Germany 1*

World Cup semi-final, 4 July 1990, Stade delle Alpi, Turin

By Rob Smyth

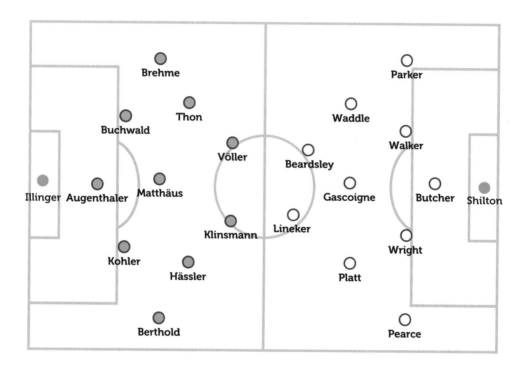

English football was reborn on the fourth of July. Umpteen factors contributed to the game in this country becoming both richer and poorer; by far the most significant was England's Italia 90 campaign and particularly the glorious failure against West Germany in the semi-final on Wednesday 4 July 1990. England's campaign started as a *Carry-On* film and ended as an operatic epic. The ultimate consequence was the Premier League, prawn sandwiches, Sky, Wags and the rest. All that may well have happened eventually, but it would have done so at a different time and in a different way.

The poetic nature of England's defeat, in which they were the sophisticated equals of arguably the greatest World Cup-winners since 1970, partially obscured what went before. The truth that is sometimes not allowed to speak its name is that, for much of the tournament, England were a bit of a mess: an increasingly endearing mess, admittedly, but fortunate to reach the semi-finals. Once they did, however, they performed in a manner that ensured their campaign would almost exclusively be recalled with misty eyes, wistful smiles and a Pavarotti soundtrack.

Their Italia 90 was far from an unmitigated triumph, but ultimately it was a triumph, of the human spirit as much as anything. In the *Express* the morning after the game, James Lawton wrote, "I cannot imagine a more honourable way for this England team, and their embattled and frankly erratic manager Bobby Robson, to take their leave of the peaks of soccer."

Both West Germany and England almost did not reach those peaks in the first place. They were dangerously close to not qualifying. Although both were unbeaten, winning three and drawing three of their games, they only got through as the best second-placed teams in a mini-league with Denmark, the runners-up in the only other four-team group.

Uefa had 13 places for the 24-team tournament, the same as for this summer's 32-team event in Brazil. The difference was that there was no safety net: no play-offs, no culture of the second chance. West Germany were in with the European champions the Netherlands, with only one team guaranteed to qualify. The Germans had to beat Wales in their final home game to get through; on a fraught night in Cologne, they came from 1-0 down to win 2-1.

England had reached the tournament a month earlier after a 0-0 draw in Poland. It was a game in which they were pummelled. Peter Shilton was sensational, repelling a stream of vicious shots from absurd distances and angles, although he could do nothing when Ryszard Tarasiewicz's 30-yard screamer hit the bar. Commentators often say "the crossbar is still shaking" when a particularly well-struck shot rebounds off it. The crossbar in Chorzów has long since stopped shivering, but English football is still reverberating from their qualification for Italia 90.

A defeat in Poland would not have eliminated England at that time. But had subsequent games — both in England's group and the other relevant groups — panned out as they actually did, a 1-0 defeat in Poland would ultimately have put England out, with Denmark qualifying ahead on goals scored.

In the nine months between that match and the tournament, English football was constantly criticised, with focus on two particular things: a lack of sophistication on the field and a lack of humanity off it. In the early part of 1990 there was a clamour for Bobby Robson to adopt the voguish sweeper system. (There were football hipsters in those days too; they just didn't make a scene.) Fifa's technical report of Italia 90 says a sweeper was used by 19 of the 24 teams. Even Jack Charlton tried it in training before deciding against it. England were seen as neanderthals for playing 4-4-2.

Off the field, their fans were compared unfavourably to animals by the minister for sport Colin Moynihan. Hooliganism remained an enormous problem, while Hillsborough had accentuated the almost apocalyptic mood surrounding English football. The prime minister Margaret Thatcher called the hooligans a "disgrace to Britain" and discussed pulling England out of the tournament. England, the team nobody wanted to come to the party, were dumped on island of Sardinia when the draw was made.

Thatcher's don't-send-them-there-in-the-first-place idea found an inevitable cousin once the tournament started. After a desperate 1-1 draw in the opening game against Ireland, in which statisticians said the ball was only in play for 49 minutes, the *Sun* officially went beyond satire with a "SEND 'EM HOME" headline. *La Gazzetta Dello Sport*'s headline was: "NO FOOTBALL PLEASE, WE'RE ENGLISH." It's a good job the papers didn't know that Gary Lineker had soiled himself during the game, or they would have had a field day.

With the circulation war at its most desperate, England, and particularly Robson, had been the subject of unpleasant abuse from the British tabloids since losing all three games at Euro 88. "ENGLAND MUSTAFA NEW BOSS" was one *Sun* headline after a draw in Saudi Arabia. Then, when the tabloids got their wish, when it was leaked that Robson would take over at PSV Eindhoven after the World Cup, they called him a traitor. "ROBSON SELLS OUT FOR A POT OF GOLD" and "PSV OFF BUNGLER BOBBY" were two of the headlines the following day.

Accusing a decent and patriotic Englishman of treachery was among the more preposterous accusations ever to appear in print, and that was even without knowledge of the situation. Robson had already been told that his

England contract would not be renewed when it expired in 1991. The FA had given him permission to discuss a new job, with no plans to announce it until after the tournament. A generous description might be that it was pathetic and infantile. Robson, who almost exclusively responded with extreme dignity, finally cracked and accused the press of trying to "ruin" England's World Cup campaign. He also sued the *Today* newspaper and settled out of court.

The players were next in line, with some accused of having sex with a hostess. "It was all bollocks," said Gascoigne, who lightened the mood by introducing a song of "Let's all shag a hostess" for the team to sing on the bus for the rest of the tournament. The players were filmed ripping up a tabloid and most stopped talking to the press. It was all used successfully to foster a siege mentality. They needed such a mentality after the first match. In his autobiography, Robson says the Ireland game "was portrayed, by the *Sun* in particular, as just about the end of civilisation".

Five days later, everyone in England was heralding a new age of civilisation. England drew again, this time 0-0, but this time it was with the European champions the Netherlands, and after a brilliant performance in which they had two goals correctly disallowed and missed some fine chances. Bobby Robson had unexpectedly put Mark Wright as sweeper, the first time he had used the system in eight years as England manager. Almost all of the squad deny that it was the result of player power, although there were certainly discussions between the team and manager about its potential use. Robson says it had been in his mind from the moment the draw was made the previous December, such was the damage Marco van Basten and Ruud Gullit had done to his flat back four in 1988.

Wright played superbly, and over the tournament he would reintroduce the word "elegance" to the English defender's dictionary. There was even the occasional comparison with Bobby Moore, the ultimate tribute for an English defender. It made it even more fascinating and strange that he had not made a single appearance for England between June 1988 and April 1990.

After the match there were plenty who loved to say they had told you so, and attributed England's performance almost entirely to their tactical switch. The reality was inevitably more nuanced. Paul Gascoigne, whose role did not really change, was outstanding and almost created a goal after symbolically Cruyff-turning Ronald Koeman. (The *Guardian*'s Barney Ronay later said Gascoigne was "selling the Cruyff turn back to the Dutch like the Beatles peddling rock and roll to America".)

It's often said that you have four years to prepare for a World Cup. It rarely works like that and, as in 1966 and 1986, England significantly changed their team once the tournament had started. Robson had tinkered on the eve of the tournament, too. "Robson didn't build a team in this World Cup so much as eventually let it happen," wrote Lawton in the *Express* after the semi-final, referring to the late introduction of Gascoigne, Platt, Wright and Parker. "For this he goes with considerable honour."

Robson went back to 4-4-2 for the 1-0 win over Egypt which enabled England to top the group (had Egypt equalised, and they had a good chance, lots would have been drawn to decide all four positions in the group) and returned to a sweeper for the excellent second-round match against Belgium. David Platt changed both his life and the mood of England's World Cup campaign at a stroke — or rather a swivel, with his 119th-minute volley saving England from penalties and prompting his memorable Cheshire-cat smile. Robson danced along the touchline, Butcher and Waddle had a disco. After all that negativity there was a sudden overwhelming infusion of joy.

Not least because England had a bye in the quarter-finals. That, at least, was what Howard Wilkinson said. "We'd had a report on them, a spying report, that said, 'They've got four players missing' and pretty much, 'You've got a bye'," said Gary Lineker on the BBC's *Match of the Nineties*. "Bobby Robson said: 'I shouldn't be telling you this, I know I shouldn't be telling you this ...' and he was right, because they were fantastic." In the same programme, Robson recalled Wilkinson saying, "Look it's a bye. Tell the players: it's a gimme!"

What the players were given was the mother of all chasings. They were eight minutes from going out after a wonderful performance from Cameroon — particularly their substitute Roger Milla, who continually dropped into the hole between defence and midfield to devastating effect — yet somehow sneaked through 3-2. This despite ending with their old-fangled formation and Mark Wright playing right-wing because of a serious head injury. Robson's verdict was simple: "4-4-2 saved us."

The World Cup, as Ferris Bueller might have said, moves pretty fast. If you don't stop and look around once in a while, you could miss it. All of a sudden England were in the semi-final. On the day of the match, the *Guardian*'s David Lacey said it was "difficult to come to terms with" the idea of England in the final. There was also the usual discussion of 5-3-2 and 4-4-2 in the build-up, although it seemed not even 5-4-4 could save England, so superior had West Germany been to everyone else in the tournament except the now eliminated hosts Italy.

The Germans reversed their usual tournament approach of starting slowly and getting better: in the opening match they slaughtered an excellent Yugoslavia side 4-1, with their captain Lothar Matthäus scoring two individual goals of terrifying purpose. Matthäus, in his absolute prime, seemed like a different species to everyone else in the tournament, an omnipotent footballer-cyborg.

Not that Germany were a one-machine team. Their side was full of all-time greats: Andreas Brehme, Jürgen Kohler, Jürgen Klinsmann, Rudi Völler and perhaps Guido Buchwald. They did not quite have the Ramba-Zamba stylings of the wonderful 1972 West Germany side, yet they could certainly play and they were the ultimate power team.

In the second round, they thrashed the Dutch 2-1. The game is remembered almost exclusively for Völler and Frank Rijkaard being sent off. Völler's punishment is almost certainly the harshest in the history of mankind: he was scythed down, spat at, picked up by the ear, sent off and then spat at again, yet somehow resisted the urge to go all *Falling Down*.

Klinsmann would be castigated for falling down after the quarter-final, yet in the second round, without Völler, he gave one of the great centre-forward performances, scoring the first, thumping the post and running himself to exhaustion. The second was scored by Brehme, a wing-back so good that he was effectively man-marked by Holland winger John van't Schip.

West Germany were aiming to reach their third consecutive World Cup final, having lost in 1982 and 1986. That's where the comparison between the sides ended. Their coach Franz Beckenbauer, who had been in charge four years earlier, would later laugh at the memory of his 1986 side: "Can you believe we got to the final with these players?"

In 1990, it would have been unbelievable if they had *not* got to the final with their players. For Robson, by contrast, the thought of getting to the final was almost unthinkable. In an interview shown before the match, he seemed almost in pain at the thought. "Well... I've been in the game now 40 years... it, it would be lovely to, to win the, the biggest prize the game has to offer, which is the world championship. It is the prize of all time. Erm..."

Around the country, hope tended to wipe the floor with logic. The reality of German superiority was only occasionally discussed, shouted down by the idea that 22 men were about to chase a ball for 90 minutes and that anything could happen. England were not scared of West Germany *per se*. At that stage they actually had a better head-to-head record, even if most of England's wins had occurred in previous generations. It's a recognition of how dominant England once were in this fixture that, before

Germany's victory in the 1970 World Cup quarter-final, the *Observer*'s Hugh McIlvanney wrote that, "the Germans have to ignore more omens than Julius Caesar on assassination day."

Twenty years later West Germany not only had the better team, they had the fresher team. "We were exhausted," said Lineker in a *FourFourTwo* interview. "Even on the morning of the game, my legs felt almost gone. We'd had extra time against Belgium and Cameroon. Physically we'd been running on empty. Despite all that, we did enough to win." The England players said, and still say, they were very confident before the game despite the tiredness. Their subsequent performance suggests we should believe them.

In a sense, this was not a semi-final but a final. A limited Argentina side, who had seen off Italy with their one decent performance of the tournament, had four players suspended for the final. "We know, that if we can win tonight — but Germany do too — you're in the final," said Robson. "With a great chance of beating Argentina. Great chance of beating Argentina. This is the one. Germany's the big one."

The bigger the game, the more likely Robson was to return to his sweeper system. Butcher's lack of pace meant he was used as the spare man, with Wright marking Klinsmann and Völler faced with the task of beating Des Walker. Peter Beardsley came in for the injured John Barnes. Beckenbauer made three changes. Völler, available after suspension, replaced Karl-Heinz Riedle, and Matthäus had two new partners in midfield: Olaf Thon and Thomas Hässler came in for Pierre Littbarski and Uwe Bein.

The status of the game was reflected by the seriousness of the faces in the tunnel beforehand. With one exception. Gascoigne larked about, smiling and kissing Beardsley. It was not so much that he was calm; more that the significance of the game had not registered. He might as well have been in a park in Dunston.

England started the game superbly. They won a corner after 15 seconds, two more inside the first 90 seconds, and it is a reasonable interpretation that their first-half dominance was a simple consequence of them running with the mood of those first few minutes. Other interpretations are that they played with the freedom of the apparently damned, and that the manner of their victories over Belgium and Cameroon had created a sense of destiny which in turn created the pre-match confidence of which they have spoken.

When the first of those corners was only partially cleared, a backpedalling Gascoigne hooked an excellent left-footed shot from 20 yards that was palmed behind by Bodo Illgner. It was going slightly wide anyway, though that does not especially detract from an adroit effort.

England troubled West Germany considerably in the early periods. Beardsley, starting for the first time since the Ireland game, twice broke beyond the defence, once in each inside channel, only to pick the wrong option once he entered the box. After five minutes, Gascoigne shimmied superbly inside Augenthaler on the edge of the area before lashing a shot that was desperately blocked by Kohler.

Gascoigne was full of it, and in the 15th minute he Cruyff-turned away from

Klinsmann near the halfway line to prompt lusty cheers from the England fans. Moments later, his even more callow sidekick Platt — making only his third start for England — collected a loose ball 30 yards from goal, magnetised six defenders, and pushed a fine pass behind them all for the marauding Pearce. His firm low cross towards Lineker was put behind superbly by the sliding Kohler. This was the story of the game: there were not many clear chances but both sides were forever finding promising positions. The defences, both outstanding, were like batsmen on a pitch where they are never truly 'in'. The match is legitimately called an epic, despite that relative lack of chances, because of the quality of the attacking and defensive play, and the intense theatrical drama contained therein.

There was another reason why the match lingers in the memory: the level of sportsmanship, extreme by the standards of the day and startling today. As the match approached the quarter point, Stuart Pearce and Brehme both made a point of helping Thomas Berthold and Paul Parker, whom they had just fouled, to their feet. The match was full of handshakes – instinctive and sincere, not the meaningless, staged PR of the contemporary pre-match handshake. The mood was briefly altered when Gascoigne, after being fouled from behind by Brehme, lifted Brehme to his feet by the shirt. Hässler gave the referee a slightly appalled look, though it should be noted that this was not really a case of Gazza's mania: it was an outlier in a performance of largely striking serenity.

At that stage, Germany's only vague opportunity had been a Hässler shot that spun wide off Pearce, though they were starting to have more of the ball. Nonetheless, England continued to have the better attempts at goal. After 24 minutes, Waddle's free-kick was headed clear by Klinsmann to Gascoigne, who chested down and flashed a fine strike from just outside the area that was well held by Illgner. If such excellence was normal from Gascoigne, the intervention of Butcher three minutes later was not. He came out from defence stealthily to nip a German attack in the bud, then ran to the halfway line before backheeling the ball to Gascoigne and sauntering back to his station as if it was the most normal thing in the world; not so much Terry Butcher as Terry Beckenbutcher.

After the backheel came a nutmeg, Gascoigne on Matthäus. It was barely noticeable, because of the camera angle, the whirl of legs and its essential insignificance, near the halfway line and with Gascoigne losing the ball seconds later. But it was a reflection of his intrepid approach. "You would say, 'You're going to play against Rijkaard,'" recalled Waddle in *Three Lions Versus The World*. "And he would say, 'Who? Who's he?' He didn't care who he was playing against, and it wasn't an act. He would say, 'I'll introduce them to Paul Gascoigne.'"

Gascoigne was the face of England's tournament: the boyish face, the gurning face and of course the crying face. "In that World Cup squad," said Robson, "he was the focal point of everything." He should have known it would be his World Cup even before England played a game. On the opening day he put a bet on Cameroon to beat Argentina "just to be sociable, join with the lads" and won £800. Yet six weeks earlier, there was significant doubt as to whether Gascoigne would be in the squad, never mind the team. Robson had regularly shared his concerns as to Gascoigne's tactical discipline. "We need two balls, one for him and one for the team," he said after a game against Albania in 1989, when Gascoigne scored after coming on as substitute. "At one stage I thought he was going to play in the front row of F stand because he played in every position except the one I told him to play in."

Robson's concerns were considerable, although at times it seemed like pantomime exasperation. His affection for Gascoigne — who was both problem child and teacher's pet — was obvious. Robson did not doubt Gascoigne's talent. Nor did anybody else. In 1988, the Newcastle legend Jackie Milburn was particularly effusive "I think it's about 35 years since I've seen a kid as good as this lad. There's no holding him. He's the *best in the world*. Honestly. He's the best in the world."

Robson, assuming Bryan Robson would be a certainty in his midfield, and with Neil Webb and Steve McMahon almost sure to make the squad, decided to give Platt and Gascoigne a game each: Platt at home to Brazil in March, Gascoigne at home to Czechoslovakia in April. It was Gascoigne's second start for England, and he had only played 30 minutes for England in the previous 11 months.

The Czechoslovaks were a strong, canny team, full of classy midfielders who would take them to the quarter-finals in Italy. Gascoigne beat them on his own, producing one of the great England performances in a 4-2 win. He made two goals for Steve Bull, one with a marvellous raking pass over the top and another with a run and cross, before sealing the match with a lovely solo goal. "That's fantastic," said a po-faced, finger-wagging Robson.

"Well done son, you've made three goals," said Robson after the game. "Four" replied Gascoigne, taking credit for a corner that flew around the box before being put into the net by Pearce.

"It was the match that changed Bobby Robson's view of him," said Barry Davies, who commentated on the game for the BBC. "I'm convinced, and I've said it to Bobby's face — he didn't deny it, nor did he say it was true — that he put him in so that he could say, 'Well, I gave him his chance.' And Gascoigne ran the match. He ran the match in the way that Netzer did against Alf Ramsey's England in 1972."

After that, Gascoigne was not only away to get his suit measured; he was in Robson's first XI. He still managed to forget his passport when England gathered to fly to Italy. With the flight going early in the morning, Jimmy Five Bellies had to drive through the night to get it to Gascoigne in time.

Once he arrived in Italy, Gascoigne did unto the World Cup as Vinnie Jones had done unto him. He was in perpetual motion and that was just off the field. His brain couldn't sit still, never mind his body. "Gazza was a pain in the arse early in the competition," said Butcher. "Chris Waddle was his roommate and he was always in our room because Gazza would drive him mad." Waddle occasionally got his own back along with Barnes. "We'd bore the arse off Gazza talking tactics, formations and foreign football."

Gascoigne had other ways to entertain himself. Throwing soap at chickens, shouting "Look at my wad!" like Harry Enfield's Loadsamoney character, after a sting during one of the race nights that were run by Shilton and Lineker; playing tennis, table-tennis, snooker, golf or anything else with anyone he could find (the story goes that, late on the night before the semi-final, he was playing tennis with some Americans before Robson pulled him off the court).

Then there were the pranks. With England's injury list reaching absurd proportions, Gascoigne staggered towards the team emitting chilling screams, covered in bandages (which were actually toilet paper). "Don, he's fallen off the bloody balcony!" said Robson to Don Howe, at which point Gascoigne dived head first into the swimming pool. Before the first game, Gascoigne and the team appeared live on *Top of the Pops* via satellite before a playing of "World In Motion". When the presenter Mark Goodier asked an inane question about how preparations were going for Monday's game, Gascoigne prompted lusty laughter among his teammates by replying imperiously, "Well that has absolutely nothing to do with the record!"

England's team spirit was unusually strong. "It was like a lads' six-week bender," said Butcher. "But when it came to training, the football, it was like a switch, the lads just turned it on." One of the few times Gascoigne lost his temper in the comedy style was when the lads were taken away from him. He didn't have a girlfriend at Italia 90, and got the hump when the players were allowed to have a short break with their Wags (or, as they were called in those days, partners) — not because he wanted a girlfriend, but because he felt the wives were taking his mates away from him. When the group had a big game of charades and it was Gascoigne's turn, he announced "two syllables". Then he stood up, shouted "Fuck off!" and stormed out.

Gascoigne started the tournament well, particularly against the Netherlands. Against Cameroon he was England's best attacker — he made the third goal, and almost created an equaliser for Platt at 2-1 down with a sumptuous turn and through pass — but a defensive liability, most notably when he conceded the penalty from which Cameroon equalised.

"Gascoigne had strayed in the match against Cameroon," said Robson in a BBC interview years later. "I said to him, 'Listen, if you do that against Germany Matthäus will come striding through our midfield and stick two goals past Peter Shilton from 25 yards, because that's what he can do, so you can't chase the ball.' 'Boss', he said, 'sit back and enjoy it, I know what I have to do.' This is Gascoigne talking to me like this! So I looked at him and said, 'I know you know what you have to do, but will you do it?'"

He did it. "The fact he was going to play Matthäus thrilled him," said Robson. "He was going to adore that challenge and he was going to win it. And he did. He was better than Matthäus." His defensive discipline was firmly evident after half an hour, when he blocked Völler's cross from the right of the area with Shilton out of the game. Völler was injured soon after, continuing his hitherto miserable tournament, and Riedle replaced him in Walker's pocket.

West Germany played with 10 men for six minutes, and in that time Waddle hit the bar from 45 yards. Such a statement would normally be accompanied by one or more exclamation marks, though in this case a foul had been given a moment earlier for an off-the-ball offence by Platt. Waddle, who had not heard the whistle, instinctively lofted a golf shot that was tipped onto the bar by Illgner, leaping backwards. In a sense, the foul was irrelevant: it did not change Waddle's imagination and execution. In the eyes of most this was the moment that symbolised England's New Continentality. (In reality Waddle always had the capacity for such brilliance, and it was the subtler passing movements that were perhaps worthier of praise, but that is an argument for another time.) The goal from either side of the halfway line has been increasingly devalued since David Beckham's in 1996; at the time it was something magical. Even Pele hadn't managed it.

At that stage England had been incontrovertibly the better team. The *Times* said they had outplayed West Germany to "an astonishing degree" in the first 40 minutes. Then the dormant monster stirred so suddenly and so terrifyingly that it was England who did not just need half-time but were desperate for it. There had been a slight sign when, after 38 minutes, Thon hit a 25-yard shot that was held well by Shilton despite a difficult bounce. A much more difficult save from Shilton started Germany's surge. When Parker sent Matthäus flying — prompting another handshake as Matthäus got to his feet — the free-kick was laid square to Augenthaler, whose swirling 25-yard shot knocked Shilton off his feet as he moved to his right to push it over the bar.

For the remainder of the half England's defenders, thus far in the box seat, were on the seat of their pants, repelling some intense pressure around the edge of the area. Respite came after four seconds of added time. It would have been thoroughly unfair had England gone behind at half-time. In the BBC studio, Jimmy Hill said it was "a pleasure to see an England team give such a display in the arts and crafts of the game. It's been delightful. We look a classy, stylish international side."

West Germany *were* a classy, stylish international side, and legitimate pride in England's performance was accompanied by the doubt that the Germans would surely play better after half-time. So they did. Their start was such that it was as if they had simply paused the game at 45.04 rather than had an actual half-time break. Matthäus was crowded out by four defenders after a one-two with Riedle, although there was brief respite when Parker overran the ball slightly in the area after a delicious lofted return pass from Waddle. It was a reflection of Parker's tournament: admirable gameness despite his limitations in a role he had never played in his life. He probably got forward more than Pearce. He had not been in England's plans at the start, but counter-intuitively benefited from the switch to a sweeper (Gary Stevens, the man he replaced, was probably a better attacker and Parker a better defender). After feeling nervous before his first game, against Holland, Parker developed a calming ritual of listening to "Soul 2 Soul" on his Walkman before the match. He was never an England regular before or after, just three happy weeks in 1990.

Parker's quarter-chance was one of the few decent attacks England had in the first 15 minutes of the second half. Yet even when they did attack they were in danger. A 53rd-minute corner led to the best chance of the match thus far. It was half-cleared to Pearce, who lost the ball 35 yards from goal to spark a rapid counter-attack. Walker's tackle on Klinsmann diverted the ball to Thon; he ran to the edge of the box, shuffled away from the last man Parker and hit a left-footed shot that was blocked by Shilton.

Wright then made a crucial interception from Riedle; Lineker was flattened by Kohler, who helped him to his feet and patted his sweat-drenched head; Thon shot well wide from 25 yards after a nice set-up from Matthäus, who then surged imperiously past Waddle, Gascoigne and Walker down the left wing only to slip over when he entered the box. "England are under siege now," said John Motson on the BBC. A goal was not in the post; it had been sent by recorded delivery.

It came in the 59th minute. Pearce fouled Hässler, 22 yards out to the right of centre. It was touched off to Brehme, whose low strike hit the outrushing Parker ("the kamikaze man," as Robson called him) and looped in the most awkward parabola towards goal. Shilton backpedalled desperately but could only push it into the net as he fell backwards. Shilton, continuing the inadvertent war theme, said he was "in no-man's land". There has never been consensus as to whether he could have done better. Some felt Shilton — aged 40, only four years younger than the West German manager Beckenbauer — was slightly too slow on his feet, and ended up going backwards like a falling tree to help the ball into the net, rather than having the spring to push it into the net.

Unsurprisingly, he doesn't agree. "You're going to get people making comments, but they don't know what they're talking about," he said in the 2010 ITV documentary *Gazza's Tears*. The affronted pride almost comes at you through the screen. Shilton's argument is that, by reacting so quickly to the spin of the ball and moving backwards, he made himself look bad; that most keepers would been still for longer and watched it sail over their head. It's a persuasive view, not least because Shilton's crazy dedication was such that he came as close as is humanly possible to nurture nature and develop a sixth sense about goalkeeping. His view is supported by Brehme. "Shilton," he said, "reacted like no other goalkeeper I had seen."

West Germany reacted like few other teams would to going ahead in a World Cup semi-final — they kept pushing forward, and soon after the goal Matthäus ignored a challenge from Butcher before shooting wide from 25 yards. Even if England had the inclination to feel sorry for themselves, fate would not allow them to do so. It is striking how often the mood of a match changes entirely by chance. Four minutes after the goal, Gascoigne's superb free-kick from the left wing found Pearce, six yards out, and his backheader drifted just wide of the far post. Illgner had not moved. The chance seemed to remind England that their task was emphatically surmountable and for the next 10 minutes they were superb.

Gascoigne could strip a defence naked, taking off one layer at a time as he went past player after player in the centre of the pitch, and gave a reminder of that rare ability when he swerved classily away from Augenthaler on the edge of the area before being fouled. The free-kick hit the wall.

With England starting to press, Stefan Reuter was brought on to add defensive ability in midfield. It was a consequence of the goal in two ways: one because Germany, at first intent on making it 2-0, now needed to protect the lead in view of England's backlash, and also because Hässler, the man he replaced, had been injured in the tackle by Pearce that produced the free-kick.

Gascoigne, in an unspoken arm-wrestle with Matthäus all night, was now the dominant midfield figure again. He was acting like he owned the ball. Germany's attempts to get it off him were such that Gascoigne was fouled seven times, more than twice as often as anyone else on the pitch. In the 68th minute Gascoigne's through ball was tantalisingly ahead of Waddle, who had made a brilliant angled run.

Waddle's contribution in this match, in a fairly unusual central-midfield role, is generally forgotten because of what happened in the penalty shoot-out. He was one of the best players on the pitch and was inexplicably denied a penalty in the 69th minute. He was on the left of the box, when he received the ball from Beardsley. Waddle duped Augenthaler without touching the ball, using sleight of hip, and when he then dragged the ball to his left he was taken down. Yet the offence was only obvious on replay, and the referee José Ramiz Wright may well have felt that Waddle simply fell over. Replays ended that argument. The slight strangeness of the incident — which is

scarcely ever referred to in discussion of this match, even though it was a clear penalty — was compounded by the fact that Waddle and England barely appealed.

While replays were being shown, Robson made what was becoming his trademark substitution: Trevor Steven on for Butcher, and a switch to 4-4-2 once again. (Steven and Butcher both played for Rangers, who had more players in the squad — four, with Chris Woods and Stevens — than any other team. Arsenal, English champions in 1989 and 1991, had none.)

As is so often the case in football, England did not score when they were on top and did when they weren't. For a ten-minute period after the substitution the clock seemed to eat itself, with little of note happening: England pressed but West Germany were pretty comfortable. Robson was preparing his final substitution, with Steve Bull stripped off, when Lineker scored in the 81st minute. It was certainly not against the run of play, but it was not particularly with it either.

Parker, on the halfway line, tossed a nothing angled ball towards the edge of the area, where Lineker was up against Kohler, Augenthaler and Berthold. It was one against three, but the one had the most important weapon, clarity of purpose, whereas the three defenders did not seem to know what to do or even which one of them should do it. The ball hit the thigh of Kohler and went to Lineker, who kneed it away from Augenthaler and Berthold before swinging his left foot to direct the ball across Illgner and into the far corner. Lineker has talked about swinging and hoping with his weaker left foot, with which he had scored score just three

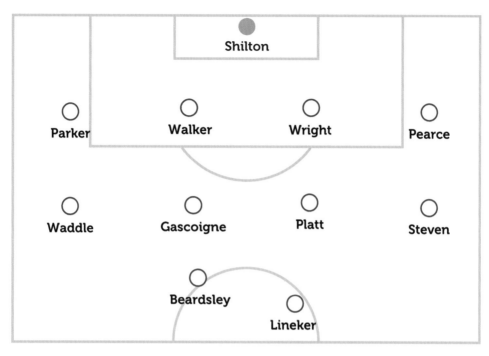

How England finished

of his 34 England goals before that. Whether by accident or design, it was an extremely precise finish.

The goal, Lineker's fourth in the tournament, made him only the eighth man to reach double figures in the World Cup overall. Lineker was seen as the boy next door of English football but he was fiercely single-minded and mentally tough. His tournament had started poorly. He was bothered by a toe problem and missed excellent chances against Holland and Belgium — both with his left foot — but in this match he looked as sharp as anyone, even if his "legs felt almost gone" on the morning of the game.

Lineker was put clear again straight after the goal, this time on the left wing after an exhilarating 60-yard cross-field pass from Gascoigne, only for Platt to be penalised for an offence in the centre with Lineker about to cross. Thereafter the game meandered towards extra-time, a timeout in nature if not name as both sides considered their changing circumstances and the prospect of another 30 minutes.

England thus became the first side to go to extra-time in three consecutive World Cup matches. Waddle and Bull, whose tracksuit went back on after Lineker's goal and would stay on, stood around laughing. Robson issued some instructions to his kamikaze man Parker. Gascoigne applauded the England fans, entirely oblivious to the trauma he was about to experience.

First, England's defence had to withstand the most intense pressure of the match.

Klinsmann led a two-on-two break, only to be almost contemptuously dispossessed by Walker, and then missed two excellent chances in two minutes. The first, a thumping six-yard header from Brehme's excellent left-wing cross, was splendidly saved by the diving Shilton. The header was not right in the corner but it was still a superb piece of goalkeeping. Shilton was not required to repel the second chance. Wright came deep to challenge Klinsmann, who ran into the space as Wright followed the ball. Augenthaler drifted a lobbed pass over the defence, and Klinsmann dragged a left-foot volley wide of the far post from 12 yards. It was an awkward chance, because of the flight of and lack of pace on the ball, though he should have worked Shilton.

When Beardsley gave the ball away on the halfway line, there was barely time to blink before Walker had to get in front of Riedle at the near post to clear Brehme's dangerous cross. England needed a breather. They got one, though not in the manner they would have hoped: in the 99th minute, Gascoigne was booked and ruled out of a possible final. He moved past Reuter and Matthäus near the halfway line but overran the ball and, with naivety and a surfeit of adrenaline, lunged through Berthold. His explanation for the tackle was simple. "I just wanted my ball back."

It was probably a yellow card seven times out of 10 in the climate of the time. The potential consequences hit Gascoigne immediately. As Berthold rolled over and the German bench jumped to their feet in faux outrage, a desperately contrite Gascoigne put his hands in the air and apologised to Berthold. It was too late. Robson called it "half a yellow";

Gascoigne legitimately cited Berthold's disproportionate rollovers — which might be seen as especially callous given that he was also on a yellow and knew the consequences — and the reaction of the German bench. Both were incongruous in the context of an exceptionally sporting match. Yet it was a poor lunge. "I still don't think I touched him," said Gascoigne in *Gazza's Tears*, 20 years after the event. "The guy was 6'4", rolling about like a little kid. Drives us nuts when I still see it." In the same programme, Berthold disagreed. "No, I'm not the type to make that kind of stuff. It was a foul. You don't care whether the player gets booked."

Robson said "my heart hit my shoes" when it happened. Gascoigne's was on his sleeve. Often grief takes time to seep in. Not here. Gascoigne's face was excruciatingly scrutable. In the 15 seconds after the yellow card was shown, his features betrayed so many different emotions: confusion, anger, regret, distress, fear. There will never be a greater antonym of the poker face.

"The World Cup was a special time," he told *FourFourTwo*. "When I was a young kid playing at my youth club, every night I used to dream about playing football at the World Cup. I lived that dream in Italy, but when I was shown the yellow card I knew it had come to an end. When things are good and I can see they're about to end I get scared, really scared."

With a beetroot-faced Gascoigne struggling to suppress tears, Lineker famously signalled to the bench to "have a word with him". Lineker, who scored 10 World Cup goals, 48 goals for England, a Clásico hat-trick and took one of the worst penalties in history against Brazil, is asked about it more than any other moment in his career.

Gascoigne was on the pitch only in body for two or three minutes, though he had composed himself and was doing diligent defensive work by the end of the first period of extra-time. He almost had reason to lose it again, this time because of England taking the lead. With the last touch of the first period remaining, Waddle hit the post.

By now Waddle and Steven were playing as inverse wingers, though both found themselves on the left in this attack. Steven's cross was partially cleared, and he leapt above Berthold to head it back towards the area. Waddle, 16 yards out on the left side of the box, hammered a first-time shot across Illgner and onto the inside of the far post. At one stage the ball was heading just inside the post before a slight change of direction. There is a small chance it brushed Illgner's fingertip, though it seems far more likely that the deviation came in the air or off the pitch. The pace of the shot probably cost England a goal: it bounced off the post so quickly that Platt, following up, was beaten for pace eight yards out.

Platt was involved again in England's next, and final, chance after 111 minutes. Gascoigne, shielding the ball down the right wing, was booted up in the air by Brehme — an appalling foul that might warrant a red card these days. He was booked. With all that had gone, it would have been a great surprise had Gascoigne taken it out on Brehme's chin. Instead Gascoigne shook his hand and patted him on the head.

The resulting free-kick, taken by Waddle, was headed expertly into the net by Platt,

eight yards from goal as the Germans pushed up. He was flagged offside just before the ball hit the net, and jogged straight back to his station, with nothing resembling a complaint from any of the England players. The commentators also suggested it was a clear offside. Like the foul on Waddle it is never told in the story of this match, yet it was seriously close. In those days level was offside and the interpretation surrounding players interfering with play was different, which makes watching historical offside decisions a slightly confusing experience. Platt was couple of millimetres behind Berthold, the deepest defender, although Gascoigne on the near side of the box was a fractionally ahead of both of them. The fact he was not directly involved in the play was irrelevant in 1990. Gascoigne might have inadvertently cost England a place in the World Cup final.

Extra-time ended with another intense spell of German attacking. For much of the match they seemed to play within themselves, yet there were four spells of between five and ten minutes — either side of half-time, the start and end of extra time - in which they put England under the most extreme pressure.

It started when Thon shaped a 25-yard shot that was held well if showily by the plunging Shilton, the first of four opportunities in five minutes. Brehme, moving infield from the left, played a one-two with Riedle and thrashed a vicious rising shot not far over the bar. After an England corner, Augenthaler drove a fine cross-field pass to Klinsmann on the halfway line; he headed it beyond the last man Walker and seemed set to go through on goal, only for Walker to move thrillingly through the gears. Finally, with two minutes to go, Matthäus's shot was blocked by Pearce and came to Buchwald 20 yards out. He used Steven as a screen and sidefooted a precise curler that bounced up onto the post with Shilton beaten.

The loose ball came to Berthold, who was tackled with feeling by Gascoigne to give West Germany a corner. At the age of 23, it was Gascoigne's final touch in a World Cup. That was because, when the game finished five seconds before the end of extra-time, he was not fit to take a penalty, despite being on the provisional list before the match. "My head wasn't there. I was nowhere, I was in another world."

After a brief burst of mutual respect at the final whistle, with both sides seeming to recognise that each did not deserve to lose, they prepared themselves for the business of a penalty competition. "I wasn't worried about penalties," said Robson. "We'd practised penalties, we'd talked about penalties. We had good guys who were going to keep their nerve. Any volunteers? Hands up straight away. Lineker, Beardsley, Platt, Pearce, Waddle… couldn't beat it."

England, who'd had two penalties in eight years under Robson, would now take a minimum of seven in four days. It was their first penalty shootout and Germany's fourth: they lost to Czechoslovakia in Euro 76 final before beating France in the 1982 World Cup semi-final and Mexico in the 1986 quarter-final. At this stage there was none of the contemporary fatalism that comes when a team meets the Germans in a penalty shootout. In many ways, the attitude towards penalty shootouts was naive. They were still relatively unusual in those days; this was only the 12th in

the history of the World Cup, European Championship and Copa América.

It was an adventure, and it often seemed as if, like children going on a trip to the hospital, people did not quite realise the seriousness — that if you lost that was it, it was over. At half-time in this match, when the BBC's Jimmy Hill criticised the format in reference to Italy's defeat by Argentina the night before, Des Lynam said, "Penalties are so *exciting*".

Hill proposed awarding the game to the team who had conceded fewer fouls. Other suggestions included disciplinary record over the whole tournament, corners, corners within the width of the penalty area, the golden goal (with eight-a-side in some cases) and — probably the most popular — allowing a player to run towards the goalkeeper from the halfway line with a certain number of seconds to put the ball in the net.

Hill's criticism stemmed from the widespread belief that a penalty shootout was unfair. Given the contemporary perception of the skill and nerve involved in such a contest, it is striking to see how differently it was viewed in 1990. "Some people are willing to see the shoot-out as a serious extension of the game, to be dignified by detailed analysis," wrote McIlvanney in the *Observer*. "In fact, it is first cousin to a roll of the dice and should be done away with without delay." In the *Guardian*, Lacey described it as "a sadistically cruel way for any team to be beaten at this stage. Russian roulette should be left to the Russians … penalty shoot-outs are always a lottery."

The word lottery was so commonplace in this context — even ITN used it — as to become a cliché. Yet when the shootout started, there was nothing lucky about the first four penalties. Lineker, Brehme, Beardsley (not always a safe penalty taker for his club) and Matthäus scored with varying degrees of excellence. Brehme, a man with two right feet, placed his into the side netting with his right foot, having drilled one with his left foot in the quarter-final shootout against Mexico four years earlier.

By now there was barely a dry nail in the house. The first scare came when Platt put England 3-2 ahead with a rising side foot that was not in the corner. Platt, having originally decided to go his right, changed his mind during his walk from the centre circle. On the way back he swore he would never change his mind again. Illgner went the right way for Platt's penalty but, close to full stretch, could only fingertip it into the net.

At the same end, Shilton kept going the right way but was never close to getting hands on the ball. The two were not unrelated. He was waiting as late as possible before diving. It might have been a good tactic against normal penalty takers but, as the world would come to realise, such a description did not apply to West Germany's players. "Every penalty the Germans took was a cracker that no one would have saved," said Robson, though that was not strictly the case. And Shilton — like a few of the truly great goalkeepers, strangely, including Peter Schmeichel — did not have a great penalty record. "I can't remember him saving one!" said Wright, who played with him for nine years at Southampton and Derby as well as with England.

The keeper ordinarily has a bit of a free pass in a shootout, but as time as gone

on Shilton — generally the subject of deferential, respectful praise in the press at the time — has been tentatively criticised. It is all rather unusual. Attitudes to Shilton, more than with most players seem to be a generational thing: the older you are, the more likely you are to be in his corner. There is certainly a case that his approach in the shootout was flawed, yet he had a superb tournament and to blame him when he only had a chance of saving Thon's penalty is a desperately unfair way to recall an astonishing goalkeeper. Some have suggested Robson should have brought on Dave Beasant just for the penalties, a tactic that was used by Martin O'Neill in the 1996 first division play-off final (in fact Leicester scored a last-minute winner). It was a non-starter: in those days sides had to nominate five substitutes for World Cup games, and Woods rather than Beasant was on the bench.

When he was growing up as a Leicester fan, Lineker's hero was Shilton. "During the tournament Peter and I noticed how many penalties went down the middle," he later said. "We said: 'Why doesn't the keeper wait and see? If the ball goes anywhere near him, he can save it.' Shilton decided that if we got to a shootout, he'd stay on his feet. And every German penalty went in the corners!" Shilton's plan was to increase the already asphyxiating pressure on the taker by not giving him any clue as to which way he might go. He said he had "no chance" with any penalty.

That was certainly true of Riedle's, whipped high into the net, it was 3-3. Stuart Pearce was next. Even though he had never taken a penalty for England, he had been the nominated taker for a couple of years, but England did not get a penalty in that time. Just before the tournament, Lineker asked to take the penalties and Robson agreed but still regarded Pearce as "my best penalty taker". As Pearce walked up he thought, "This'll be 4-3."

Pearce's penalty was firm, low and pretty straight; Illgner dived to his right but was able to save with his legs. "It's quite a biggun to have on your conscience," said Pearce, who had to wait 2180 days for the most violent public exorcism. (In the short-term he used it as fuel, playing with absurd purpose for Forest the following season and scoring 16 goals.)

Thon confirmed Germany's advantage with numbing inevitability, although it was the weakest of their four penalties and might have been saved by a keeper who had guessed and gone early to that side. Waddle, who 10 minutes earlier had no idea he would be taking a penalty, and whose only penalty at senior level had been in a pre-season friendly for Spurs, had to score to keep England in the tournament. You know the rest.

"It was probably about six inches from being one of the best penalties ever seen," he said in *FourFourTwo* years later. "Unfortunately those six inches made it one of the worst penalties ever seen." Weirdly, Waddle's point was proven the next time he took a penalty, for Sheffield Wednesday in an FA Cup tie at Wolves in 1994-95. The Wednesday goalkeeper Kevin Pressman slashed an unsaveable penalty into the postage stamp in the top-left corner for which Waddle had been aiming. Soon after, Waddle, with sad inevitability, missed the decisive penalty in sudden death. The only penalty shootout he ever won was in

France, an individual contest with Völler to decide who should be awarded Mullet of the Year.

The demand for electricity just after Waddle's kick against West Germany was the highest for six years, since the final episode of *The Thorn Birds*. As the German team ran to put Illgner at the bottom of a bundle, Matthäus went straight to console Waddle, a nice end to a match defined by its sportsmanship. "You know," said Trevor Steven, who was down to take the sixth penalty, "at the end, they almost felt upset for us, It was one of those games." Waddle says it was "a magnificent gesture", and it probably deserves to be recalled every bit as much as Andrew Flintoff and Brett Lee during the 2005 Ashes. "Everything was there in that game," said Brehme. "Either team could have won. The players had real comradeship. Even now, if I meet one of the England players, we could go and have a drink and talk about it." He said it was "the final before the final".

After the game Robson smiled ruefully and gently punched the air as if to say: Bugger our luck. "Under all the circumstances," he would later say, "I think England played one of the best games they've played for 25 years." It was one they did not deserve to lose. "We did not have the rub of the green," said Parker in his autobiography, "but then, in my view, we had used it all up in the previous two fixtures."

Gascoigne almost used up all his tears after the game, dissolving with distress and inadvertently providing one of English football's more famous photographs. The tone of his autobiography suggests something far more complex and heartbreaking than was evident at the time. Gascoigne did not cry because England had lost, or because he was out of the final, the latter being irrelevant by this stage anyway. He cried because he instinctively realised life would never be this good again, that his nature and mental illness — even if he did not recognise it as such at the time — would not allow him to live the life everyone assumed for him after Italia 90.

"I loved being at the World Cup," he says in that autobiography. "It was everything I wished for, how I wanted life to be … I wanted it to go on forever, and then I'd never have to face real life." He was the kid who could not bear to going home from the best summer holiday he ever had. There is a similar romance for England fans of a certain age when they reflect. Gazza and Italia 90 is their first kiss, their prom night, their lost girl or boy, a Proustian rush of a mood of hope, youth and innocence that can never be replicated.

"Desolate. Bereaved." That's how Robson described his feeling after the match. "It still rankles," said Lineker. "I don't care about Bobby Charlton's scoring record, but we were within a whisker of a World Cup final. We'd have won it too. Argentina were shot." England, by contrast, seemed to have peaked at the right time. Their Italia 90 campaign is still open to considerable debate. Dissenters point out that they won only one of seven games in normal time and only played especially well against Holland and West Germany; disciples say that nothing became them like the manner of their leaving, and that all bar the very best teams who reach a World Cup semi-finals stumble a little en

route. The most accurate interpretation acknowledges both.

There are two interpretations of the eventual champions, too. One is that they only scored three goals — none from open play — in their last three games; another that they were in complete control of every game bar the semi-final against England and the dead rubber against Colombia, and are the best side to win the World Cup since 1970. It is notable that they did not even need recourse to a German team's most powerful weapon: stung pride. Many of Germany's most famous triumphs, and some of their failures, have involved startling comebacks. The 1990 team are one of only three World Cup winners not to go behind at any stage. (The others were Italy in 1938 and 1982.) After two defeats in two finals, this World Cup was even bigger for them than it was for England. They were worthy, brilliant champions.

With the Berlin Wall falling in 1989, there was a sense that the unified Germany would dominate football. It did not work out like that, and Euro 96 is their only subsequent triumph. Nor did England excel in the manner that was naively assumed after Italia 90. "Bobby Robson's legacy to Graham Taylor is the nucleus of an England football team to take on the world," said the *Express*. It would be wrong simply to blame Taylor for that not happening.

English clubs were readmitted to European football on July 10, two days after the World Cup final, and the 1990-91 English season started on a beautiful day with a mood of almost unprecedented optimism. It was not the first day of a new season; it was the first day of a new era. That has largely been a disaster, the consequence of avarice and other human failings, though nobody was to know as much at the time. In England, football was fashionable again. And abroad, England footballers were suddenly fashionable.

After the tournament, English players became the latest must-have accessory in Serie A, which at the time was comfortably the strongest league and probably as strong as any domestic league has ever been. Wright turned down offers from Roma and Fiorentina. Bull rejected Torino — "after six weeks of going up and down Italy I decided I would miss my English breakfasts" — while Tottenham would not sell Lineker to the same club. "If it was up to me," said Lineker, "I would transfer to Italy right away." The *Express* estimated that Gascoigne's value had increased from £860,000 to £6m. He was principally linked with Juventus, who ensured they had no chance of signing Des Walker by announcing they *had* signed him, thus engaging the wicket of Brian Clough. "They will never get their hands on Walker," he said with approximately 100% finality. Others were linked too. The Genoa president generously said, "I would say that John Barnes can count himself as 90% a Genoa player."

In fact no English player joined Serie A that summer, though Platt, Gascoigne and Walker would later do so. What none of the 22 men in the England squad for that semi-final would do — unimaginably at the time — is play in a World Cup again. The only man to do so was Seaman, who was in England's original squad but left with a broken finger. Twelve of the squad were 27 or under at the time, but England failed to reach the 1994 World Cup and Gascoigne was infamously omitted in 1998.

"The magnitude of it didn't sink in," said Platt later. "You're only young and you think, 'I'll have another World Cup in four years' time'. You don't realise how quickly your career comes to an end relative to World Cups." It lends extra poignancy to the words Bobby Robson said to Gascoigne on the pitch at the Stadio delle Alpi that night. "Don't worry, you've been one of the best players of the tournament. You've been magnificent. This is your first World Cup — you've got your life ahead of you."

Bobby Robson's life came to an end of 31 July 2009 after a 17-year struggle with cancer. Five days earlier, the 1990 semi-final was replayed at St James' Park in the Bobby Robson Trophy match. He defied doctors' instructions and came to the game in a wheelchair, shaking the hands of each player beforehand. The teams included 10 from England's 1990 squad and three from West Germany's, all with hairlines and waistlines that had changed a little in the intervening 19 years. This time England won 3-2.

The word the players — Parker, Gascoigne, Wright, Butcher and others — use to describe Robson is not respect, affection or admiration: it's love. The feeling was mutual, particularly with regard to one player. On the way home after the game, the first question Robson asked his son was: "How did Gascoigne play?" Ⓑ

179

Eight Bells

"It was pointless to stay at Ajax
and sit on the bench, just to be
at the same club with Frank."

Non-identical Twins

A selection of twins who looked the same but played very differently

By Michael Yokhin

Identical twins supposedly have similar characteristics. If they are footballers, you expect them to occupy similar positions on the field, as the recent examples of Vasily and Aleksey Berezutsky of Russia or Lars and Sven Bender of Germany show. Such assumptions don't always hold true. Here are eight curious cases of identical twins who were not identical on the pitch at all.

 ### Erwin and Helmut Kremers, born 24 March 1949

Looking at the stats of Bundesliga's first pair of twins, you might think they were quite similar. Helmut scored 67 times in 331 games in all competitions, while Erwin amassed 69 goals in 321 appearances. However, while Erwin played as a winger who sometimes drifted into the penalty area, Helmut was a left-back occasionally used as a holding midfielder. Both were quick and possessed good dribbling skills and a quality left foot, but their talents were employed in completely different fashions.

As Helmut, the younger brother by 10 minutes, remembered, "Ever since we joined Borussia Mönchengladbach at the age of eight, Erwin always loved playing as a striker, but I preferred to see the pitch in front of me, develop the game from behind and join the attacks every now and then. Coaches never questioned that throughout our careers." Helmut was famous for roaming forward and scored a number of goals from open play, as well as specialising in taking free-kicks and penalties.

The great coach Hennes Weisweiler gave the brothers their debuts for Gladbach in the 1967-68 season, and he always liked them, but they fell out with the team's equally legendary manager Helmut Grashoff and chose to leave for Kickers Offenbach. After winning the DFB Cup, they moved on to Schalke 04 in 1971 and became talismanic for the Gelsenkirchen club as it recovered from the infamous match-fixing scandal. Extremely charismatic, they were instantly loved by the fans, and their first season at Schalke was nothing short of phenomenal. Schalke narrowly lost out on the title to Bayern Munich, but won the cup, after Helmut scored three penalties in the semifinals against FC Köln.

The coach Ivica Horvat proclaimed Erwin to be "the best left winger in the world", and Helmut Schön duly called him into the West Germany squad for Euro '72, where he played a major role in winning the title. Two years later, both brothers were supposed to be included in the squad for the World Cup that took place on the home soil, but Erwin didn't make it. Five minutes from the end of the last Bundesliga game of the season, as Schalke were thrashed 4-0 by Kaiserslautern, the emotional striker, having been wound up by the referee Max Klauser throughout the match, erupted when another decision went against him. "Shut up, you stupid pig!" he shouted. Klauser was aware that sending off Erwin would, thanks to Schön's strict disciplinary rules, mean he was out of the World Cup, so he tried to avoid showing the red card. "I didn't understand," he said. "What did you say, Mr Kremers?" Erwin repeated his rant. Klauser gave him a third opportunity, again pretending he didn't hear the words, but the obscenities were uttered for the third time he had no option. "I was unlucky that Helmut was injured that day," Erwin said. "He would have stopped me if he'd been on the pitch." His brother went to the World Cup alone, but didn't play a single minute in the tournament.

In 1974, the twins also became famous for performing a song called The Girl of My Dreams as a duet. To their surprise, it became very popular, and was even ranked third on the list of radio hits for a while. The producers were happy, so other songs were recorded, and one of them, No Hello No Goodbye, was eventually picked up and performed by Julio Iglesias. The brothers continue to claim that they performed it better than the Spaniard, who could himself have become a footballer, once starring as a promising goalkeeper at Real Madrid's academy.

The Kremers brothers turned down numerous offers from Bayern to stay at Schalke, where they always felt at home. Erwin retired aged 30 and left the

game for good, while Helmut continued playing for a couple more years, eventually moving to Canada. He later served as Schalke manager, and even had a short and unsuccessful spell as the club's president.

 ## Andreas and Thomas Ravelli, born 13 August 1959

Thomas became famous around the globe at the age of 34, when he starred at the 1994 World Cup for the bold Sweden team that claimed third place. The balding goalkeeper peaked in the quarter-final clash with Romania, making saves from Dan Petrescu and Miodrag Belodedici in the penalty shoot-out, and producing a funny little dance at the end. Thomas was also outstanding in the semi-finals, when limiting Brazil to a single goal and keeping his team in with a fighting chance until the final whistle.

In those days, few people outside Sweden even knew that Thomas had a twin brother, let alone that Andreas was actually considered much more talented when the siblings started playing football. Until the age of 12, both were defenders — Andreas played at centre-back, whereas Thomas was a right-back — or at least he aspired to be, but the coaches thought differently and, more often than not, he was watching his brother from the bench. Then the revolutionary idea came: the team needed a keeper and Thomas was asked to try his luck. He never looked back.

The Ravelli brothers' illustrious career started at Östers, in the southern Swedish town of Växjö, one of the best teams in the country at the time.

Andreas was the first to make his debut and played in the side that won the title by a distance in 1978. Thomas followed him into the first team in 1979, and the perfect understanding between the twins helped to make Östers' defence almost unbeatable under Bo Johansson, a coach best known for managing Denmark in the late 90s.

"Our partnership was fabulous because we always felt and understood each other without words," Thomas said. The team conceded just 16 goals in 26 games when finishing first in Allsvenskan in 1980, and Thomas picked the ball out of his net only 20 times when Östers were crowned champions again in 1981 in what had become a very attack-minded league.

In 1980, Andreas became the first to be capped by Sweden, before Thomas got his call in 1981. As the defender put it, "I am the older brother. I showed Thomas the way when we were born and continued to open the doors for him." He did that again when moving to IFK Göteborg in 1988. As Östers gradually faded away in the 80s, the temptation to move to a bigger club was too difficult to resist. Göteborg naturally wanted to sign both brothers, but could only afford one of them. Thus it was Andreas who left, and Thomas reflected: "It was a good thing for us to get some rest from each other, since we were always together and started to get a bit tired."

The separation proved to be disastrous for Östers, who were relegated despite the best efforts of Thomas. The keeper then joined his twin in Gothenburg. Sadly, they only played one more season together. By that time, Andreas was already suffering from serious knee

problems and he was forced to retire from the professional game at the age of 30. He attempted a comeback with Östers but eventually gave up in 1992, just as his brother represented the country at the European Championship that took place in Sweden.

Two years later, Thomas had the summer of his life in the States, but Andreas preferred to stay at home and watch the games on TV with his mother. He still regrets that decision. The stopper might have been the best in Sweden in the 80s and amassed 41 caps, but that's not much compared 143 international appearances by the keeper — a Swedish record recently broken by Anders Svensson. Thomas played until the age of 40, and he admitted, "When I switched to goal, I knew that goalkeepers tend to have longer careers." Andreas was never jealous, though. "Everywhere I go, people think that I am Thomas, so I'm just as famous, because of him," he joked.

3 Hossam and Ibrahim Hassan, born 10 August 1966

As far as international caps are concerned, the Hassans are the most successful pair of brothers in football history. Hossam represented Egypt 169 times, with more than two decades separating not only his first and last appearance, but also his first and last medals at the African Cup of Nations. He won the tournament in 1986 as a 19 year old, and repeated the feat in 2006, having celebrated another title in between, in 1998. Ibrahim wasn't part of any of those triumphs. He made his debut for Egypt in 1988 and wasn't called up after 2002, while missing the

1998 tournament because of injury. Nevertheless, he has 127 games for the Pharaohs to his name. Between them, the incredible Hassan twins amassed 294 matches, a record extremely unlikely ever to be surpassed.

They will always be remembered together, but they could hardly have been more different on the pitch. Both started playing as strikers, but while Hossam proved to be a natural scorer, Ibrahim was far less successful in front of goal. The youth coach at Al Ahly tried him in defence instead and the gamble worked out perfectly. Ibrahim remained at right-back for the rest of his career.

Hossam based his game on intelligence, good movement and had that uncanny ability to be in the right place at the right time. Ibrahim, on the other hand, was a tough no-nonsense marker, feared by opponents for his physical, never-say-die approach. His technical qualities were not outstanding, but in his prime he still was one of Africa's finest defenders.

Of the two of them, Hossam was always the leader, taking his brother with him along the way. The striker was the favourite player of Egypt's most famous coach, Mahmoud Al Gohary — the man who, in 1990, took the country to their only post-war World Cup. The twins were key players for Egypt in Italy that summer, and European teams became interested in them. PAOK of Thessaloniki signed the pair, and Hossam became an idol of black-and-white fans, scoring one of the team's most iconic goals with an overhead kick against Panathinaikos. They only wanted to keep the striker for the following season, though, so both twins signed for Neuchâtel Xamax.

With Al Ahly in trouble in 1992, the twins took an emotional decision to come home and took their beloved club back to glory. As years passed, their value to the team was very different. Hossam, whose game was never too physical, remained in brilliant form, seemingly ageless. Ibrahim, on the other hand, couldn't perform on the same level on the wrong side of 30. The inevitable moment came in 1999 when Al Ahly wanted to re-sign only Hossam, but that was impossible. The brothers never separated, and they moved to Al Ahly's Cairo rivals Zamalek. In 2004, when Zamalek tried to retain Hossam only, the siblings signed for Al Masry. Eventually, Ibrahim played until the age of 38, thanks to his twin who retired a year later. Between them, they won 13 league titles, two African Champions League trophies and four African Cup Winners' Cups.

They have continued to work together as coaches in recent years — Hossam in charge, Ibrahim as his assistant. They were both on the bench of Al Masry in 2012 when the tragic Port Said massacre took place, and coached Jordan as the Asian team lost to Uruguay in the 2014 World Cup play-offs. Hossam's ambition is to become the coach of Egypt sooner rather than later, and his twin will surely be by his side when that happens.

 ### Frank and Ronald de Boer, born 15 May 1970

It might come as a surprise now, but as a child Ronaldus de Boer was thought to be a more promising player than his brother Franciscus. They were born not far from Alkmaar, where their father Cees used to play before a poor tackle ended his career prematurely. At their first club, De Zouaven, Ronald was a versatile striker, while Frank played as a left winger. When the twins joined Ajax at the age of 14, they met the legendary youth coach Dirk de Groot, who soon decided that Frank's place was in defence. The mentor was certain that Bryan Roy was a much better prospect on the wing, as Frank lacked pace and wasn't a great dribbler.

Thus Frank became a left-back, and later on moved into central defence. He never regretted it. Ronald might have been the first one to make a debut for the first team, aged 17, but he remained a bench player for his first three seasons, while Frank soon made a starting place his own. Eventually, when Louis van Gaal took charge in 1991, he made it clear that Ronald would have to leave in order to play regular football, and off he went to Twente Enschede. "It was pointless to stay at Ajax and sit on the bench, just to be at the same club as Frank," he once recalled.

The Amsterdamers left themselves the first option to re-sign Ronald, and used it 18 months later after he'd found his feet and become a regular first division player. The versatile attacker, who was often used in midfield, was never a prolific scorer, his best tally in all competitions standing at just 11 in the glorious 1994-95 season when Ajax stunned Europe by winning the Champions League. The brothers played together in the final against AC Milan, and they also won five Eredivisie titles together.

As most of the youngsters nurtured by van Gaal left the club, the de Boers remained stalwarts, but in the summer of 1998 they opened controversial legal procedures against the club, claiming a verbal promise had been made that they would be released if a suitable offer was received. The twins lost the case, but their presence became problematic and they were sold to Barcelona in January 1999, being reunited with Van Gaal. Those were not happy times for them, though, with Frank being banned after a test suggested he had used nandrolone and Ronald struggling for form.

In the end, Ronald accepted a generous offer from Rangers, and the pair were separated for three and a half years before Frank also arrived at Ibrox, his twin advising the management that he was available. There was no happy ending for their European career as Celtic ran away with the title, and the brothers eventually hung up their boots after a spell in Qatar.

Since his professional debut, Frank had been the leader of the pair, and he was a very important player for the national team as well, accumulating 112 caps. Ronald only played 67 times for the Netherlands and is mostly remembered for missing the crucial penalty in the 1998 World Cup semi-final shoot-out against Brazil. Frank, visibly frustrated, wasn't supportive of his sibling that day, but then he himself missed two penalties against Italy in the semi-final of Euro 2000.

5 Arnar and Bjarki Gunnlaugsson, born 3 March 1973

When one of Gunnlaugsson twins scored a hat-trick for Iceland Under-16 team, the coach ran on to the field to check which one it was. They were absolutely identical and he didn't want to make a mistake. The hero was Arnar — the one who had played as a midfielder as a kid, switching to a more advanced role as years went by. Bjarki, on the other hand, started as a striker and gradually moved into a midfield position.

They became famous very early in their homeland, making their debut for ÍA Akranes at the age of 16 in the same game: Arnat was in the starting lineup, Bjarki came on as a substitute. The winning formula was to give the ball to Bjarki in the midfield — more often than not he found his brother, 15 minutes older than him, who would score. Bjarki was more visionary; Arnar had a better eye for goal.

Rumours of their talent reached the Netherlands and the duo signed for Feyenoord in 1992. The Rotterdamers had a fine team in those days, winning the Eredivisie title under Wim van Hanegem, and the youngsters found it difficult to get a game. Growing impatient, they chose to leave two years later — a decision they now regret. "We were too young to understand what was good for us," Arnar said. "Look at Giovanni van Bronckhorst who played with us for the reserves: he stayed and became a big star. We should have done the same and waited for the opportunity. The Dutch league was perfect for us."

So they went to FC Nürnberg, who had just been relegated to the second flight and initially things looked promising, even though Bjarki was played out of position on the wing. The team didn't meet their expectations, though, and Rainer Zobel, the coach who had signed the pair, was forced to leave. His replacement, Günter Sebert, was

reluctant to play both twins at the same time. "Sometimes people thought we didn't work hard enough defensively and only one of us could be on the pitch," said Arnar. "That's why we only started one game together for the national team during the whole of our careers. Our perfect mutual understanding wasn't really used, and that's a great pity." Eventually, Nürnberg were relegated again and the pair went back to Akranes.

From there on, their roads parted. Bjarki went to SV Waldhof Mannheim, continued to Molde and Brann Bergen in Norway, and then Preston North End. Arnar chose to join Sochaux in France, but left a more significant mark in England, playing for Bolton Wanderers, Leicester City and Stoke City. Both were somewhat unlucky with injuries. Bjarki even retired at the age of 29 because of his bad hip, but eventually returned to the field, as the pair spent long years in Iceland before actually hanging up their boots.

They were always popular in their homeland — humorous, easy-going, dressing well and starring in various stories on the back pages. Having played for KR Reykjavík together, they twice tried a joint player-coaching position at ÍA, without real success. Their only game against each other took place in 2010, when they were 37. "That felt really strange, especially because we were direct opponents on the pitch," said Arnar. "I was the playmaker for Haukar, Bjarki was the defensive midfielder for FH Hafnarfjörður." FH won 3-1 that day, but Arnar scored the only goal for the losers, so their parents couldn't have been happier.

They went out on a high note, Bjarki winning the title with FH, and Arnar being the top scorer for Fram. Since retirement, they have worked together as football agents, representing young players and teaching them patience, trying to ensure this generation never makes the mistake they did.

6 Guillermo and Gustavo Barros Schelotto, born 4 May 1973

The Barros Schelotto brothers aren't well known outside Argentina, largely because of a lack of exposure in the national team — Guillermo only won 10 caps, while Gustavo was never called up. In their homeland, though, they are household names, especially among the fans of their first team, Gimnasia La Plata, and Boca Juniors.

The twins, following the footsteps of their older brother Pablo, were accepted into the Gimnasia academy, and it was soon evident that their talents were rather different. The youth coach saw that Gustavo was a cool-headed player who was able to fill various positions in midfield, using his vision. He was also better developed physically, whereas Guillermo was a flair player, light on his feet, always willing to take on defenders and score goals. Eventually, Gustavo established himself as a holding midfielder, playing long passes to his sibling. He rarely stood out, but had a huge influence on his teammates. Guillermo, mainly a playmaker in the youth squad, ended up as a tricky winger, easily stealing the limelight from his twin.

The differences off the field were also significant. Gustavo was always an outgoing personality, ready to speak to everyone and friendly with journalists.

Guillermo was shy and less talkative, but changed on the pitch, where he enjoyed being a troublemaker. Both brothers loved to provoke, raising the temperature by constant trash-talking and getting a number of their rivals sent off. Nice guys in the dressing-room , they were perfect teammates, even becoming friends with Martín Palermo at Boca Juniors, despite the fact that he had been raised at their local rivals Estudiantes de La Plata. Their opponents, however, hated to play against them.

There was never any rivalry between the duo. When Guillermo got the nod to make his debut for Gimnasia in 1991, it was Gustavo who called to break the good news to their parents. As their contribution grew, the team became a significant force in the league, missing out on the title by a single point in the Clausuras of 1995 and 1996. During the latter, Gimnasia recorded one of their most famous wins ever, thrashing Boca 6-0 away, with Guillermo scoring a phenomenal hat-trick.

That was the moment at which the Boca board decided to sign the twins and the deal was done a year later. Guillermo went on to become one of the most beloved players of los xeneizes, spending a decade at La Bombonera, scoring 62 league goals, winning six league titles, and lifting the Libertadores Cup four times, not to mention two triumphs in the International Cup.

Gustavo was less fortunate, falling out with the coach after being benched. He left Boca in 2000 and started wandering, spending some time at Racing Club and Rosario Central, as well as short spells at Villarreal in Spain and Allianza

Lima in Peru. He had retired by the time Guillermo moved to MLS with Columbus Crew before finishing his career at Gimnasia at the age of 38. Nowadays, they are thriving as joint coaches at Lanús, with Guillermo formally in charge and Gustavo his assistant.

7 Marcin and Michał Żewłakow, born 22 April 1976

When playing for youth teams, both brothers were forwards. Marcin was mostly used centrally, whereas the two-footed Michał was sent to the wing and supplied the crosses for his sibling. Coaches at Polonia Warsaw, though, spotted other talents in the pair. Since both were sound in tackling and possessed good vision, it was suggested that the twins should move backwards and be involved more in build-up play.

The brothers' reactions couldn't have been more different. Michał pragmatically decided to play to his strengths, as he moved to the left-side of midfield, then to left-back, eventually becoming a dominant leader in central-defence. Marcin just wanted to score goals and saw directives to play in midfield or at right-back as punishment. He was ready to sacrifice the chance of a more prominent career for his passion for putting the ball into the net.

As they moved to the Belgian club Beveren in 1998, Marcin presented himself as a striker and proved the point when scoring a brace on his debut. The brothers were transferred to Excelsior Mouscron a year later and proceeded to have a very solid career. However, despite having a

decent scoring record, Marcin was never considered first choice for Poland, while Michał, who made his debut for the national team before his twin, went on to become the most-capped player in Polish history with 102 appearances.

Both brothers, the first twins to play for Poland, were included in the squad that went to the World Cup in 2002 — Michał a certain starter, Marcin a substitute. "Poland is the only team where I could quietly accept being left on the bench," he said, and would proudly note that eventually he played in all three games in the tournament, whereas Michał was pulled out after two defeats. Marcin's international career was over soon after and he will never know what would have happened if he had accepted a switch to midfield in his youth. He doesn't care, though: "I have no regrets. I wouldn't give up a single goal in exchange for more caps or better recognition. Scoring is the greatest feeling in the world, it always gave me all the satisfaction I needed."

As the more established player of the duo, Michał went on to play for bigger clubs, signing for Anderlecht in 2002 and leaving Marcin at Mouscron. Being separated for the first time in their lives was tough for the twins — both lost form and needed half a season to regain confidence. Marcin was even benched by the coach Lorenzo Staelens, who blamed the World Cup for his tiredness, although the real reason lay elsewhere.

The hardest experience, though, was playing against each other, as clashes in the penalty area were unavoidable. Both twins thrived in physical battles and were never afraid of crunching tackles, but had to change their attitude when facing one another — they couldn't stand the thought of accidentally injuring their brother. "We had absolutely no secrets. It was impossible for me to surprise Michał, and Michał couldn't surprise me," Marcin said.

He did, nevertheless, score twice against his sibling, and the second goal proved to be of huge importance. The game in question took place in the Polish Ekstraklassa, after both brothers returned to their homeland. Michał, who won two Belgian titles with Anderlecht and three Greek championship trophies with Olympiakos, signed for Legia Warsaw. Marcin, whose only title was in Cyprus with Apoel, went to the less fashionable GKS Bełchatów.

The twins had always dreamed of finishing their careers at the same club, but that didn't work out, and when GKS played at Legia in March 2012 the capital team were considered favourites to finish first. Michał's team lead 1-0 at the break, but Marcin netted the equaliser in the second half, derailing Legia's challenge. They eventually finished third, three points from the top, and Marcin was jokingly "blamed" by his brother for the collapse.

The happy ending for Michał came the following year, as Legia were crowned champions in his last season before retiring. Marcin also retired in 2013 and now the brothers have more opportunities to spend time together. "We were always the same," Marcin said. "Sometimes I went out shopping and watched a movie, and it turned out that Michał bought exactly the same things at the same time and then watched the same film." So similar in life, but so different on the pitch.

 Hamit and Halil Altintop, born 8 December 1982

The Altintop twins were born in Gelsenkirchen to a family of Turkish immigrants. Their father died of cancer when they were just two years old. According to local journalists, their characters tended to be quite different. Hamit, older by 12 minutes, is a bit more 'Turkish' — talkative, open hearted and impulsive. Halil is a bit more 'German' — he favours long-term planning and can be shy, especially with strangers.

They started their careers at SG Wattenscheid 09, a proud club that had had a few decent seasons in the Bundesliga, but was playing in the third division by the time the Altintops joined their youth academy. In 2000, aged 18, the brothers were promoted to the first team by the coach Hannes Bongartz. "They are completely different players with different skills," he said. "Hamit has always been strong defensively, an aggressive fighter on the pitch and a leader by nature. Halil was better technically, cool and clever, always looking to score goals."

That's how they played from the very beginning. Hamit, originally a holding midfielder, is very versatile, and so was used in many positions, including at right-back. Halil has always played up front, a penalty-area predator.

At the age of 17, the twins had a decision to make as to which national team they wanted to play for. Halil was seriously thinking of representing Germany, but Hamit didn't want to hear about that. "Do you want to play against me?" he asked. Halil clearly didn't and both went on to play for Turkey. They did, however, play against each other on numerous occasions, as their careers saw them separated as they progressed to the Bundesliga.

In 2003, Hamit stayed at home to join Schalke 04, while Halil moved south to sign for Kaiserslautern. Hamit's career was much more impressive from there on, as he had an absolutely sensational debut, scoring a brace with phenomenal long-range shots in the Ruhr derby against Borussia Dortmund. Bold and fearless, he took his first opportunity with both hands and his place in the starting line-up was never in doubt. Halil had to wait much longer for his breakthrough, as Miroslav Klose was calling the shots at Lautern. He eventually proved himself as well, though, scoring 20 goals in the 2005-06 season and earning a transfer to Schalke.

2006-07 was the only season in which both brothers played for the same team and Schalke came agonisingly close to winning the title, eventually losing out to VfB Stuttgart, beaten by Dortmund in the penultimate match. Hamit was then signed by Bayern Munich, and won two league titles and two DFB Cups before moving on to Real Madrid in 2011. Had he enjoyed better luck with

injuries, he would surely have had an even more illustrious career. He now plays for Galatasaray, and his only goal in the 2012-13 season was scored against Schalke in the Champions League.

Halil stayed at Schalke for two more years, but never found his true form and was eventually forced to leave for Eintracht Frankfurt, where he had a disappointing 2010-11 season without scoring a single league goal. He put his career back on track at Trabzonspor and is now at Augsburg.

The twins became used to facing each other and never changed their style on such occasions. "We are both fair players, who rarely get yellow cards. It's just a duel that I want to win," Hamit said ahead of one of the games between Bayern and Schalke.

Their biggest dream was to play together for Turkey at a major tournament. They came very close to achieving it, having been regulars in qualifying for Euro 2008. However, the coach Fatih Terim controversially omitted Halil from the final squad. Hamit, positioned at right-back, overcame an injury and was excellent throughout, as Turkey dramatically reached the semifinals, where they lost to Germany, of all teams. In his mind, he wasn't there alone. He played for both of them. Ⓑ

Contributors

The Blizzard, Issue Twelve

Philippe Auclair is the author of *The Enchanted Kingdom of Tony Blair* (in French) and *Cantona: the Rebel Who Would Be King*, which was named NSC Football Book of the Year. His biography of Thierry Henry has just been published. He writes for *France Football* and *Offside* and provides analysis and commentary for RMC Sport. Twitter: **@PhilippeAuclair**

Robin Bairner is a French football writer primarily found working for *Goal*. He also holds a keen interest in the Scottish game. Twitter: **@RBairner**

Paul Brown is the author of *The Victorian Football Miscellany*. He is also the editor of the *Goal-Post: Victorian Football* anthologies. He has written for publications including *FourFourTwo* and *When Saturday Comes*. Website: www.stuffbypaulbrown. com. Twitter: **@paulbrownUK**

Matthew Campelli is a tech and telecoms journalist for *Mobile Magazine* and *Mobile Today*, as well as a football writer and researcher. Twitter: **@MatthewCampelli**

Miguel Delaney is an Irish-Spanish football journalist based in London, who writes for ESPN, the *Irish Examiner* and the *Independent*. He is the author of a history of the Irish national team called *Stuttgart to Saipan*, which was released in 2010. In 2011 was nominated for Irish sports journalist of the year. **@MiguelDelaney**

Brian Homewood is a freelance journalist who, after living in Colombia, Brazil and Argentina, decided to be really adventurous and moved to Switzerland. He writes for Reuters and World Soccer. Twitter: **@brianhomewood**

Graham Hunter is a journalist of international reputation and covers Spanish football for Sky Sports, the BBC and newspapers and magazines across the world. He writes and interviews for uefa.com and has been a TV producer for Fifa. Twitter: **@BumperGraham**

Richard Jolly is a football journalist for ESPN, the *National*, the *Guardian*, the *Observer*, the *Straits Times* and the *Sunday Express* and has covered Premier League matches for 10 British national newspapers. Twitter: **@RichJolly**

Alex Keble is a freelance journalist who has written for FourFourTwo.com and the *Guardian*. Twitter: **@alexkeble**

Sergio Levinsky is an Argentinian sociologist and journalist. He is the author of three books and the editor of a World Cup encyclopaedia. He is a columnist for *Jornada* (Argentina) and Yahoo in Japan and works for *Kicker*, *Footballista* (Japan) and *Clasico* (Dwnmark). His blog is at www.sergiol-nimasnimenos.blogspot. com. Twitter: **@sergiole**

Felix Lill is a German freelance journalist who last September moved from London to Tokyo, where he now works as an author for *Die Zeit*, *Die Presse*, *Der Spiegel*, *NeueZürcherZeitung*,

Tagesspiegel, Zeit Online and others. He was awarded the Austrian Sports Journalism Award in 2010, 2011 and 2012. He was awarded the Austrian OEZIV Media Prize 2012.

Sid Lowe is a Spanish football correspondent for the *Guardian, World Soccer* and ESPN FC. He is the author of *Fear and Loathing in La Liga* and of *Catholicism, War and the Foundation of Francoism*. Twitter: **@sidlowe**

Iain Macintosh is the author of *Football Fables* and the *Everything You Ever Wanted To Know* series of sports guidebooks and a co-author of *Football Manager Ruined My Life*. He writes for the *New Paper* in Singapore, ESPN and anyone else who'll pay him. Twitter: **@iainmacintosh**

Steve Menary is a regular contributor to *World Soccer, When Saturday Comes* and playthegame.org. He is also the author of *Outcasts! The Lands That Fifa Forgot* and *GB United? British Olympic Football and the End of the Amateur Dream*.

James Montague writes for the *New York Times* and *World Soccer*. He can also be heard regularly on the BBC World Service's World Football Show. His first book, *When Friday Comes: Football, War and Revolution in the Middle East* was updated and released this summer. His second, *Thirty One Nil: On the Road With Football's Outsiders, a World Cup Odyssey* will be out in May 2014. Twitter: **@JamesPiotr**

BartoszNowicki is a freelance photographer and a trustee and curator of Third Floor Gallery in Cardiff. He is

the author and publisher of the *City — The Season* book. Website: www. bartosznowicki.co.uk

Scott Oliver is an honorary research fellow in Nottingham University's Department of Latin American Studies, where he completed a doctorate on Peronist Argentina. He has written about cricket for the *Guardian*, cricinfo, *Spin* and Wisden India and football for BT and ESPN. Twitter: **@reverse_sweeper**

Javier Sauras is a nomadic journalist and photographer who has been wandering from Asia to Latin America during the last four years. He has written about Japan, the Philippines, Spain, China, UK and Bolivia. He is still on the road. Twitter: **@jsauras**

Rob Smyth is a freelance sports writer. He was co-written two books that will be released in April — *Danish Dynamite: The Story of Football's Greatest Cult Team* and *And Gazza Misses The Final*, a collection of minute-by-minute reports on classic World Cup matches.

Tim Vickery writes and broadcasts on South American football for the BBC, *World Soccer*, ESPN, SBS and TalkSport.

Jonathan Wilson is the author of *Inverting the Pyramid*. He writes for the *Guardian*, the *National, World Soccer* and *Sports Illustrated*. His latest book is *The Anatomy of Liverpool*. Twitter: **@jonawils**

Michael Yokhin is a European football writer with a keen interest in the history of the game. He writes a regular column for ESPN and contributes to the likes of *FourFourTwo* and *Champions*. Twitter: **@Yokhin**

Blizzard **Subscriptions**

Subscribe to the print version of The Blizzard, be the first to receive new issues, get exclusive Blizzard offers and access digital versions of all back-issues FREE

Subscription Options

Set Price for Four Issues

Get a four-issue subscription to *The Blizzard* — for you or as a gift — for a flat fee including postage and packing (P&P):

UK:	£35
Europe:	£45
Non-Euorpe:	£55

Recurring Pay-What-You-Like

Set up a quarterly recurring payment for each edition of *The Blizzard*. The recommended retail price (RRP) is £12, but pay what you like, subject to a minimum fee of £6 plus P&P

See www.theblizzard.co.uk for more

Digital Subscriptions

If the cost of postage is prohibitive, or you just want an excuse to use your new iPad or Kindle, you can set up a subscription to digital versions of The Blizzard for just £3 per issue.

See www.theblizzard.co.uk for more

Information for Existing Subscribers

The Blizzard is a quarterly publication from a cooperative of top class football journalists and authors from across the globe, enjoying the space and freedom to write about the football stories that matter to them.

Free Digital Downloads for *Blizzard* Subscribers

Whether you have taken advantage of our set price or pay-what-you-like offer, for the duration of your subscription to *The Blizzard* you are entitled to download every issue FREE.

See www.theblizzard.co.uk for more

We very much value the commitment of our print subscribers and have a policy to make available new issues, special offers and other limited access events and benefits to print subscribers first.

About *The Blizzard*

Distribution & Back Issues
Contact Information
About Issue Twelve

Buy *The Blizzard*

We want as many readers as possible for *The Blizzard*. We therefore operate as far as we are able on a pay-what-you-like basis for digital and print versions.

Digital Version (Current & Back Issues)

All issues of *The Blizzard* are available to download for Kindle, Android, iOS and PC/Mac at: *www.theblizzard.co.uk*.

- *RRP: £3*
- *Pay-what-you-like minimum: £0.01*

Printed Version (Current & Back Issues)

Purchase a physical copy of *The Blizzard* in all its luxurious, tactile, sensual glory at: *www.theblizzard.co.uk*. If you haven't felt our rough textured cover-varnish and smelled the inner genius, you haven't properly experienced its awesome true form. Read it, or leave it on your coffee table to wow visitors.

- *RRP: £12 (+P&P)*
- *Pay-what-you-like min: £6 (+P&P)*

Contact *The Blizzard*

All advertising, sales, press and business communication should be addressed to the Central Publishing Office:

The Blizzard
Ashmore Villa,
1, Ashmore Terrace,
Stockton Road,
Sunderland,
SR2 7DE

Email: info@theblizzard.co.uk
Telephone: +44 (0) 191 543 8785
Website: www.theblizzard.co.uk
Facebook: www.facebook.com/blzzrd
Twitter: @blzzrd

About Issue Twelve

Editor Jonathan Wilson
Publisher The Blizzard Media Ltd
www.theblizzard.co.uk
Design Daykin & Storey
www.daykinandstorey.co.uk

Copyright

SPIEL POSTER SHOP

This selection of posters is a collaboration between SPIEL, Well Made Studio and the contributing artists to Field. Each print is available in a limited edition of 100 copies and is printed on high quality fine art paper.

£25+p&p. Prints are available at:
www.spielmagazine.co.uk/shop